Making Thinking Visible

Making Thinking Visible

Writing, Collaborative Planning, and Classroom Inquiry

Edited by

Linda Flower
Carnegie Mellon University

David L. Wallace
Iowa State University

Linda Norris
Indiana University of Pennsylvania

Rebecca E. Burnett
Iowa State University

National Council of Teachers of English
1111 W. Kenyon Road, Urbana, Illinois 61801-1096

Manuscript Editor: Hilary Taylor Holbrook

Production Editor: David A. Hamburg

Interior Design: Doug Burnett

Cover Design: Cameron Poulter

NCTE Stock Number 30399-3050

Library of Congress Cataloging-in-Publication Data

Making thinking visible : writing, collaborative planning and classroom inquiry /
    edited by Linda Flower . . . [et al.].
        p.   cm.
    Includes bibliographical references and index.
    ISBN 0-8141-3039-9
    1. English language—Composition and exercises—Study and
teaching—United States—Research.   2. English language—Rhetoric—
Study and teaching—United States—Research.   3. Action research in
education—United States.   I. Flower, Linda.
    LB1576.M3616   1994
    808'.042'07—dc20   93-5976
                                                                    CIP

Contents

Members of the Making Thinking Visible Project, 1988–1992

Linda Flower, Project Director, Carnegie Mellon University

Linda Norris, Educational Coordinator, Indiana University of Pennsylvania

Jean A. Aston, Community College of Allegheny County, Allegheny Campus, Pittsburgh, Pennsylvania

Nancy Atkinson, University of Pittsburgh, Pittsburgh, Pennsylvania

Joyce Baskins, Community Literacy Center, Pittsburgh, Pennsylvania

Michael A. Benedict, Fox Chapel Area High School, Pennsylvania

Marlene W. Bowen, Iroquois High School, Erie, Pennsylvania

James R. Brozick, North Hills High School, Suburban Communities, Western Borough and Ross Township, Pennsylvania

Rebecca E. Burnett, Iowa State University, Ames, Iowa

Linda Carey, Carnegie Mellon University, Pittsburgh, Pennsylvania

Kasey Cole, Pittsburgh High School for the Creative and Performing Arts, Pittsburgh, Pennsylvania

Leonard R. Donaldson, Peabody High School, Pittsburgh, Pennsylvania

Leslie Byrd Evans, Steel Valley High School, Munhall, Pennsylvania

Philip Flynn, Community Literacy Center, Pittsburgh, Pennsylvania

Jane Zachary Gargaro, Peabody High School, Pittsburgh, Pennsylvania

Karen W. Gist, Peabody High School, Pittsburgh, Pennsylvania

Thomas Hajduk, Carnegie Mellon University, Pittsburgh, Pennsylvania

Russell Kuehner, Pittsburgh High School for the Creative and Performing Arts, Pittsburgh, Pennsylvania

Elenore Long, Carnegie Mellon University, Community Literacy Center, Pittsburgh, Pennsylvania

Theresa A. Marshall, Iroquois High School, Erie, Pennsylvania

Andrea S. Martine, Allderdice High School, Pittsburgh, Pennsylvania

Patricia McMahon, Community College of Allegheny County, North Campus, Pittsburgh, Pennsylvania

Sharon Michael, Westinghouse High School, Pittsburgh, Pennsylvania

George Mower, Community College of Allegheny County, Allegheny Campus, Pittsburgh, Pennsylvania

Wayne C. Peck, Community Literacy Center, Pittsburgh, Pennsylvania

Lois Rubin, Penn State New Kensington, Pennsylvania

continued on next page

Nancy N. Spivey, Carnegie Mellon University, Pittsburgh, Pennsylvania

Pamela Turley, Community College of Allegheny County, Allegheny Campus, Pittsburgh, Pennsylvania

James Vincent, Robert Morris College, Moon Campus, Coraopolis, Pennsylvania

David L. Wallace, Iowa State University, Ames, Iowa

Dolores Weaver, Woolslair Elementary Gifted Center, Pittsburgh, Pennsylvania

Patsy Williamson, Community College of Allegheny County, Allegheny Campus, Pittsburgh, Pennsylvania

Mario Zinga, Woolslair Elementary Gifted Center, Pittsburgh, Pennsylvania

Acknowledgments

This book is the result of several kinds of collaboration. Collaborative planning is about people making meaning together—about providing a supportive social context for students or other writers to develop their ideas. Thus, this book is based on students' collaborations, and it is about what happens when students are given the opportunity to support each others' writing processes and to reflect on what they learned through the process.

Not surprisingly, this book is also the result of collaboration between students and teachers; collaborative planning provided the teachers and community literacy leaders involved in the Making Thinking Visible Project with a window for observing students' thinking about writing. We provided our students with a supportive context for developing their plans for writing and for reflecting on what happened when they did that. They, in turn, surprised and taught us with their insights. This book tells many stories about what we as teachers learned by observing our students' thinking and by listening to their observations. Thus, we gratefully acknowledge the contributions of our students, our partners in the investigations reported here.

This book also tells the story of collaboration between educators and researchers (who were also teachers themselves). In one sense, this book is the story of the collaborative relationships that developed among the junior high, high school, community college, university, and community educators in the Making Thinking Visible Project. We came together with the understanding that educational innovation depends on both systematic observation and sensitivity to diverse contexts in which learning takes place. Thus, in a real sense this book belongs most directly to the members of the Making Thinking Visible Project, thirty-three teacher-researchers who conducted the classroom inquiries reported in this book. As editors, we would like to thank our colleagues for sharing not only their successes and failures but also the process of their inquiry.

These collaborations were made possible by support of many others whose stories are not told in this book but whose contributions were critical to the project's success. This four-year school/university/community collaboration was supported by the Howard Heinz Endowment of the Pittsburgh Foundation and the Center for the Study of Writing at Carnegie Mellon University. We thank Joseph Dominic at the

Pittsburgh Foundation, who encouraged us to expand our horizons and to rethink the structure of our schools. Early enthusiastic support for the goals and purposes of the project was given by Richard Wallace, superintendent, and JoAnne Eresh, director of Writing and Speaking, Pittsburgh Public Schools. Paul LeMahieu, Stanley Herman, and Phil Parr at the Pittsburgh Board of Education provided helpful suggestions and encouragement, as did JoAnn Doran and Gregory Morris at the Teacher Training Center.

We would also like to thank the reviewers of this manuscript for their insightful comments.

Part I Frameworks for Discovery

1 Teachers as Theory Builders

Linda Flower

Carnegie Mellon University
Pittsburgh, Pennsylvania

Teaching is a theory-building enterprise. That is, it is a hypothesis-creating, prediction-testing process that leads to the framing and reframing of action. Theory building is an act by which teachers construct an imagined frame for actual pedagogy.

Sitting here, starting to work up my syllabus, I jot down a book list and go over the topics and ideas I want to cover in the course. I am *reviewing information*; it's business as usual. But as I begin to construct an assignment, this planning process takes a new, "theory-building" turn: I begin to *build a hypothesis* about my students, to spin out a scenario of how their learning process will unfold as they encounter these ideas. For example, the assignment is a reading-to-write task that asks students to "apply their readings" (in this case Freire, Plato, Bazerman, and others) to their own experience, for a purpose of their own. However, in the scenario I *envision*, this task will, in fact, be asking my students to alter their normal approaches to reading as a way of "banking" information. My hypothetical version of the process *assumes/predicts* that my students will bring certain reading strategies with them, which this assignment will challenge. And that challenge will *offer a rationale* for us to work on new strategies for reading with a rhetorical purpose and for transforming information as a writer rather than merely "telling" it. However, *as I envision this process playing itself out*, I begin to see a small dark cloud of trouble forming—a prediction that my fine instructions and insightful feedback alone will be inadequate as students try this new task. At this point in the unfolding scenario, I decide to introduce the practice of collaborative planning in my class, so each writer can develop his or her plan with a supportive partner. I do this *because I predict* that I will need to scaffold this new process of both transforming information and applying "authorities." In the process, as I imagine it, students will need to talk over what it means to "apply a reading," to test *their* theory of the task in a planning session where they can talk out their interpretation and where they might bump up against someone else's image. And in the back of my mind, I hope (predict) that collaborating on this "shared problem" will, in turn, defuse the threat of trying a new strategy and motivate a desire to move beyond the comfortable strategies of banking and knowledge telling.

As a teacher, starting to run this complex scenario through my mind, I am spinning out a model of my students—the assumptions, habits, and strategies they bring—predicting a dynamic interaction between these students, the task, the ethos of the course, and other students, and then projecting the cognitive process and intellectual stance I hope to teach and support. Even though the class I eventually teach will also be shaped by material realities outside my control (e.g., class size), I have a strong hypothesis about the shape of this event and the ways my interventions might affect it. And yet, even here in the safety of syllabus writing, I know my theory is only that—a strong working hypothesis that the resistant, empirical reality of teaching will rewrite.

An Educator's Situated Theory

What is this construction that I am dignifying with the name "theory"? Despite the hard knocks and radical revision that knowledge of this sort is sure to take, it is not a slender or speculative construction. Though based on practical experience, it is not the inevitable product of mere hours in the saddle. Rather, it is an intentionally created representation that is firmly situated in the experience of teaching— it is based on specific scenarios that come to mind as the teacher plans the class, on swift vignettes of talks with last year's students, on an image of previous papers, on a diagnosis of the strategies and as- sumptions that produced them, on the evidence of past success (or failure), on students' reflections, and on the teacher's interpretation of what all of those meant. A situated theory is not a repository of lore, but a new construction, a scenario of possibility that in being articulated, even privately, can be tested against what comes next.

A qualification: This is not a pollyanna view of teaching. I do not suggest that anytime we plan a class we become paragons of virtue and intellect engaged in such theory building. In fact, it is only too easy for prevailing ideology, unexamined assumptions, ossified theories, and business-as-usual attitudes to take over and dictate a fine, familiar curriculum. It is only too easy to "cover" topics. However, the process I have tried to sketch exists. We might choose to call it an instance of praxis, of reflective action, or an example of an expert teacher's problem-solving process. That might be accurate, but it would also be inadequate in that it glosses over the fact that the thinking to which I refer is, in large part, an act of theory building. That is, it is *the construction of a coherent explanatory account that rests on critical assumptions and generates essential predictions—a self-conscious interpretation designed both to guide action and to be tested by the actions it produces.*

To call such a plan a theory may seem a striking departure from the formal or highly abstract statements we often associate with the term. So, let me explain the context for this argument and why I think it is worth making. For the last four years, I have been part of a group of high school and college teachers in the Making Thinking Visible Project. We have been using collaborative planning in our classrooms, both as an instructional technique and as a way to gain insight into the thinking of our students and ourselves. As a classroom inquiry group, we have focused our monthly seminars on the questions we were framing and even more on the observations and discoveries collaborative planning had allowed us to make about our students. As these observations became articulated in monthly, informal discovery memos, it became clear that this collaborative experience was fostering the creation of a distinctive kind of "situated theory," which differed from both the lore of teaching and the abstract discourse of formal research or theory. By way of a preface to this book, which is a fruit of that project, I would like to explore the nature of these situated theories and the distinctive way in which they appear to connect theory and practice.

The Knowledge Teachers Create: A Controversy

What sort of knowledge do teachers create? Louise Phelps (1991) notes that in defining practitioner knowledge as "lore," North offered little room for critical or inventive thought; Phelps and the other writers we will look at set out to map the relationship between teaching and capital "T" Theory in broader terms. In *Composition as a Human Science,* Phelps argues that teachers play a critical role in the development of theory in two ways. The insistent skepticism and objection of many teachers to "theory" force composition scholars to defend the value of their theories in the face of "practical" questions and to examine assumptions that privilege theory over practice (Phelps, 1988, p. 207). More important, she says, the reflective thinking of teachers is a source of "practical wisdom" (Aristotle's notion of *phronesis* by way of Gadamer). It is a form of reasoning triggered by a concrete situation and a dialectic use of knowledge directed toward making judgments about a course of action. Practical wisdom is a response to the tension between the general rule and the particular instance (p. 216). In experimenting with Theory, Phelps says that teachers' actions are a process of evaluating and validating or revalidating Theory (p. 235). Her account of practical wisdom replaces the polarized options of either accepting or rejecting theory with a dialogic engagement that combines critical judgment with constructive appropriation or affirming use of theory (p. 220).

However, a later paper notes that this focus on the "process of appropriating others' theories neglects the more independent roles that teachers play as thinkers and inquirers in their own right" (Phelps, 1991, p. 865). On the basis of her own writing program experience, she adds an important new role for teachers, one in which, as members of an effective practitioner community, they interact face-to-face on the development of a curriculum. Struck by the impact of collaborative reflection, she wonders aloud if these theories of practice can even "arise or speak deeply to teachers except in the context of participation" (p. 867).

The practical wisdom teachers create depends on reflection. Phelps's account draws on a continuum Schon has called the "ladder of reflection" that starts with unreflective *knowing-in-action* which, like North's "lore," is rarely self-critical and preoccupied with "what works." At the other end of this ladder is the *reflection-on-action* that leads to formal inquiry and metatheory. In the middle is a process that Schon calls *reflection-in-action*, which is both "experimental and highly responsive to the 'back-talk' of the situation," leading teachers into testing alternative "moves" and hypotheses (p. 872). Schon (1987), however, identifies this process strongly with "artistry" in which reflection is bonded to performance moments of in-process insight and problem solving—and to a process that resists articulation, examination, or discussion. It would seem, then, that the sustained sequence of written reflections we observe in classroom inquiry exists somewhere else on this ladder, closer to formal theory.

However, a ladder of more or less reflectivity may not give us a really substantive portrait of the different kinds of knowledge teachers actually construct in different situations. Zeichner and Liston (1990), members of the National Center for Research on Teacher Education, criticize the popular work of Schon for its generic approach to reflection:

> After we have agreed that thoughtful teachers who reflect on and in action are more desirable than thoughtless teachers who are ruled by tradition, authority and circumstance, there are still many unanswered questions. . . . [Schon and others have little] to say about what it is that teachers ought to be reflecting about, the kinds of criteria which should come into play during the process (e.g., technical or moral), the degree to which teachers' reflections should incorporate a critique of the institutional contexts in which they work. . . . In some extreme cases, the reader is given the impression that as long as teachers reflect about something, in some manner, whatever they decide to do is okay, since they have "reflected" about it. . . . We do not think it makes much sense to attempt to promote or assess reflective practice in general without establishing some clear priorities for the reflections that emerge out of a reasoned educational and social philosophy. (p. 24)

The situated theory building that we observed at times in the Making Thinking Visible Project appears to be reflective, collaborative, and goal-oriented like the effort of Phelps's curriculum developers. However, it differs from Phelps's account in some other important regards. These differences, I believe, warrant a closer look at this process of knowledge construction in the hope that we can add another possibility to Phelps's "geography" of teachers' knowledge and Schon's "ladder" of reflection.

The term "situated theory" calls up aspects of "situated cognition" (Collins, Brown, & Newman, 1989), "teacher's self-reflection" (Kagan, 1990), and "grounded theory" (Spradley, 1980)—concepts used to describe acts of knowledge making by students, teachers, and researchers. Like Giroux's (1988) vision of teachers as "transformative intellectuals," it presumes a theory maker who links reflection and action. But perhaps we should also consider what this process is not: Situated theory is not a simple statement of belief, a body of comfortable generalizations, or the sort of intriguing speculations we can all generate about students. It is not reducible to the contents of a "teacher-research" essay, even if such an essay springs from this process (Goswami & Stillman, 1987; Mohr & McLean, 1987). Nor are we referring to the underdefined notion of "teachers' lore" or the vaguely honorific category of tacit, unarticulable intuitions known as "practitioner knowledge," since I believe these two categories set up invidious and often inaccurate distinctions between theory and practice (North, 1987; Schon, 1987).

Concepts like these are part of a genuine effort to understand (and value) what teachers know. Yet, as one educator asks, "How can we gain entry into what teachers know if such knowledge is seen as idiosyncratic, tacit, or intuitive?" (Freeman, 1991, p. 439). Shulman takes a stronger stance: "While tacit knowledge may be characteristic of many things that teachers do, our obligation as teacher educators must be to make the tacit explicit" (Schulman, cited in Freeman, 1991, p. 439). Many educators see reflection as a way to bridge theory and practice, especially when it is embedded in a situation that supports experimentation (Calderhead, 1991). Watson, however, makes a stronger claim from rhetoric for the value of articulated reflections: "Our writing improves our learning; it obliges us to reflect on what we are learning, and it invites us to reflect on how we are learning it" (Watson, 1991, p. 133).

Some Features of a Situated Theory

In short, to understand the unique contribution that a situated theory can make to education, we need to distinguish this way of representing "what teachers know" from both formal theory (i.e., a broadly inclusive, abstract philosophical or scientific statement of rules and general principles) and everyday claims (i.e., simple maxims, tacit patterns of belief, and the unexamined statements of presumption or causal speculation we often preface with the words, "Well, my theory is that . . .").

The situated educator's theory to which I would draw your attention is recognizable by a set of features.[1] It is, first of all, a *construction:* a complex and elaborated scenario, a series of "if–then" images, a network of expectations about what students in this class/ in this situation will bring, and predictions about what might be produced by alternative moves on the part of teacher or student. This conceptual construct—which is made, not found—functions as an intricate web of hypotheses and contingent predictions about the course of learning and teaching—an integrated explanatory account. And because this understanding is articulable rather than tacit, it is more fully subject to the test of the classroom and the accounts of others.

Second, this construction is an *informed prediction,* grounded in both research and observation. Unlike "lore," which is sometimes set up as the practitioner's alternative to research, situated theory making engages in an energetic dialogue with prior research. At the same time, it is driven by its own agenda to generate, test, and refine its predictive hypotheses about the course of teaching and learning for individual students. It feeds on careful, question-driven observation.

A field guide for recognizing an educator's situated theory when we see it would look for the following:

- a problem-driven construction—a scenario of teaching and learning that functions as a working hypothesis and set of situated predictions
- an account with significant explanatory power to provide a rationale and guide for decision making
- an articulated understanding that is not only open to rival hypotheses and disproof, but that invites its own transformation
- an informed construction shaped in a dialogue with prior research, which not only validates or resists research, but builds on, appropriates, and transforms the insights of research into its own practice
- an observation-based account that grows out of planful, question-driven observation (of an in-the-act process or a record of that process)
- a reflective account that steps back to draw inferences about its own actions and observations

Let us be clear: Some of the situated theories teachers build will be far more coherent, complex, and open to interrogation than those of other teachers (or the same teacher in a different situation). Like any predictive scenario, the quality of such accounts will reflect the knowledge that we as teachers bring to the situation in question and our engagement in this demanding constructive process. However, I would like to suggest that this form of knowledge making is not only important, but a form of inquiry that is worth understanding in its own right.

A Meeting Ground for Observation and Research

We think this kind of inquiry goes on in many settings, in many collaborative teacher groups. What was interesting about the Making Thinking Visible Project was the way it created a context in which at least a part of this process of theory building became more public and shared. An end-of-term discovery memo by Jean Aston, for instance, traces her attempt to interpret a change in LaRhonda, a woman in her community college class. LaRhonda had been coming to her planning sessions "with no more than a few phrases written on a sheet of tablet paper. What triggered the change" was the copy of other students' notes that Jean distributed to the class:

> At the end of the class, LaRhonda stopped to tell me how excited she was to see Ann's "head on paper" as she phrased it. She told me she had not understood what I really meant about coming with plans until she saw the notes of Ann and others. As she said, "We can really think things out ahead of time."

Jean showed us the page of notes covered with arrows, boxes, and ideas LaRhonda brought for her next planning session and pointed out the way certain notes LaRhonda wrote to herself (e.g., to develop a thesis, to compare and contrast, to show how and why) were repeated on different parts of the sheet.

> When I asked her why, she told me that the idea of taking assignments apart was new to her and that the repetition in her notes was a way to help her remember the various tasks she needed to address. This redundancy was a form of control. . . . Her reminder list seemed to be a way of asserting conscious control over writing problems that she was not conscious of in prior papers.

Jean Aston is a gifted and experienced writing teacher, but building a more grounded theory, a more insightful hypothesis about the experience and needs of students like LaRhonda is not easy.

> Watching her development has made me all the more conscious of how little I really know and maybe we know as a profession about the development of novice writers who, like the students described here, are adults from working-class backgrounds. We can describe what they don't know in relationship to expert writers, but the transformation is still very sketchy to me, *which is why this work continues to hold my attention* [italics added].

The Making Thinking Visible Project brought together a group of research-sensitive teachers from high schools, community colleges, colleges, universities, and the community who were committed to a cooperative inquiry into collaborative planning as both a teaching practice and a way to learn about our students. Out of this experience came two insights into how teachers construct such theories:

- When teachers engage in a dialogue with prior research, they engage in an interpretive act; that is, they *adapt and transform the observations from research in order to build their own situated theories.* (In this case, that means adapting and transforming not only the practice of collaborative planning but the principles and hypotheses with which the project started.)

■ And at the same time, when teachers engage in a process of observation-based theory building, they engage in another interpretive act that *uses observation to test and transform their own theories.*

Finding this generative place to stand, this place where prior research and theory are balanced with close observation, is not always easy. As our experience confirmed, one must confront deep-seated tensions between teaching and research as well as the power relations in academia that narrow the definition of theory and restrict theory making to the practice of an elite. However, at its best moments, this balancing act leads to a cycle of informed, creative thinking about teaching, followed by testing, and then reformulating hypotheses and practice. Moreover, I will argue, situated theories are able to do what current published theory often fails to do: Go beyond simple dichotomies that oppose social and cognitive practices and construct images of cognition in context. Let me offer a context for this book and the papers, discovery memos, and reflections you will read by raising some of the issues that surround this process of classroom inquiry and situated theory building.

Situated Theories and Research

What is the role of research in teaching? The educator's theory building I wish to describe is caught up in a continuing dialogue with research, with both formal, systematic studies and the informal but deliberate inquiry we conduct ·as teachers. "Dialogue" implies an interchange among different ways of knowing. My own experience illustrates how classroom inquiry can lead to formal research (with its more abstract theoretical claims) and how both can contribute to the situated theory making sketched at the beginning of this chapter. In that situation, the reading-to-write assignment and the cluster of expectations/predictions surrounding it came out of an extended conversation with research, which prompted the question: How can I help students to look at their own writing/thinking process, to see it for themselves as researchers have the opportunity to see it? For two years I had been experimenting with ways to let students observe and reflect on their own thinking. Those classes surprised us all (students and teacher) when we began to hear the dramatically different ways students were approaching a common reading-to-write assignment and when we began to discover what students (and their teacher) could learn when they reflected on short think-aloud tapes of their own planning and writing process.

This glimmer of insight (and a workable method of inquiry) led to more questions about these differences and to a formal research project investigating the reading-to-write processes of a larger group of college freshmen—a study using "dorm room protocols," interviews, self-analysis sheets, and texts to seek patterns behind this process. Formal studies have "results"; this one showed us how students were, in fact, building their own representation of the task, influenced in many ways by their prior experience in school, their assumptions about writing, and their reading of their current context and class (Flower et al., 1990). Students' "theories" of what a college-level reading-to-write task called for influenced what they wrote (leading some students to careful summary, for instance, others to inclusive synthesis, and still others, to selective interpretation). These representations differed in significant ways not only from one another, but, in many cases, from their instructor's image as well. Moreover, there was little indication that students realized their own agency—that their representation of the task was a thing they constructed, that their representation had a history and assumptions behind it, or that there were other live options and different choices being made by the student next to them in class. Finally, this study showed that when students became aware of their own decisions and options, many could, in fact, do different, "more sophisticated" versions of the task.

Research of this sort, which grows out of teaching and offers a close analysis of what students are doing in a specific context (e.g., a reading-to-write task in a freshman course), would appear to enter into an easy dialogue with teachers' theory building. However, the theory of task representation developed in a study like this does not replace or even dictate the teacher's working theory, which must operate at a different level of abstraction. The specific ways students behaved in that formal study do not generalize to all students (and were not intended to). In fact, the formal theory of task representation that emerged from the reading-to-write project argues that these representations are something writers construct in response to a rhetorical, social, and cultural context. Therefore, the patterns that were typical in one study/setting may not be typical for other groups in other settings, even though the principle of task representation does generalize. For the same reason, the "results" of successful teaching experiments cannot offer reliable directives for how to teach one's own students, even if they illustrate some powerful principles at work. In short, the observations, results, and theories that emerge from research can indeed contribute to informed, critically aware teaching— but they do so as an input into the teacher's own adaptive planning. Research enters into the teacher's theory building as a voice in the discussion. It challenges comfortable assumptions. It functions as a hypothesis or an image of possibilities that must be transformed into a new image of action.

The relationship between my own reading-to-write research and the reading-to-write assignment was, for me, a compelling case in point. Here was a body of research with which I was on intimate terms, which had documented a lot about my students, from the insightful strategies of "expert students" to some of the problematic assumptions and conflicts these freshmen faced moving from high school to college. But what was I to do with this news? Give a lecture on it? Make a handout? Obviously not. How do you make such insights vivid, motivating, and usable to a student? How do you locate such practices within the pulse of a student's own academic culture and writing process? It is the teacher's theory of instruction—a contextualized theory molded around the contours of the present class—that must translate both descriptive theory and the results of educational experiments into a theory of present practice.

This teacherly dialogue with research draws attention to the extended constructive process that is required to create a dynamic, predictive model of learning in this setting. Attempting to use one's own formal research only makes the distinction between these different forms of knowledge more vivid. Switching from researcher to teacher is one of those unremarked, extraordinary sea changes that punctuate the everyday life of teaching. One's published claims are suddenly no more than a starting point; the translation to action may resist one's best efforts. Moreover, the cognitive and social scenario finally envisioned in a teaching theory comes with no guarantees. As chapter 3 will suggest, the collaborative planning practice we describe in this book had a long and slow gestation, emerging out of perhaps ten years of formal research and efforts to teach planning. Yet every time teachers use it, it is still a theory in the making, a hypothesis about what student writers know, need to know, and might learn. The old distinctions between theory and practice simply do not hold. To use research well is to build an interpretive situated theory of practice.

Tensions in the Conversation

In valuing the empirical evidence of the classroom, teaching and research have much in common. However, the discourse of research is sometimes the source of misunderstandings about what research is saying in the dialogue with teaching—and what it cannot say. In talking about its observations, the language of research sets great store by concepts such as "reliability" and "validity." Within the discourse of research, these concepts are not abstractions but are, in fact, procedures that the research community insists on as a way to test evidence and weed out claims or analyses that can not be replicated by someone else (that are not reliable) or that do not measure or describe what they purport to be measuring (that are not valid). Within the research community, "results"—that troublesome concept that conjures up images of the scientific elite in white coats promoting certainties about pain relievers—are not certainties at all; rather, they are hypotheses supported by evidence. To report a result is to make a probabilistic argument supported by (stronger or weaker) evidence that is still and always subject to disproof (Flower, 1989).

Some humanists who are skeptical of such "certainties" continue to see them under the bed and misread this language of results or the concerns for reliability and validity. They view results as implicit claims that the observations reported are assumed to be reliable and valid for everyone else, for all settings. And clearly the experimental claims made in the hard sciences and the historical ethos of science offer a basis for such misreading. But the ethos for many educational and cognitive researchers centers on building convincing arguments from evidence—their stance is openly exploratory and committed to rival hypotheses, their goal is to discover more general patterns within particular contexts. Notice how this argument cuts two ways: Once we recognize that research is a way to build strong but conditional hypotheses—not universal truths—we can no longer posit uncritically "research has shown" as a sufficient justification for a given teaching practice.

The issue is not what research tells us, but how we as teachers read and use it, recognizing it to be an argument based on evidence. The careful investigation of even a single group of students can be a gold mine of insight: It may open up new images of what students are doing, why they do that, what the context offers or imposes, and how different teaching practices influence learning. A careful study can also force us to rethink some of our comfortable assumptions or see things we had happily ignored for years. And most of all, it can offer us strong hypotheses that help shape our models of our own students.

Another obstacle to a fruitful dialogue among research, theory, and practice is more clearly a political one. As a profession, we have restricted theory building to a few privileged places, associated with a certain kind of publication rather than a certain kind of thinking. In educational research, theory is identified with the cutting-edge research that has the luxury of sustained inquiry; of piloting, replicating, and carefully analyzing a question in a cumulative sequence of studies. In contemporary literary studies in English, theory making has become identified with the work of a group of continental writers, which a second group of literary theorists then explicates, extends, and debates. In rhetoric and composition, theory is largely identified with classical and contemporary scholars who have proposed systematic theories of rhetoric or discourse, or with writers applying literary theory and its social critique to composition. In all these cases, theory building as an intellectual act is identified with a certain power structure in the discipline, with people who publish, who receive grant money, or who are so difficult to read and interpret that they must be explicated to the rest of us by a community of intermediate theorists.

But theory building as a serious intellectual enterprise goes on in other parts of education. Moreover, except for the genuinely innovative ideas that grip the imagination of the profession, much of the formal discussion of theory tends to exist within a painfully limited sphere of influence. Theorists publish in small-circulation journals, talking to a circle of friends and enemies, or they come before a larger readership, many of whom will only skim the article. I do not want to dismiss the potential value of such work at all. (I, too, have written theoretical arguments that I continue to believe are significant, but which I am equally certain have been skimmed by readers not in that particular conversation.) What I want to argue is that the other theory building that goes on in the conduct of teaching is not only an equally significant, equally demanding intellectual act, it probably has a much wider sphere of palpable influence than much of the theorizing done by the academic establishment. It leads to the real action of teaching; it leads to the reshaping of current practice. For good or for ill, it makes a difference.

For significant theory building to occur in teaching, it must overcome another obstacle, which is the complacency that affects any practice—the complacency of the recycled syllabus supported by the tendency to romanticize knowledge based on experience. It is possible to operate for years with comfortable, conventional, hackneyed images of one's students and with firmly held "theories" about how they think and learn, serenely untainted by careful observation or rival hypotheses. As others have argued, the self-awareness of "strategic teaching" is strongly associated with the effortful professionalism of teachers (Jones, Palincsar, Ogle, & Carr, 1987). It is easy to opt out of the dialogue with other research that might extend or even challenge one's theories. Speculation and assertion come naturally. Theory building is a more demanding enterprise.

Building on Research

The Making Thinking Visible Project brought some of the possibilities and the tensions of theory building into focus. It was soon clear that formal research and theory could be stimulating partners in the attempt to build strong instructional hypotheses. However, the need to adapt and transform that research was even clearer. It began with adapting the practice of collaborative planning itself (developed with college freshmen) to fit the diverse abilities found in a high school classroom or the ethos of practicality in a junior-level college business course. For Leonard Donaldson, collaborative planning had to fit the critical thinking goals (and high school curriculum) of his social studies class. In his translation of the practice, students used their experience as purposeful, rhetorical planners and writers to then read primary source texts—to uncover the rhetorical intentions behind historical documents such as the *Communist Manifesto*. Down the hall, Jane Zachary Gargaro used collaborative planning to help her high school students mine literary texts for techniques such as imagery and dialogue and then use them in their own autobiographies.

It is hardly surprising, of course, to see teachers adapt a new teaching practice to their own goals or students—even though that is in itself an important kind of educational experiment. However, building a situated theory in this project also meant questioning and transforming some of the central insights about planning and collaboration with which we started.

For example, it was apparent from our first experience with students at Pittsburgh's Creative and Performing Arts High School that collaboration in principle and in practice are two different things. As David Wallace shows (see his project paper in section 1), some students embrace collaborative planning as an extension of the way they already write, depending on a supportive network of friends and family. But for some students, collaborative planning may come in conflict with some deeply held notions about writing as an intensely personal, private, and expressive act. Collaboration may contradict their own history of success going it alone on short essay assignments that rewarded a distinctive style. For some teachers, this new practice challenges the assumption that planning stifles individual creativity, and it may trigger fears that collaboration will lead students to borrow (steal) ideas (and violate the grading system).

It was in the face of discoveries like this that each of us had to develop a "theory of teaching collaborative planning" that could adapt the powerful principles sketched in our research to the equally powerful schemas and assumptions we and our students were bringing to writing. And as Linda Norris's project paper shows (section 4), the same process happens in teacher education—the way future teachers understand and use new practices is strongly shaped by their own experience as writers. Teacher education courses that "hand out" new ways of teaching writing as a theoretical practice, without immersing would-be teachers in an experience that transforms their own assumptions, are probably doomed to failure. In both these cases, the theory of collaborative planning had to be complemented by an equally sophisticated, teacher-generated theory of instruction that anticipated the chemistry of new ideas and old practices.

Building on Observation

The situated theories that teachers develop not only adapt and transform research, they have the power to extend and transform themselves. That is because the "what if" scenarios that constitute a teacher's plan are shaped not only by intuitions, assumptions, and suggestions from research but by close observation. By that I mean close, analytical observation of students in acts of talking, thinking, composing, and in the process of planning, drafting, evaluating, revising—especially if these acts are in some way recorded and open to later reflection. Speaking more generally, teachers are engaged in a form of *observation-based theory building* when they use systematic observation to generate hypotheses (in the form of scenarios about the process of teaching and learning) and to examine and test those expectations in teaching (Flower, 1989). Although there are many ways to create theory, observation-based theory building has a particular value for teaching: It helps us build grounded theories that reflect the experience of at least one group of real students (Spradley, 1980). And instead of polarizing or separating the acts of thinking, feeling, and social interaction that make up writing, observation-based theory stands right at their point of intersection. It allows us to see cognition in context and to build theories of interaction and negotiation.

Although our project was organized around the practice of teaching collaborative planning, it was named the Making Thinking Visible Project because our larger goal was to use collaborative planning as a platform for observation and reflection. Collaborative planning sessions (which students often tape) give teachers an opportunity to observe student thinking in action, to catch a glimpse of strategies, attitudes, and strengths, and to discover problems. And because these sessions spotlight rhetorical concerns and let writers verbalize their own problem-solving process, they help students come to see themselves as thinkers. As the chapters in this book suggest, the process of observation-based theory building we observed had three important effects: It made our hypotheses open to testing, open to reflection, and open to consideration by students as well as teachers.

Open to testing. One of the most inescapable features of a teacher's situated theory building is that (more than other sorts of theory) it is subject to the rigorous tests of the classroom. Teachers cannot afford to indulge in armchair theorizing or in hypotheses too complex, abstruse, or fragile to withstand the crucible of a classroom. Situated theories must exist in a context that continually tests and refines or attempts to dismantle them. This is not to say that as teachers we always know when our theories fail or that it is not possible to ignore at times the way "reality butts in." But in articulating expectations, we make it possible to compare the dream of the syllabus maker with the empirical evidence of students' comments, writing, problems, and growth. *Situated theory building is an extended process that tests and transforms its descriptive hypotheses over the course of teaching.* However, it is careful observation that makes this process possible.

In this group, one of the first observations to be made by teachers and students alike was that a good supporter makes a large difference in what a writer is able to do, but being a good supporter requires more than a friendly attitude. College students who asked roommates to fill in as partners came back to complain that their friend turned into an advice giver rather than an informed supporter. Teachers began to see how they needed to teach careful listening and to scaffold this process for both partners. As we observed the different roles supporters were taking, the skills they needed, and the effects that support had on writers, a new view of how to support this relationship grew, which is documented by Rebecca Burnett in chapter 5 and by Theresa Marshall and Marlene Bowen's discovery memos (see section 2).

Open to reflection. Acts of collaboration and insight, moments of problem solving that we try to support, that we want students to recognize in themselves and others, fly by like shadows. There are few things more difficult than recalling the swift passage of one's own thought. The act of informally structured collaboration helped put some of that thinking on the table: Asking students to write reflections about their own experience as collaborators, planners, and writers created a body of valued, common knowledge. But the real insights came when teachers and students had the opportunity to replay the experience on tape or to talk about selected transcripts. Although tape recorders make everyone nervous initially and undoubtedly affect some of what is said (even in dorm room sessions), we found high school students becoming disappointed when they could not tape a session, and teachers seeing important issues crystalized in small segments of a transcript that they could use with their class. As Michael Benedict describes it (section 4), when collaborative sessions go beyond question-asking to genuine dialogue, they often open up a "window" to concerns beyond the immediate topic of discussion. Others, however, function more like a "mirror," creating a space for reflection and reconsideration that students use to think over who they are, both as writers and as people.

Leslie Evans's discovery memo (section 1) documents one of those small but transformative moments in which a young woman, unsure of her own ideas and fearful of asserting herself with others, reflects on a small segment of her own planning tape. Though the partner dominates the discussion, with Leslie's subtle prompting, the young woman begins to find in the dialogue evidence of her own creative and independent (if tentatively stated) thinking.

Open to students and teachers. Leslie Evans's memo documents a teacher's reflection (which we hope helped that young woman revise some hypotheses about herself as a writer). In other cases, this process of observation and reflection was clearly shared by teachers and students in a way that transformed the working theories of both. Jean Aston's inquiry (section 3) began with a clear-cut, teacher-generated question about the differences between the "rigid" and "adaptable" planners she had seen in the previous term. It was a good question, but the inquiry took a whole new direction when she began to ask why so many students in her community college basic writing class were resisting both the process of collaboration and the premise on which it was based—that writing is a purposeful act, in which one adapts knowledge to his or her own uses. Her paper traces a collaborative inquiry with her students into their own assumptions about education as "banking"—dictated, it turned out, by their own prior experiences in the "non-academic" track of high school. In recording the anger and the dismay that came with the discovery of what they had been socialized to do, Jean shows how some students came to grips with this legacy, transforming not only images of themselves but, as her tapes showed, their own practice as planners.

Observation, based on the independent record of a tape or transcript, is a great leveler. It makes reflection both possible and the prerogative of students as well as teachers. Because collaborative sessions are under the writers' control, students find themselves in an unusual position: They are the authority on their own thinking. Their reflections show this new control as they begin to articulate, question, and in some cases transform, their own "working theories" about writing.

This chapter started with some strong claims about the enterprise of teaching and the ways research and observation can contribute to building and transforming educators' situated theories. This book is both a tribute to and an inquiry into that process. The story of the Making Thinking Visible Project joins a growing body of work calling attention to the intellectual activity of teaching, to teacher research, to strategic teaching, to the potency of collaborative inquiry, and to the role critical awareness, close observation, and reflection can play in education (Goswami & Stillman, 1987; Jones et al., 1987; Schecter & Ramirez, 1991). The special contribution of this book is to show one distinctive path that process can take and to document the results of a collaborative inquiry into the act of collaborative planning—a writing and teaching activity with roots in cognitive and contextual research.

United by a common interest—and a curiosity about our differences—we ended up building for each other a richly contextualized image of collaboration and planning that somehow accommodated those differences. At the same time, this group practiced the collaborative practice we preached, using a series of monthly discovery memos to push our own inquiries forward and document what we were seeing. On one level, then, this book is about a project to make thinking more visible for our students by teaching collaborative planning and reflection. But on another, even more important level, it is a portrait of the process of inquiry that crosses the apparent boundaries of research and teaching as well as high school and college, suburban and inner-city, school and community teaching. It is the thinking of teachers as well as students that this collaboration helped to make apparent.

The chapters that follow in part I, Frameworks for Discovery, build that framework for the rest of the book, with a thumbnail history of the project, some snapshots of the research and theory on which we were building, and an introduction to the principles and practice of collaborative planning and supporting. Part II, Observations across Contexts, which consists of five sections, presents some of the observations that came out of the project. Some take the form of project papers, reporting in-depth observational studies in which the writer took a sustained, systematic look at a particular setting or event. But most reflect what we saw as the trademark and accomplishments of this project—the genre of the discovery memo. For members of the Making Thinking Visible Project, this monthly memo was the reflective act that pushed each of us to translate observations to insight; it was also the basis for a dialogue with three or four other teachers or the group as a whole. Memos often led to written response; many lived on in memory of the group as touchstone observations. And many became the basis for a more sustained inquiry. However, as we soon came to see, the real power of a discovery memo lay in the way it differed from the longer papers included above. Focused on critical incidents in the life of a class, these memos start with questions and telling observations: They crystalize an experience and, in doing so, they make it open to reflection. The memo then becomes the basis for dialogue, not just about this observation, but about what it reveals about collaboration, planning, or learning. The memo elicits both shared experiences and rival hypotheses about what this "telling event" can, in fact, tell us.

Because the discovery memo became a text to talk from, it is both a written and oral genre, an individual and a collaborative act. In presenting some of the memos from these four years (edited to supply missing contexts), we have tried to include some sense of this context and to represent the diversity of issues they raise. For some, the very process of engaging in this inquiry was as intriguing as it was problematic. Others record the sequence of question, hypothesis, and observation: A September memo ponders some alternative ways to set up collaborative partnerships, and a November memo reflects some surprising observations of what happened. Other memos are out and out sites of struggle—teachers posing possibilities, reviewing options and attitudes. Still others tell us about students, what they did or what they discovered. Although we often found it helpful to compare teaching techniques across our differences in student age and context, it was these vignettes of students' thinking, collaborating, or reflecting that elicited the greatest sense of shared discovery. In many ways, the essence of this inquiry is in these memos which, in making thinking a little more visible, helped dissolve the boundaries among observational research, theory making, and teaching, and among high school, college, and community educators.

Note

1. Although I do not mean necessarily to limit the notion of "situated theory" to the features described here, I want to be explicit about the kind of thinking that this situation appeared to foster.

2 Creating a Context for Collaboration: A Thumbnail History of the Making Thinking Visible Project

Linda Norris
Indiana University of Pennsylvania
Indiana, Pennsylvania

Linda Flower
Carnegie Mellon University
Pittsburgh, Pennsylvania

To see yourself as a thinker is an important part of being one. To see yourself as a writer who steps back to reflect, as a problem solver who can see options, as a student who can take control of meaning making, and as a teacher who can combine inquiry with teaching is not just an attitude. It is the potent knowledge that one's own flow of talk and thought—that rapid, tumbling, sometimes surprising, sometimes confusing flow of thought—is also the rapid and generative creation of plans, goals, strategies, and decisions. A "making thinking visible" project of the sort we carried out in our own classrooms is a teaching project dedicated to making the grand mystery of thought even more wonderful by being less mystifying and more visible.

In the Making Thinking Visible Project, we used *collaborative planning* as a way to teach writing and as a platform for observation and reflection by both students and teachers. Listening to students think aloud with the help of a supporter opened up a window on the processes of planning and collaboration, giving us all new insight into writers' needs, strengths, strategies, and assumptions. This observation, in turn, opened up the door to *reflection*—to the sets of student reflections, monthly discovery memos, collaborative sessions, presentations, case book papers, dissertations, and formal studies that stand behind this book.

Grounding this inquiry on collaborative planning allowed us, as a group, not only to ask some shared questions (about planning, thinking, and collaboration), but also to create diverse answers that responded to our individual needs as educators. There was a synergy in this shared concern/independent inquiry that let us collaborate across the boundaries that often separate high school and college, teachers and researchers, school and community. In an insightful paper on interaction among school and college writing teachers, Schultz, Laine, and Savage (1988) claim that although high school and college English teachers have a long history of trying to work together, college teachers have attempted to dominate their colleagues in the schools and have ignored the fact that high schools and colleges are two cultures with different beliefs and different agendas. They claim that three beliefs prevent successful collaboration: (1) high schools and colleges exist in a hierarchical relationship with each other; (2) knowledge is created at the advanced levels of the educational system and is then applied or carried out at lower levels; and (3) high schools and colleges have language and discursive practices that are mutually exclusive, that is, they do not speak the same language (pp. 147–149).

They note further problems: It is difficult for school and university teachers to find time to get together; because universities contribute financial backing, the high schools are less invested in programs and are reluctant to criticize them; and, finally, the professional rewards for high school writing teachers (such as salary increases, department headship, and advanced placement classes) are not based on participation in collaborative projects.

We wanted to form a project group that celebrated the fact that school teachers and university researchers have different cultures, beliefs, and agendas; when we initiate programs that encourage school and university writing teachers to work together, we have to recognize these differences up front. But these differences do not mean that we do not or cannot understand each other, and they are not necessarily deterrents to the success of collaborative projects between schools and universities. On the contrary, we believe that when high school and college writing teachers engage in a partnership in which they create their own projects and where their diverse cultures are recognized, discussed, and challenged, all teachers involved can experience a new level of professional growth and awareness. The most meaningful way to explain how our project made this kind of collaboration possible is to share some of the products of this collaborative effort.

We, the authors of these papers, speak from our experiences with high school students from the inner city, from computer-rich suburban classes in a community north of Pittsburgh, from the struggling ex-steel towns on Pittsburgh's south side. We speak from experience with college freshmen and future teachers; with women going to community college while educating and nurturing their own children; with business students eager to engage the workplace; with teenagers coming to see themselves as thinkers, writing about teen pregnancy in a community literacy center. Across these differences we were asking: What are we trying to do as thinkers and writers? How can we add to what we already know and to what we already do? The following pages also reflect the diverse styles of writing and inquiry we shared with each other, from discovery memos to dissertations, from curriculum development for the Pittsburgh public schools to staff talks and NCTE workshops. Within this circle of observation and reflection, our differences have led to some of our most provocative questions and discussions.

In this chapter we want to sketch the history of this collaboration not only to create a context for our inquiry and to share what we learned about doing a "making thinking visible" project, but also to note some of the interesting dilemmas this collaborative process raised. We begin with how the Pittsburgh project came to be and how it grew; we reflect on the issues, problems, and achievements that made up this four-year project. We share our brief history of the workings of the project and the insights we discovered with those of you who may want to conduct your own private or collaborative "making thinking visible" project.

The History of an Idea

Like all such projects, this one has a history made up of converging stories. Chapter 3 sketches the story in terms of a line of research and a growing body of ideas that put their stamp on this project. A social history would point to the newly forged relationship between Carnegie Mellon and the University of California, Berkeley, as partners in the Center for the Study of Writing—a partnership dedicated to seeing writing as a social/cognitive process and to crossing the boundaries not only of research and practice, but also of an English department and a school of education. But the immediate catalyst was a conversation between Richard Wallace, superintendent of the Pittsburgh schools, and Linda Flower that led to an informal, "let's see what happens" experiment in looking at thinking. With the help of JoAnne Eresh, the director of writing and speaking for the Pittsburgh public schools, and an enthusiastic film crew from the media division of the Pittsburgh public schools, two groups of students (one from Carnegie Mellon and one from Pittsburgh's High School for the Creative and Performing Arts) created two student-produced videos for each other, showing and reflecting on themselves as writers and thinkers. It was in the midst of this wonderful, if rather wild-eyed, experiment that collaborative planning took its first shape in each class, both as a teaching practice and as a source of insight for teacher and student (and scriptwriter). The idea of a collaborative inquiry across institutions took shape out of conversations with Joseph Dominic of the Howard Heinz Endowment of the Pittsburgh Foundation. A four-year grant from the Howard Heinz Endowment supported our monthly seminar gatherings and allowed each teacher in the project a small budget for collecting information, making transcripts, and attending conferences to share their work with colleagues.

This thumbnail sketch emphasizes the underlying goals, the spirit of inquiry, and the degree of uncertainty with which we embarked on this adventure in 1988. We were influenced and encouraged by reviewing the work of those who had pioneered the notion of teacher as researcher (Atwell, 1982; Bissex & Bullock, 1987; Calkins, 1985; Emig, 1971; Graves, 1983; Murray, 1985; Perl & Wilson, 1986) by reading books on teacher research by Goswami and Stillman (1987) and Mohr and Mclean (1987), and by following the growing number of such projects supported by the National Writing Project, including the project at the Center for the Study of Writing at Berkeley (Schecter & Ramirez, 1992). We have also been informed by writing-across-the-curriculum consortiums such as the Bay Area Writing Project and the exciting Baltimore group conducting a naturalistic study of students in four disciplines (Walvoord & McCarthy, 1990).

Inspired by reading accounts of others' projects and by talking to teachers at local and national conferences, we began to sketch our own ideas for a workable consortium. We were particularly impressed with educators like Lucy Calkins and a community of teachers and parents who told us at an NCTE conference how they came together on a regular basis to talk intimately about what they read and how they and their children reacted to the great books they were reading. We were impressed with this notion of a community of readers and with the collegiality of talking to and learning from one another about a shared topic. We decided that we wanted to create an experience much like Sam Watson's "community of writers" (1989) and his letter exchanges with his writing classes (1991), with writing teachers exchanging discovery memos at our monthly seminars. Also, conversations with Shirley Brice Heath and Juliet Langman helped us clarify the goals for making thinking more visible in community literacy projects in nonacademic settings. In short, we wanted our project to build on the experiences of a host of exemplary teacher-research projects—projects that take as their central assumption that teaching is a way of effecting change. We agreed with Miles Myers's assessment:

> [D]eveloping a research tradition among classroom teachers is a way of changing institutional roles and shifting more of the responsibility for teaching expertise to teachers themselves. . . . Teacher research is one of the ways not only to inspire and renew teacher commitment but also to enable teachers to appreciate the complexity of their own classrooms. (1985, p. 2)

As part of this tradition, we also wanted to do some things that none of these other projects was doing. We wanted to work as a collaborative group united by an inquiry that revolved around collaborative planning, that is, around a research-based, theory-driven effort to both teach writing and highlight thinking. Such a relationship would give us the shared language and goals—the synergy—of a research team, where the discoveries of each member are relevant to the others, where diversity yields converging evidence. If it worked, we would be able to create an unusually rich portrait of an educational idea in practice. On the other hand, this project was also dedicated to celebrating our differences. We were all teachers, working in radically different contexts, with our own fish to fry. Our students had a wide variety of needs, and the kinds of "writing" we had in mind ranged from a fifth-grade Christmas play, to a research project on Marxist theory, to revising technical documentation for a solar energy unit. Within this common concern about collaboration and planning, it was necessary for all the students to shape their own questions, make their own discoveries, and find a way to make this group a relevant, productive experience for themselves.

Goals and Skepticism. When the Making Thinking Visible Project officially started in 1988, we articulated several key goals:

- To help students develop a repertoire of strategies for planning and writing

- To help students to become more reflective about their own writing process and more aware of themselves as thinkers

- To discover ways classroom inquiry by teachers and students can support teaching and learning

Just beneath these official-sounding goals, however, were a number of equally important questions and uncertainties:

- What can one really do—in the context of normal classes and the grip of a curriculum—to make thinking more visible and students more reflective? Videotapes, collaborative planning, mini-protocols, written reflections were all possibilities, but what would pass the test of the classroom?

- What makes us think that we, as a group, can cross the institutional, political, and practical boundaries that separate teachers in public schools, colleges, universities, and the community, not just to talk to each other, but to carry out a genuinely collaborative inquiry? In particular, how do we deal with the legacy of curriculum developers "using" schools and the stream of educational "experts" arriving to dictate practice?

- And how will research find a meaningful place in the already delicate balance of such a collaboration? That is, how do we avoid that political line drawn in the sand between research and practice and find ways to value one without invalidating the other? Given our commitment to shared-questions-but-independent-inquiry driven by one's own teaching, what form(s) could this inquiry take?

Setting out to answer these large questions, fourteen people from a variety of different backgrounds launched the Making Thinking Visible Project in Pittsburgh with some fruit, cheese, wine, and a common bond: We were all writing teachers curious to know about each other, interested in growing professionally, and ready to learn more about what we and our student writers were doing. During the pilot year, we got our feet wet. We met monthly to see what discoveries would come from doing collaborative planning and conducting classroom inquiry.

We all came with assumptions about what this technique might help student writers learn and do, and we came with apprehensions as well. Some of us assumed that collaboration between students was good because it gave students authority and voice; some of us thought that planning was an important part of the writing process and that more time should be spent planning writing in and out of class. However, a mixed bag of questions and problems also emerged from our discussions at the initial planning meetings. Some of us were not sure what collaborative planning would do: Would it make our classes noisy and unruly? Would it allow students to "steal" ideas from one another? Would it take "control" out of our hands? Would it put us farther behind what we had to "cover" for the year? Would our students really learn anything from it? We all questioned whether collaborative planning and conducting classroom inquiry would fit in with our schedules, our curriculum, our students, and our notions of what the teaching of writing was all about.

Finding a Structure for Inquiry

After the pilot year, we were ready to start our inquiries in earnest. The final section of this chapter provides a brief overview of the progress we made during the three main years of the project (referred to as year one, year two, and year three).

Getting Started. Our first seminar in September of year one was a two-day colloquium, where we explained, modeled, and did collaborative planning with each other. To work as a group and figure out how to teach this process in our varied classroom contexts, we found it was important to do collaborative planning ourselves. Working in pairs, we voiced our goals to each other, and we discussed the questions we wanted to answer by observing our students using this process. We tape-recorded our first attempts at being writers and supporters for each other and reflected on what happened in a large-group discussion. We helped each other formulate and focus what we wanted to study.

In year one, some of us just wanted to try collaborative planning first and see how our students responded to it; others had specific assignments they wanted to use it for, such as a brochure about the city of Pittsburgh, writing about a hero, a problem analysis, a research paper on World War II, a family narrative, or a discussion of Freire's "banking" concept of education.

The initial assumptions, questions, and misgivings we had about this undertaking began to be played out as we moved from doing collaborative planning as a project group to observing what was happening in our own classes. We began with what each of us intended to find out. Andrea Martine questioned whether her ninth graders would write more elaborate comparison papers if they had planning sessions and if they also took notes on important points during their sessions. She decided to compare these notes with the papers they wrote to see if the planning notes helped with elaboration of details. She concluded that they did. Jim Vincent wondered if it would be worth his college business students' class time to do some collaborative planning for their semester projects—brochures about Pittsburgh. Walking around the room, talking to his business writers, he observed how collaborative planning was prompting them to generate exciting things to see and do, things that he felt they would not have included had they written their brochures without consulting one another. Leslie Evans, a high school writing teacher who wondered if her students would understand what text conventions meant and if they would even consider them in their planning, listened to and later transcribed tapes of students discussing specifically how they were going to organize their papers on Conrad's *Heart of Darkness*. As it turned out, those first two years were devoted to discussions and writing about how to teach collaborative planning in our different settings and what happened when we used it with certain writing tasks to answer our specific questions.

Although initially many of us were skeptical about asking students to tape-record their collaborative planning, almost all of us decided to borrow or buy tape recorders and audiotape some of our students' planning sessions. We transcribed some of these sessions and brought excerpts to the seminars to share with one another. Some of us used the video camera the project supplied and made videotapes of students' planning sessions. We learned a great deal from these sessions: A supporter could challenge a writer whose definition of a hero did not quite match the hero she wanted to write about, and a writer could acknowledge and decide that a certain third-person perspective would give life to his personal narrative. Some students ignored suggestions from well-meaning peers or were not very well prepared to discuss their plans. Some went away with an expanded, purposeful plan for the task, while others clung to limited surface-level intentions. We witnessed how some students just go through the motions of collaborative planning, needing more guidance about how to ask good questions or how to speak with authority about their key points. Planning sessions revealed a range of emotions and attitudes: Some were quiet and engaged, others were intense and almost hostile, some revealed boredom, and others, delight. These sessions, along with the verbal and written reflections our students made on their collaborations, were the basis of how we came to "see" and understand the thinking that our students were doing about their writing.

Joining the Seminar. A large part of our motivation for inquiry, besides observing the collaborative planning that was going on in our classes, was the monthly two-hour seminar to which we each brought something we had written about using this process with our students during the preceding month. We photocopied these "discovery memos" and shared them with each other. They formed the basis for small- and large-group discussions about what was happening in our classrooms when we tried collaborative planning. (See Leslie Evans's "Transcripts as a Compass to Discovery" memo in section 1, for example.) Some of the other seminars were devoted to learning more from project members who were willing to give short presentations about topics they were studying, such as the different roles of the supporter, a computer program for doing collaborative planning, and teaching collaborative planning to remedial readers and writers.

Incorporating Reflectivity. An important feature of our monthly gatherings was practicing with one another what we were asking our student writers to do and seeing what we could learn from this. We came to recognize that reflection was an essential part of the process of making thinking visible. In the following pages you will see how our student writers, when asked to reflect on their planning sessions, gained insights into their thinking and composing processes. For a few seminar meetings, we came with reflections we had written about our own collaborative planning sessions with other people in our project. Some of us used these reflections to plan and write our papers for this book. We wrote about how planning with another teacher-researcher from the group helped us clarify or elaborate our ideas, or we wrote about whole new avenues that we would take or whole new approaches we would try after we hashed them out together. In one of her reflections, Jean Aston described how the dynamics of collaboration—the listening, questioning, and explaining—led her to build a new "bridge" among her own ideas:

> I came to the planning session with Linda [Flower] frustrated and confused. She listened carefully to my description of the class, to the questions I was raising about what I was observing about the students' learning and the relationship to the students' behaviors in collaborative planning sessions, and to my uncertainty about what and which research techniques to use to gather data. Throughout the session she raised questions and offered examples from her own research that acted in the planning session to help me to make new connections in my ideas and to make my questions more specific.

> Specifically, she helped me to bridge what I felt was a chasm between the issue from the fall class—the contrast between algorithmic and heuristic users of collaborative planning—and the issue this spring—the concepts of learning held by many of the students and the consequent problems students face in acting on the concepts and in trying to change them. In particular, one question she asked let me build the bridge: "Do students have concepts for heuristic action in planning?" . . . The bridge has helped me reframe my paper to look at the concepts the students hold and possibly change about learning and the relationship to the roles they take in collaborative planning. Now in the paper, I will be looking at collaborative planning in the context of a learning environment as defined by both classroom and student. I found myself sensing links during the planning session, but I was able to understand and make better use of Linda's questions by listening to the tapes. Time to think and reflect was important to me.

Jean's session with Linda and her replaying of their tape allowed her to solidify an issue and a direction for her writing.

In another vein, Rebecca Burnett's planning session with Leslie Evans helped Rebecca deal with two issues: that the coauthoring process that her students went through was as enlightening as the documents they wrote, and that the practitioner audience for the casebook we were writing needed to be addressed so that teachers might benefit from what Rebecca and her students discovered:

> Thinking about the session I had with Leslie reinforced the notion that I really must make the information I discuss in my discovery essay understandable and relevant to teachers. Leslie was good at gently reminding me that research is valuable by itself, but it does have other benefits our audience will find more interesting. In other words, our research should help us be better teachers so that our students learn more.

From this shared insight, Rebecca developed a new plan for her paper that brings to the fore this goal of making her findings useful to other writing teachers. She decided to provide examples of students who, in planning recommendation memos, were making the wrong rhetorical decisions, even though these decisions were based on logical reasons. The paper traces their decision-making processes through their recorded planning sessions and offers these situations as a model for other business-writing teachers:

> Now here's where my teacher role kicks in. If I had depended only on the memo the students submitted (as we usually do), I would have missed an important opportunity to catch these

students' errors and the nature of their errors. They were wrong, but they had not made thoughtless decisions; they had given their decisions a great deal of thought. What allowed me to catch this was turning to their planning tapes and retrospective reactions. Not only does this information give me important points to teach, but it encourages me to reflect on the reasons students do what they do.

Some of us used our set of discovery memos as a guide for writing the papers in this book; others conducted a more formal analysis of the data they collected. Jean Aston (see her project paper in section 3), for example, traced the development of her community college freshmen, using questionnaires and oral interviews throughout the semester. Jane Zachary Gargaro (see Aston, Norris, & Turley, 1990) used the transcriptions of high school students' planning sessions to link planning comments with what the writer included in the final draft of a narrative writing assignment. Rebecca Burnett, by following students in business communications classes at Carnegie Mellon University who were writing recommendation reports, discovered characteristics of engaged supporters (chapter 5) and the potential value of substantive conflict (see her discovery memo in part 4).

Writing to Consolidate Our Learning. At the end of year one, we prepared a Project Book to keep track of what we were learning and to explain the goals and purposes of the project along with a how-to-do-it chapter on collaborative planning for our new project members and other interested teachers. This book helped us to consolidate our techniques and materials into an introduction to collaborative planning and classroom inquiry that demonstrated how teachers could use this process with their own students for their specific writing assignments and goals.

By this time, we had also written three newsletters that contained short pieces about how different project members conducted their classroom inquiries and how they and their students responded to collaborative planning. Through our newsletter, through workshops that we conducted for National Writing Project sites, and through NCTE conference presentations, we made contact with about 1,500 university and high school educators and other colleagues, many of whom became interested in this classroom inquiry. By the end of year two, we were twenty-four teacher-researchers from Carnegie Mellon, the Pittsburgh public schools, Community College of Allegheny County, the University of Pittsburgh, Robert Morris College, a wide range of suburban junior high and high schools, and the Community Literacy

Center. The next year, we compiled our first of two casebooks, in which all project members shared the discoveries they made about the questions they had asked at the beginning of the year.[1]

Finding a Genre. For the last two years of the project our vision was to be able to share our discoveries with colleagues outside of the project, even after our demonstration was over. A new goal for the seminars was to allow time for private collaborative planning and writing workshops among project members who wanted to write something for publication that they would be able to take with them to their schools, universities, and communities at the end of the project.

Although everyone was conducting a focused classroom inquiry, and some of us were doing more formal and systematic studies, we all agreed that the genre of the academic "research report" would not speak to the range of readers we ourselves represented. In fact, we struggled with the tyranny that genre exercised in our own minds, when it set up certain formal expectations for reporting methods and making and supporting claims. Published research offered a model of discourse that did not fit our real purposes and silenced some writers when they felt they should use it. The polished, personal essay was, of course, a more familiar genre for English teachers, but it brought its own baggage, including expectations for an artfully crafted, even entertaining, literary product. In the place of perfecting a text as text, we wanted to *use* our texts the way research does to document and share observations. But beyond that, we wanted a genre designed for inquiry that could stimulate observation and reflection within the timetable of being a teacher—a genre where writing was a tool for thinking, a way of talking, and a means of getting a response, not an object to be perfected.

As the second casebook developed, beginning in year two of the project, we found ourselves experimenting with different ways of presenting our observations, from tracing the twisting path of our own thinking, to analyzing students' taped sessions and written responses, to constructing a step-by-step rendering of teaching that compared ninth-grade and community college classes. But in the end, having struggled to develop texts that seemed appropriate for a casebook, we came to a striking realization. The discovery memo, which we had been using from the beginning of the project, had grown into a powerful and flexible genre. As a statement of observations and reflections, it went directly to the heart of the matter—sharing what we saw in a way that pulled others into the discussion. It invited us to speak in our own voices, to articulate uncertainties, dilemmas,

questions, as well as conclusions and decisions. And it helped coun-
teract that subtle pull such groups feel to justify their teaching practices:
It focused attention not on what we did, but on what we discovered;
not on what we knew, but on what we were in the act of learning.
This book represents our reworking of this energizing mini-genre, as
we elaborate and extend these discovery memos just enough to bring
you, the reader, into the conversation as well.

Widening the Conversation. We felt that our inquiries into collaborative planning touched several important issues that we wanted to
acknowledge and discuss publicly in the final year of the project.
Widening the scope of the Making Thinking Visible Project, we hosted
a series of seminars that provided opportunities for teachers, students,
parents, administrators, and community activists to engage in conversations about pivotal issues that affect teaching and learning. Project
members and those we invited from our academic and community
settings participated in five different dialogues centered on a host of
issues related to teaching and learning. The issues and questions
addressed at the dialogues included the following:

Collaborative Planning and the Curriculum

What happens when collaborative planning becomes part of city
curriculum? How did those who used collaborative planning in the
city schools' curriculum find that it worked for them? How do we
adapt collaborative planning to an already existing curriculum? What
happens when the technique moves out from a project to individual
pilot teachers?

Community Literacy Projects

What are the links between planning and writing in school and the
writing and planning that students do in community literacy projects?
Is there any overlap between the literate practices of school and specific
arguments and projects, such as arguing for a van to take teenagers
to places where they can learn something important or revitalizing a
senior citizens' center?

Training Teachers in a New Technique

What happens when novice teachers are introduced to collaborative
planning? What happens when expert teachers start to work with a
new technique such as collaborative planning? Are their experiences

similar or different, and in what ways? How does collaborative planning fit in with developing a repertoire and philosophy for teaching writing?

Signs of Success in Different Contexts

What constitutes success in teaching collaborative planning with a variety of students in different contexts? In other words, how did collaborative planning work for different teachers and students in different situations?

Bridges between High School, College, and the Workplace

What are the bridges between high school and college writing? Can collaborative planning help students to cross these bridges? How? How will planning and collaboration prepare students for the workplace?

Summaries of these dialogues, along with fifteen new discovery papers, were the subjects of the second casebook, *Discoveries and Dialogues* (Norris, Brozick, & Gargaro, 1992). What we learned together in the project has helped us to grow professionally; we have gained insights into our students' thinking as writers and into our practice as writing teachers. The following pages provide detailed explanations of our discoveries in the genres that we found most suited us.

Note

1. These casebooks, as well as the project book and newsletters, are available as ERIC documents (see the collaborative planning bibliography at the end of the book).

3 Writers Planning: Snapshots from Research

Linda Flower
Carnegie Mellon University
Pittsburgh, Pennsylvania

A making thinking visible project is a classroom inquiry that combines focused observation and reflection with an assertive and generative use of prior research and theory. The desire to help writers see themselves as thinkers in a social and rhetorical context, and the decision to use collaborative planning as a platform for such "seeing," grows out of a rich tradition of social and cognitive research trying to answer the question, "How do people construct meaning?" Collaborative planning itself bears the clear imprint of this research. The history of its development is a history of concepts, questions, and hypotheses coming together in a practical theory about writing and learning to write. This chapter looks at that history through six snapshots from research that form a family album of some key ideas behind collaborative planning, ideas that, in turn, became starting points for our own inquiry. Like any family history, this story is itself an interpretation and construction, but one that tries to show some of the goals to which collaborative planning is aspiring and the insights it is attempting to honor.

Snapshot 1: Constructing the World

Two children are overheard constructing with each other a plausible story about rabbits that can account for their mother's surprising advice to "pick up your bunny by its ears"—advice that seems to contradict some recent and equally firm instructions about how *not* to pick up a puppy. In studying the development of children, Piaget and Vygotsky each argued that children like these are not simply imitating or absorbing knowledge; they are in the process of constructing it (Piaget, 1932; Vygotsky, 1987). The tradition that draws on their work, called the constructivist tradition in developmental psychology, shows how learning and development are processes of appropriating information to construct the world. Children learn by using conventions such as storytelling to make sense of their experience, to carry out social purposes, and to solve problems. Piaget looked at how logical, analytical reasoning develops as children try to resolve conflicts. Vygotsky focused on the ways language develops not just by imitation but in response to a social and often collaborative context of children, peers, and adults.

Reading research has turned this powerful metaphor of knowledge construction into an even more explicit tool for describing what readers do with texts. In 1932, Bartlett asked British readers to read and recall an American Indian story—a bizarre, symbolic myth that violated readers' expectations of story structure and logical cause and effect. "The War of the Ghosts" ended with the young man returning from the seal hunt to recount the battle he witnessed:

> He told it all, and then he became quiet. When the sun rose he fell down. Something black came out of his mouth. His face became contorted. The people jumped up and cried. He was dead.

One reader recalled the ending thus:

> When they came to the battle field they heard a great noise and shouting, and a voice said: "The black man is dead." And he was brought to the place where they were, and laid on the ground. And he foamed at the mouth.

As Bartlett showed, readers used their prior knowledge to "construct" a coherent meaning—and in the process added inferences, deleting information that did not fit their sense of a meaningful story, and radically "rewrote" the text they read (Bartlett, 1932).

In Spivey's 1987 synthesis of the research that followed Bartlett, she describes three key processes by which readers construct the text that they recall: selecting relevant information (and ignoring other), organizing the information they attend to within a more global meaning-giving schema or frame (indeed, this organizing schema often directs the process of selecting what is important), and finally connecting information with bridging inferences. This theory challenges older notions in which comprehension was simply an accurate record of the text, and writing was merely the transmission of one's knowledge. Both readers and writers are engaged in constructing coherent meaning out of a rich network of possibilities in response to a variety of purposes.

The notion of *making thinking visible* has its roots deep in this constructive tradition. It asserts that people are not only constructing meaning as they read and write, but also that many parts of this mysterious process are open to observation and reflection—not only by researchers but by readers and writers themselves. In this process, readers and writers draw on a repertoire of strategies for building meaning—strategies that students are in the business of trying out and learning (constructing) for themselves.

Collaborative planning puts this constructive process on the table. It helps writers articulate alternatives and experiment with different ways to construct meaning and to give more active thought to their goals, to constraints (such as the assignment or the possible response of a reader), and to options that different text conventions (such as using a narrative or offering evidence) might give them.

Snapshot 2: Meaning Making Is a Social and Collaborative Process

In her book *Apprenticeship in Thinking,* Barbara Rogoff (1990) showed how the sociocultural context in which children grow up is itself a constant teacher. In many cultures, children learn even complex adult skills with little explicit instruction. Learners may be infants strapped to the back of a working relative; two-year-olds making small "toddler tortillas" alongside sisters; apprentice weavers in Guatemala who observe, asking no questions and receiving no explanations; or preschoolers in African American working-class communities, where young children are not seen as appropriate conversational partners, and so must gradually find ways to enter the adult discourse through performance and stories. These learners are swept into the ongoing activity of the working, adult world. They learn by participating, not in textbook exercises, but in complex events that have social and economic value.

Vygotsky (1987) showed how this collaborative, social participation with adults and more experienced peers created a form of *scaffolding* that let learners go beyond what they could do alone. Children learn to tell stories with the help of supporters who can initiate the event ("tell us about what happened at the store"), provide needed prompts ("and then what happened"), and fill in missing parts. Within these supportive social situations, children engage in a form of *cognitive apprenticeship* where thinking skills are both modeled and nurtured in day-to-day events.

When Palincsar and Brown (1984) translated this notion of a collaborative, socially supported cognitive apprenticeship into a program for teaching reading in school, they achieved some dramatic improvements in children's comprehension. In their program, called *reciprocal teaching,* the teacher initially models four powerful strategies that good readers use to monitor their comprehension—questioning, clarifying, summarizing, and predicting. But as the small reading group works through a text, the role of "teacher," who frames a question or asks for a summary, passes to the learners, who in turn model with increasing success their own monitoring and comprehension processes. The following dialogue comes from a group of remedial seventh-grade readers on the thirteenth day of instruction. At the end of fifteen days, these students had advanced from an average of 30–40 percent correct on standard tests of reading comprehension to 70–80 percent correct. The dialogue starts when Student C asks a question based on the first paragraph of a text about salt they have just read, evaluates Student A's answer and then provides her own summary:

> *Student C:* Name three different basic methods how salt is produced.
>
> *Student A:* Evaporation, mining, evaporation . . . artificial heat evaporation.
>
> *Student C:* Correct, very good. My summary on this paragraph is about ways that salt is being produced.
>
> *Teacher:* Very good. Could you select the next teacher? (Student selects another student)
>
> *Text:* The second oldest form of salt production is mining. Unlike early methods that made the work extremely dangerous and difficult, today's methods use special machinery, and salt mining is safer and easier. The old expression "back to the salt mine" no longer applies.
>
> *Student L:* Name two words that often describe mining salt in the old days.
>
> *Student K:* Back to the salt mines?
>
> *Student L:* No. Angela?
>
> *Student A:* Dangerous and difficult.
>
> *Student L:* Correct. This paragraph is all about comparing the old mining of salt and today's mining of salt.
>
> *Teacher:* Beautiful!
>
> *Student L:* I have a prediction to make.
>
> *Teacher:* Good.

Student L: I think it might tell when salt was first discovered, well it might tell what salt is made of and how it's made.

Teacher: OK. Can we have another teacher?

(Palincsar & Brown, 1984, pp. 162–163)

Collaborative planning, like reciprocal teaching, creates a scaffold for learning within the give-and-take of a supportive social situation. Engaging writers in a collaborative event that they control, it embeds meaning making within a more genuine interchange between people. At the same time, by focusing attention on issues of audience, purpose, and convention, it supports an informal cognitive apprenticeship in which writers take on the difficult but essential process of rhetorical thinking while modeling it for one another.

Snapshot 3: Learning to Do "Conceptual Planning"

What changes occur as young writers develop? Here are the notes and text from a ten-year-old writer asked to plan and then write an essay on "Should students be able to choose the subjects they study in school?"

Notes

I don't like language and art is a bore
I don't like novel study
And I think 4s and 3s should be split up.
I think we should do math.
I don't think we should do diary
I think we should do French

Text

I think children should be able to choose what subjects they want in school. I don't think we should have to do language, and art is a bore a lot. I don't think we should do novel study every week. I really think 4s and 3s should be split up for gym. I think we should do a lot of math. I don't think we should do diary. I think we should do French. (Bereiter & Scardamalia, 1987, p. 199)

Notice how the notes are complete sentences which appear in the final text with little change in wording or order. These young writers do not distinguish between planning (e.g., abstract thinking about alternatives) and drafting text. Using a knowledge-telling strategy to compose, these young writers also find it hard to believe that anyone would think of an idea and then not use it.

By age fourteen, however, students' notes begin to contain gists such as "what rights they have," which could be expanded into text, and notes on intentions such as "give my opinion," which contain no content. They are starting to *transform* their planning notes in various ways by rearranging, expanding, and condensing. Bereiter and Scardamalia (1987) described these changes as a growth in *conceptual planning*—in the ability to differentiate plans from text, to use abstract ideas, and to consider alternatives for thinking about writing.

This research revealed a key feature of growth in writing: In order to have some control over your own ideas, you had to stand back from them, turn them into gists or transform them in light of your intentions. Your ideas had to become more plastic and you had to become a more self-conscious shaper. With this and other studies, Bereiter and Scardamalia were showing how the young writers they observed were depending almost exclusively on what they called a "knowledge-telling" process. Instead of transforming information, this process allows a writer to select a topic, search memory for what he or she knows, using the rules of the genre and the assignment to filter out irrelevant information, and to turn that knowledge directly into text. Moreover, this turns out to be a highly efficient and effective strategy for writing many school papers. The catch is, it does not work for more demanding analytical or persuasive tasks, and relying on knowledge telling failed to help students develop the ability to transform knowledge.

Going beyond knowledge telling to more abstract, conceptual planning was obviously a demanding, creative act. How could instruction, we asked, support this process or help writers do it better?

Snapshot 4: Different Planning Strategies

At the same time Bereiter and Scardamalia were working in Toronto with children, research at Carnegie Mellon with college students and adults began to build a converging picture of writers' thinking (Flower, Schriver, Carey, Haas, & Hayes, 1992). This work suggests that writers depend on three major planning strategies, each with advantages and limitations: *knowledge-driven planning, schema-driven planning*, and *constructive planning*. Each of these operates as an executive-level planning strategy, which means that it guides and orchestrates how the writer goes about developing not only things to say but goals and criteria for how to say them.

In knowledge-driven planning, the writer relies on his or her knowledge about the topic to generate information, to organize ideas, and to choose what to say. Unlike the child's knowledge telling, it may involve significant conceptual thinking, but the plan is still guided by and focused on the structure of the available information. Knowledge-driven planning is a familiar and effective strategy for turning out committee reports, school themes, and letters home. It is excellent for demonstrating learning on an essay exam. But it can also lead to writer-based prose that is not adapted to what readers might need. When assignments ask writers to transform their knowledge for a new purpose or for a reader, a knowledge-driven plan (based on presenting what one knows, structured as one currently thinks about it) will not be up to the job.

In schema- (or convention-) driven planning, the writer's goals and organizing plan are provided not by the topic but by a discourse convention or format (e.g., a five-paragraph theme or a movie review). Topic knowledge always comes into play in writing, but when schema-driven planning takes over as the writer's executive strategy, the lion's share of planning can be done for the writer by available schemas or conventions. That is, the schemas and conventions help generate ideas, help in selecting the relevant ones, help set goals and criteria, and offer not only patterns of organization but appropriate language and phrasing. Experienced newswriters depend heavily on their schemas (like the 5 Ws for a news story) to guide planning; but students may also turn to conventions they know (such as summary and response) to guide their planning, even if a given assignment calls for a somewhat different plan.

Schema-driven planning allows all one's past effort to learn the conventions of a news story or school essay to pay off. Like knowledge-driven planning, it can be efficient and effective—if the conventions and knowledge one has fit the task. However, when one wants to *use* that committee report to mount an argument or to *use* a movie review to explore an idea—to write with an adaptive, individual purpose—then available topic knowledge and conventions often are not an adequate guide to planning.

In constructive planning, writers build an original plan that puts knowledge and conventions to use. With this executive strategy, writers must "read" the situation and create their own complex web of intentions. They must often consider alternatives and deal with conflicts as they develop a network of subgoals, plans, and criteria. The plan and the text develop in a kind of dialectic where each can shape the other. Because this executive strategy allows writers literally to construct the plan that will guide writing, constructive planning lets writers adapt to a rhetorical situation and transform their knowledge. It is also more difficult to do.

Planning research suggests that many people (especially students engaged in conventional school assignments) learn to rely on knowledge-driven planning as their default strategy, unless they are motivated to think in more rhetorical ways. Collaborative planning began, first of all, as a response to this problem. This research had defined a set of powerful executive strategies that older writers appeared to move among at will. Could we help developing writers expand their repertoire? In particular, how could we engage students in constructing and reflecting on their own writing plans?

Snapshot 5: Expert Writers Using Constructive Planning

It is one thing to know that experienced writers do things differently. But just how do experienced writers *construct* a plan? Are some parts of this process teachable? The transcript (figure 3.1) of a writer thinking aloud shows some expert strategies that we saw in both adults and good student writers. These writers elaborate a network of both major goals and "how-to-do-it" subgoals and plans. They also review those goals during writing, not only to monitor progress but to review and consolidate (and revise) their plan. When they hit conflicts, as all writers do, they resolve them by thinking about the plan nearly forty percent of the time, compared to the four percent by novice writers who dealt with problems at the level of text.

These experts also pay attention to more parts of the picture. They spend their time thinking about not only content, but also purpose, organization, and audience. Less experienced writers sometimes gave almost no thought to the reader or their purpose. And, on this task, the amount of planning time even predicted the quality of the paper. Extensive planners did a significantly better job on this assignment than minimal planners (Carey & Flower, 1989).

It was from this research that the Planner's Blackboard (see chapter 4, figure 4.1) took shape as a metaphor to highlight how constructive planners give themselves goals, plans, and ideas in each area. Asking writers to imagine their plan as a set of mental blackboards on which ideas were posted (or not) gave a sort of "local habitation and a name" to an elusive thought process. By visualizing ideas filling up blackboards and making links across them, we hoped to make

Clause	Comment	Analysis
46	All right, I'm an English teacher	
47	I know they are not going to be disposed to hear what I'm saying	**Audience** (draws an inference)
48	Partly for that reason and partly to put them in the right—the kind of frame of mind I want	**Goal/Audience** (prepare reader)
49	I want to open with an implied question or a direct one	**Form** (develops a structure for the text)
50	and then put them in the middle of some situation	
51	and then expand from there more generally to talk about my job more generally	
52	and try to tie it in with their interest	**Goal/Audience** (involve audience)
53	So one question is where to begin	**Form** (plans introduction)
54	Start in the middle of—probably the first day of class	
55	They'd be interested	**Audience** (draws an inference, links to his goals)
56	They'd probably clue into that	
57	easily because they would identify with the first days of school.	
58	and my first days are raucous affairs	
59	It would immediately shake 'em up	**Goals** (develops specific audience goals for the introduction)
60	and get them to think in a different context	

Figure 3.1. Analyzed Transcript of One Episode of an Expert Planner's Thinking Aloud Protocol.

these familiar abstractions more concrete, to help students see their own plan as a conceptual entity distinct from text. The Planners Blackboard also offered a way to do what good teachers often do during a paper conference—to prompt writers to extend and elaborate their ideas and intuitions of purpose into a key point and a set of other rhetorical goals; to imagine a reader and that reader's response; to consider different textual options; and to review, revise, and consolidate their plan.

Snapshot 6: Planning with a Partner—of Sorts

The Planner's Blackboard may be a useful metaphor, but it is hardly news. It reflects the kinds of rhetorical concerns composition teachers regularly teach. Although it might give writers a more integrated, memorable prompt, my own teaching experience had convinced me that presenting new strategies can open doors for some students who wonder why "no one ever taught me this before," but it can have little effect on other writers who do not see how or why to incorporate a strategy into what they already do.

Why is it that students do little constructive planning? Are we looking at a case of *can't* or *don't*? What if student writers were asked more directly to do such thinking while they were composing? To answer this question, we developed a friendly—if fictitious—computer that would write a paper, but the student had to construct the plan. In this study the computer prompted students with hard questions such as "Thank you, that was a good plan, but I was always told to consider alternatives. Can you think of another way?" and "How will you deal with the readers who disagree with you?" This Automatic Planner showed us more of what students *could* do, and with such prompting we saw college freshmen doing extended constructive planning. Those students whose freshman course had also included direct instruction in planning did even better than the rest, performing as well as master's students on some measures. But the bigger surprise was students who emerged from this demanding hour-and-a-half planning experiment saying, "This would have helped me on my paper for psychology last week," and "Can my roommate be a subject in the study?"

If even this creaky computer fiction could be such an effective prompt, how much more could students do with a live respondent encouraging and prompting their thinking? Could a partner, whose attention is not consumed by planning, help a writer by (1) prompting her to consider new possibilities and then (2) at the next moment, reflecting back to the writer the shape, the strengths, or the problems of her emerging plan?

As even these brief snapshots suggest, collaborative planning took shape in response to a tradition of research and a set of insights about how people construct meaning and about how both learning and meaning making are supported by collaborative, social arrangements. It was shaped even more directly by the series of planning studies that expanded our image of what writers were doing while raising the question of how to teach what we were learning—how to share that understanding in a way that spoke more directly to the experience of writing. But, as this book will make clear, the collaborative planning strategy we present here is itself a step in a continuing inquiry. As the writers in this group translated insights from theory and research into teaching, we were, at the same time, altering and expanding our understanding of the process we would teach.

4 Teaching Collaborative Planning: Creating a Social Context for Writing

David L. Wallace
Iowa State University
Ames, Iowa

As the previous chapter illustrates, collaborative planning took shape in response to theory and research that sees writing as a constructive activity—a social and cognitive process. It is an attempt to put some of the powerful ideas from current research into practice. Put simply, collaborative planning attempts to help writers elaborate their understanding of their rhetorical context by creating a supportive social context. In terms of turning research and theory into practice, it addresses three basic problems.

First, what do you do when students depend on a "knowledge-telling" approach to writing? One goal of collaborative planning is to provide an opportunity for students to do more planning and to devote their attention to rhetorical concerns: developing more complex senses of purpose, anticipating the reader's response, and considering and using the conventions of text itself to reach the students' goals or influence the reader. However, as the snapshots from research in the previous chapter illustrate, student writers often have trouble doing the energetic, constructive planning and testing that experienced writers do. Part of the reason for this is that many school writing tasks, particularly those in early grades, focus on storytelling or gathering and presenting information, presenting students with a rhetorically simple situation. The purpose is to tell a story or present information for a familiar audience, and the text conventions are usually well known. These assignments are appropriate for young writers who would probably feel overwhelmed by more complex writing tasks, but a problem develops if students or teachers see knowledge telling as normative: Students' attention often becomes riveted on coming up with enough things to say, ignoring rhetorical concerns (e.g., purpose, audience, and text conventions). Then, when assignments require students to address rhetorical concerns, instructions such as "think about your audience" often get translated into simple moves such as "naming" an audience that might be interested in the topic. Thus, a first step in implementing collaborative planning is to create writing assignments and situations that make aspects of the rhetorical context salient for students.

A second tough problem that teachers face is how to help students learn strategies that they will need in order to develop more complex understandings of their purposes and audiences and to manage the demands of new sets of text conventions that their audiences may expect them to use. In short, how do you teach the extended interactive planning process that experienced writers have mastered? Textbooks and class discussions may help some students to learn new writing strategies, particularly students with high motivation or students who are already aware of their writing processes. But students' needs and ability levels vary widely; the question becomes how to provide support or intervention when it is really needed—while the student is actually in the midst of planning and writing. An obvious answer to this question is to use collaboration. Most classroom collaboration is based on Vygotsky's notion of a *zone of proximal development*, assuming that learners may be able to do tasks together that would be too difficult to do individually. Collaborative planning takes advantage of the help that peers can give each other—help that is almost certain to be within their zones of proximal development. However, it also assumes that students are likely to need a push—that most often they will not attend to rhetorical issues unless prompted to do so. Therefore, collaborative planning provides a set of rhetorical prompts that students can adapt to help each other attend to issues that they might not otherwise address in their planning.

The third problem in implementing a technique such as collaborative planning is that student writers often need help becoming good collaborators. They need to develop what we call good supporting skills—learning to be active listeners, to ask for elaboration, to adapt generic prompts, to ask probing questions, and occasionally to challenge their collaborator directly. Thus, like peer editing, the success of collaborative planning depends on students' ability to provide each other with a kind of instructional scaffold within their zone of proximal development.

Defining Collaborative Planning

Socially Supported Talk. As a response to these problems, collaborative planning is a way to help students explore and develop their plans for writing. First and foremost, collaborative planning is socially supported talk. It is an opportunity for students or other writers to talk about their ideas in a supportive environment where peers will listen, prompt them to develop their ideas further, and, when necessary, press them to flesh out their purposes and their understandings of their audience or to think about how to use text conventions.

Collaborative planning needs only three things: a planner, a supporter, and a tentative plan. The planner may be at any point in his or her writing process, but planning sessions are generally most useful early in the writing process, when writers have done some serious thinking about their topic and goals but before they have made a heavy commitment of time and effort to drafting texts. The planning session provides an opportunity for the writer to talk out his or her goals before committing them to text; the supporter listens, asks questions, and encourages the writer to develop her plan. After partners have spent time developing one of their tentative plans, they often switch roles as planner and supporter.

Structured Talk. Collaborative planning is also structured talk that forces writers to develop their understanding of the rhetorical context for their writing. To help students be more effective planning partners, collaborative planning uses the Planner's Blackboard to focus the collaborators on rhetorical issues. The Planner's Blackboard (see figure 4.1) is a visual metaphor to cue writers to consider rhetorical issues as they plan. The supporter serves as a sounding board, an instant audience to whom the writer must make his or her ideas clear, and prompts the writer to address rhetorical issues.

The Planner's Blackboard illustrates the difference between plans to *say something* (focused on content alone) and plans to *do something in writing* (focused on the rhetorical concerns of purpose, audience, and the use of text conventions to achieve a purpose or communicate with a reader). The background of the blackboard represents the topic or content information that the writer plans to include. Some writers spend all their time thinking of things to say, devoting all their effort to filling their mental blackboard with topic information. In contrast, experienced writers often develop a body of supporting subgoals and "how to" plans for what they want to accomplish. Over and above the various points they have in mind, they are developing a plan

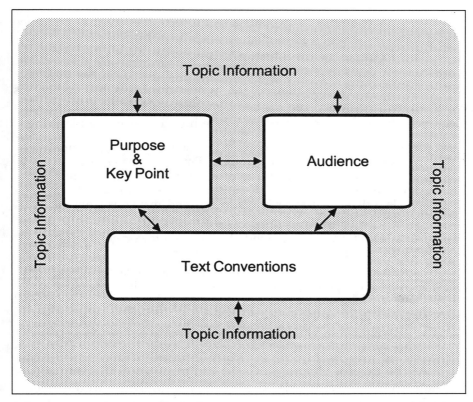

Figure 4.1. The Planner's Blackboard.

organized around the "key point" they want to make. In planning for their audience, these writers not only consider who that audience is, they imagine possible responses their readers might have. And they build plans for how they might use some of the conventions of written text to reach their rhetorical goals. In terms of the Planner's Blackboard metaphor, they are putting items on the purpose, audience, and text conventions areas of the blackboard.

Integrated Plans. The arrows between the items in the Planner's Blackboard draw attention to the way that experienced writers generate plans to link these different concerns and the way they frequently stop to assess those connections or to consolidate parts of their growing plan. For example, experienced writers may ask themselves how considering a new group of readers as part of the audience forces the writer to reconsider his or her purposes for writing. The new group may need an example to explain a point that the original audience would have understood immediately.

The example below illustrates how a student writer, Carter,[1] works with a supporter, Jenny, to identify examples that the audience will respond to. Notice that as the writer discusses his audience's expectations, the supporter not only encourages him to elaborate his ideas but also helps him keep track of where he is in the planning.

> *Carter (writer):* And my audience . . . they're probably gonna expect a lot of (writer) examples. I'm gonna have to use a lot of examples to prove, to prove it to them that different writing styles exist, and I want my audience to be able to relate their own experiences to this and maybe see how it affects them.
>
> *Jenny (supporter):* So, what kind of examples are you gonna use? Can you give me an example? An example . . .
>
> *Carter:* Um . . . Okay. I'll give you a real big example. Switching from high school writing to college writing. [The writer goes on to elaborate his idea.]
>
> *Jenny:* Great . . . It's excellent. Um . . . But . . . Okay, so that's an example for one of your points. What about an example for [your other idea of] how writing varies?

As the excerpt illustrates, Carter did some good thinking before he came to this session. He knew that his audience would expect examples to prove his point that different writing styles exist. Jenny asks a very simple question, What kind of examples are you gonna use? to get Carter to say more. After Carter explains one of his examples at length, Jenny presses further, asking to hear about an example for another point.

During collaborative planning sessions, writers and supporters work together to develop the writers' plans. Sometimes, they explore the topic information—discussing, expanding, and sometimes redefining the content that the writer plans to include. More important, they also address rhetorical issues: the writer's purpose or key point, the needs and expectations of the audience, and the text conventions that the writer will need to use in his or her text. As the planner, the writer is responsible for coming to the planning session with a tentative plan to discuss and for being open to suggestions from the supporter. The supporter's first responsibility is to listen and try to understand the writer's plan. Beyond active listening, supporters often need to ask writers for more information, prompt them to discuss rhetorical issues—

such as purpose or audience—in more detail, or play devil's advocate, pressing the writer to consider alternatives.

Reflection. In addition to helping students become better collaborators by providing rhetorical prompts and a structure for planning, collaborative planning also provides an opportunity for students to reflect on their thinking and for teachers to observe that thinking. Students get to see immediately how their ideas affect an audience, their partner, but they can also learn about their planning processes and the ways they function as a supporter by taking a second look at their planning sessions. Providing an opportunity for students to reflect on what happened in their planning sessions usually turns up some surprises. When students write reflection memos after their planning sessions, listen to audiotapes, or view videotapes of their sessions, they often see their planning and their supporting in a new light. Also, when teachers observe students' planning and supporting via students' reflection memos, audio- and videotapes, or just by eavesdropping, they can add another perspective to class discussion that reflects on planning sessions. The interplay between student reflection and teacher observation greatly improves the effectiveness of collaborative planning because both can identify problems and consider new possibilities.

Providing Opportunities for Learning

Collaborative planning provides learning opportunities in three ways. First, as instructional intervention, collaborative planning provides a supportive context in which students can develop new planning strategies. One of the primary objectives of collaborative planning is to get students to recognize their rhetorical situation and develop plans that transform topic knowledge according to rhetorical concerns (i.e., purpose, audience, text conventions). Recent research about planning in writing (Bereiter & Scardamalia, 1987; Flower, Schriver, Carey, Haas, & Hayes, 1992) has shown that many student writers concentrate on the topic—thinking of things to say. However, to be strategic thinkers and effective communicators, they need to consider the whole problem in a writing task: to think about their purpose and audience, to anticipate how other people will respond, and to use their knowledge of text conventions to achieve a purpose. If writers, particularly student writers, are to learn to address these rhetorical concerns, they may need the opportunity to hear how another person responds to the plans they have developed for a writing assignment. Thus, as a pedagogical intervention, collaborative planning makes the thinking that student writers have done for an assignment visible by making it accessible for discussion. Collaborative planning also gives the instructor access to the thinking that students have done before they begin writing; audio- or videotapes of students planning sessions allow the instructor to observe some of the thinking behind students' writing and, if necessary, to intervene early in their writing process.

Ultimately, the success of collaborative planning depends not on success for a single assignment but on students' ability to apply what they learn about themselves as planners and writers in other situations. Learning new strategies to deal with the problems that they face for a writing assignment is not enough if students are unable to transfer those strategies to new situations. Collaborative planning provides a second kind of opportunity for learning when students are invited to reflect on what happened in their planning sessions, to look beyond the immediate instructional intervention and consider what they might learn about themselves as thinkers and writers. Thus, another objective of collaborative planning is for students to examine what went on in their planning sessions and discuss what they are learning about planning and writing.

Collaborative planning also provides a third kind of opportunity for learning: the opportunity for teachers to learn from the experiences of other groups of students and teachers. The planning sessions allow teachers to observe and learn from their students. In the Making Thinking Visible Project, we have used self-interviews, taped collaboration sessions, video letters, and a computer program developed for collaboration (see Tom Hajduk's discovery memo in section 1) to help students observe their own planning. This book is testament to the power of teachers sharing in the insights drawn from close observation of their students. As a project group, we found it essential to meet monthly to share our problems and discoveries. Sometimes we shared important procedural ideas: The group discovered the power of modeling actual planning sessions for students when, as an experiment, Tom Hajduk and Pam Turley teamed up to model a planning session in their classes and were overwhelmed by positive response. Sometimes we griped about the hassles of getting tape recorders for all of our students or wondered aloud how we would make sense of the mountains of data we collected. The moments we enjoyed most were the unexpected success stories: We were all moved the first time Leslie Evans read us her discovery memo that tells Sharon's story (see Leslie's discovery memo in section 1). We have put much of what we learned as a group into this book, but the book is no substitute for a partner or group of people who share insights, provide moral support, and, most important, serve as an interested audience for thinking through tough problems.

Teaching Collaborative Planning

Unless students are already fairly sophisticated writers and collaborators, they will not automatically have productive collaborative planning sessions. There is nothing magical about the technique; as in peer review, placing students in pairs or groups for planning does not suddenly make students able to do together what they could not do alone. Successful collaborative planning sessions usually depend on good preparation.

In general, preparing students for a planning session means three things: (1) introducing them to the principles of collaborative planning, (2) discussing how to use the Planner's Blackboard terms as prompts, and (3) explaining and demonstrating the roles of writers and supporters in planning sessions. In the remainder of this section, I discuss briefly each of these topics, sharing the collective experience of the teachers who have participated in the Making Thinking Visible Project. Our experience has convinced us that teachers must adapt collaborative planning to the needs and abilities of their students; therefore, what follows should be read as guidelines rather than prescriptions.

Introducing the Principles of Collaborative Planning. The creative tension that teachers face when they introduce collaborative planning involves giving students a sense of what is expected of them without prescribing a lockstep procedure. Collaborative planning can take many forms—conversations in the hall, informal sessions in a dorm room or in class, scheduled meetings or conferences where a writer presents ideas to a group. Also, students can use collaborative planning before they write, in the middle of a draft, or as part of reviewing a text. However, for their first session, most students do best if they plan before they create a draft and if they understand the basic principles of collaborative planning.

The principles are rather simple. First, *authority (the "floor") belongs to the writer as a planner and thinker.* Unlike peer review sessions, where the writer is often a recipient of information about his or her draft, collaborative planning offers the writer a chance to talk, think, and explore options. Focusing on the writer as a thinker (rather than on the text) encourages the writer to articulate and elaborate ideas, to recognize problems, and to build a plan based on his or her own ideas and emerging intentions.

The second principle is that *the aim of this planning process is to build a richer network of goals, plans, ideas, and possibilities that are interconnected.* The Planner's Blackboard can help students become more aware of their own ideas and planning process. It also prompts them to elaborate their goals, to build "how-to" plans for the text, and to discover connections among their ideas.

The final principle is that *the supporter creates a collaborative social context that encourages the writer to shape his or her purposes and build a more reflective plan for turning those goals into text.* Although the supporter may see problems and offer criticism or suggestions as well as draw the writer out, the supporter's primary job is to work in a spirit of collaboration to help the writer develop the writer's plan.

Using the Planner's Blackboard Terms as Prompts. For students or other writers learning how to do collaborative planning, the Planner's Blackboard provides a common vocabulary to use as they discuss a writer's plans for a text, particularly for discussion of rhetorical issues. The Planner's Blackboard also serves two important prompting functions. When students are preparing for their planning sessions, they can use the blackboard items as prompts for the thinking and planning that they do before they come to a collaborative planning session. During a planning session, a supporter may use the Planner's Blackboard as a reminder to discuss rhetorical issues during the planning sessions. For example, if a supporter notices that a writer has focused primarily on topic information or has ignored one of the blackboard areas, the supporter may ask a question based on one of the blackboard areas, such as audience ("You haven't said much about your audience or their needs yet") or purpose ("How are you going to focus all this information to make it interesting for them?").

The term *text conventions* is the most difficult for students to understand. It covers a broad range of the text features writers can consider. Many of these conventions are familiar: the genre features of a journal entry or an editorial; organizing plans such as comparison/ contrast; rhetorical techniques such as examples and quotations; and ways to format and present a text such as using headings to organize, italics to emphasize, or bullets to list. The difference is that experienced writers talk and think about these features as if they had an extensive repertoire of alternative conventions they could use in this text to carry out their multiple purposes, develop their key point, and adapt to their readers. Less experienced writers may have a much smaller repertoire and may not realize that they have such alternatives.

Some writers start by using the Planner's Blackboard as a kind of outline—actually writing little notes to themselves in the different boxes. In doing so, they usually turn the metaphor into a simple checklist, like a short-answer test, which quickly becomes a straitjacket on their ideas. The Planner's Blackboard functions best when writers take control of this collaborative process, structuring it to fit their needs and using the blackboard areas as a general-purpose prompt for invention and critical reflection on their current plan. Despite the danger of turning collaborative planning into a checklist procedure, students sometimes need to see samples of the kinds of questions that they can use to get started planning. Often, simple questions that focus on rhetorical issues provide a beginning point for discussion. Simple questions—for example, "What point are you trying to make (purpose)?" "How do you think your readers will respond to that (audience)?" or "What kind of support are you planning to use (text conventions)?"—can be very effective if they are followed up with questions that push the writer to provide more detailed information. See figure 4.2 for a list of generic questions that students can modify to fit their planning partners' needs (Burnett, 1990).

Explaining and Demonstrating the Roles of Writers and Supporters. Depending on their previous experience with collaborative activities, students and other writers often need some help learning how to be effective collaborators. There is no substitute for time and experience in learning to be an effective collaborator, but at least two issues are worth talking about up front. First, students need to know what is expected of them. Outlining the main responsibilities of writers and supporters (see figure 4.3; from Burnett, 1990) gives students a sense of what they need to do to prepare for planning sessions and what to do while they are meeting with their partners.

As students gain experience with both planning and collaboration, some will naturally extend these basic roles and find more sophisticated ways to help each other. However, most students need help developing their supporting skills. (Figure 4.4 provides a more detailed list of strategies and questions that supporters can use.) A second way that many of the Making Thinking Visible Project teachers helped their students prepare was to model a planning session. This modeling took several forms. When they could arrange it, some teachers invited a colleague to class to be their supporter as they let their students eavesdrop on a planning session for something that the

Content

What more can you say about _____ ?

What additional information might you include?

Tell me more about _____ .

Have you considered including _____ ?

What additional information might you include?

I think _____ will be a good thing to include.

Purpose/Key Point

What do you see as your main point [purpose]?

Am I right that your key point [or purpose] is _____ ?

What did you mean by _____ ?

Could you clarify your point about _____ ?

I can't quite see why you've decided to _____ .

Could you explain why? (asking for justification)

A point you haven't mentioned yet is _____ .

I see a conflict between _____ and _____ ? How will you deal with it [resolve it]?

Audience

Who is your intended audience [reader]?

What does the reader expect to read [learn]?

How do you think your reader will react to _____ ?

Why is this the appropriate audience?

How will your audience connect _____ to _____ ?

What problems [conflicts, inconsistencies, gaps] might your reader see?

Text Conventions

Consider both (1) document design elements and (2) global and local elements of organization, development, support, and style.

How do you plan to *explain* _____ ?

How will you *organize* [develop, explain] this?

What *support* [or evidence] will you use? What *examples* will you use?

Have you considered using _____ [text convention]? How do you think it would work?

Couldn't you also try _____ [text convention]?

How does this [convention] let you deal with _____ ?

continued on next page

Figure 4.2. Generic clarifying, extending, and evaluating questions for supporters (Burnett, 1990).

Figure 4.2 continued

Is your paper going to have a _____ [convention]?

I like _____ better than _____ as a way to explain this idea.

Consolidation (separate or incorporated)

How does _____ relate to [develop, clarify] _____ ?

Given your purpose [audience], will you use _____ text convention?

How are you going to connect _____ and _____ ?

Is there a conflict between using _____ and _____ ?

I'm not sure _____ will make sense to this audience.

I think _____ is a good way to explain your key point to this audience.

---

teacher was planning to write. This kind of modeling has the added advantage of helping students to see their teacher as someone who struggles with writing problems. Others demonstrated planning with one of their students, inviting the class to join in as supporters. As Leslie Evans's discovery memo illustrates, when these sessions get rolling, students often take over completely, and the teacher can often sit back and take notes about what kinds of strategies or questions the students used.

Another effective way to get students to see different ways to act as supporters is to use examples of different kinds of planning sessions. Videotape clips or transcripts of previous students' planning sessions can help students to see not only what collaborative planning is all about, but also highlight specific kinds of things that supporters can do to help writers. For example, Rebecca Burnett has developed

Writer	**Supporter**
■ have a preliminary plan that you can explain	■ be an active listener so you can understand the writer's plan
■ be open to suggestions that may help you to improve the plan	■ offer comments that help the writer think about the plan's strengths and weaknesses
■ give thoughtful responses to questions	■ encourage exploration by asking probing questions
■ be flexible so you can improve your plan	■ be interested, attentive, and engaged

Figure 4.3. Basic Responsibilities of Writers and Supporters (Burnett, 1990).

The role of supporters. Supporters help the writers develop and elaborate their own plans. Good supporters listen carefully to the writer's plan and figure out how to help the planner keep thinking. We have found that the following comments and strategies, addressed directly to students, are effective for introducing the supporter's role.

Strategies for supporters. Because you are the one who gets to sit and listen, you will be able to keep the goals of the Planner's Blackboard in mind. Try to figure out how you can encourage your planner to build a better or more developed plan, especially in the key areas of the blackboard. Here are some things good supporters do. But you will have to decide which of these supporting strategies will help your planner most.

■ *Reflect the writer's talk:* Listen carefully and reflect the "gist" of what you heard back: "What I hear you saying is that _____ . Am I hearing you right?"

■ *Ask for more information:* Ask the planner to elaborate. "You just said ____ ; tell me more about _____ [what you mean or why you said that]."

■ *Check the blackboards:* Ask about key parts of the blackboard that the planner has only explained in a sketchy way. "If your purpose is _____ , how are you going to do that? What are your other goals?"

■ *Look for connections:* Ask—from time to time—how different parts of the plan are connected, especially when you see possible links or problems. "If your key point here is _____ , how do you think your readers will respond to that?" Or "Is there any link between your purpose and the format you plan to use?"

■ *Note important differences:* Share your perception of the task or alternative strategies the writer might consider. "I saw the assignment a little differently; let's talk about what our options are." Or, "You might use an example here." Or "That's an important point you could emphasize."

■ *Expressing confusion:* Let the writer know when you feel confused or see a problem. You don't need to have a solution; just give feedback about how the plan works for you. "I feel lost at this point; why did you say that?" "I don't know what you mean when you say _____ ." "Can you tell me how this part of the paper is linked to that part?" Your feedback as a "live reader/listener" (rather than as a critic or advice-giver) can help the writer begin to imagine how other readers might respond and start to plan with them in mind.

Figure 4.4. Supporter Strategies.

a set of excerpts from her students' planning sessions (see appendixes at the end of this chapter) to illustrate the different roles that supporters can play. She has pairs of students read these excerpts aloud and asks the class to observe how engaged the supporter is in each case. In the first excerpt, figure 4.5, the supporter contributes very little; in the second excerpt, figure 4.6, the supporter contributes some ideas; and in the third excerpt, figure 4.7, the supporter directly challenges the writer. The point of these kinds of exercises is for students to see that supporters can help their partners by active listening (encouraging the writer to develop ideas), by contributing ideas, or by directly challenging the writer to consider alternatives.

It is sometimes useful to give students some vocabulary for talking about supporter moves. For example, when viewing videotape clips or reading transcript excerpts, students can use the following list of supporter moves to answer a simple observation question such as "What types of questions or responses did the supporter use?"

> *Query:* Requests for clarification such as "Can you tell me how what you are planning to do relates to the assignment?" or "It sounds to me like you are writing an argument, not a definition."
>
> *Exploring:* Comments that ask the writer to develop ideas, such as "That's interesting. Can you tell me more?" or "You've said a lot about what you plan to say in this paper. Can you tell me more about your purpose?"
>
> *Solving problems:* Comments or questions that focus on particular problems, such as "It seems to me that you really don't know what your purpose is yet" or "It seems to me that your audience already knows most of the things that you are planning to say. What will be new and interesting for them?"
>
> *Challenging:* Comments or questions that confront writers, asking them to consider an alternative point such as "I don't think that your decision to leave out an example will work because your audience needs to see what you are saying."

Conducting Inquiry Projects

One of our strongest convictions about collaborative planning is that teachers must adapt it to the needs of their students and the constraints of their settings. The successes that we have seen in the Making Thinking Visible Project have convinced us that collaborative planning can provide a means for students, even those who have been judged at risk, to get some control of at least one aspect of their education. Our failures and the difficulties that each of us has faced with our students remind us that collaborative planning is not a panacea: We have resisted the impulse to shrink wrap it and market it as the new composition cure-all. Another of our convictions is that using collaborative planning to tap our students' potential is hard work: it requires

Writer:	I need a summary write up. I need that.
Supporter:	Right.
Writer:	I need something to introduce it and to summarize it.
Supporter:	Right. And I thought that—
Writer:	And also something to try and sell it a little better, I think.
Supporter:	Right.
Writer:	And really talk about why, why solar heating is for you and why this system is more efficient than other systems. And then once, once I've introduced that and said, ok, like, uh, "We have a two-speed summer-winter operation." You know, just generally state all these things that make ours better. Then go into detail below, have, like, a picture of the thermostat system, uh, you know, schematics of how that connects the—how it's different for summer and winter, and explain it better.
Supporter:	Mmuh.
Writer:	But start with the picture.
Supporter:	Aah, that's interesting.
Writer:	You know, of course, as a new employee, I would have to find out, like, how our company deals with graphics, like, do we have people who—
Supporter:	Right.
Writer:	—would do that or do I have to send out and have the pictures made? Do I have to do all the pictures?
Supporter:	Right.
Writer:	Or do we have, like, a publication artist to work on all that?
Supporter:	Right.
Writer:	Which is another reason not to revise the whole memo, I guess. Just to kind of, uh, you know, get started; save my ideas for what I want in the drawings.
Supporter:	So, you couldn't do it all yourself anyway.
Writer:	Right.
Supporter:	Right.
Writer:	But I wouldn't want to, like, you know, go into the whole thing and, uh, have someone else working on it with me and doing all this without consulting my supervisor.
Supporter:	Right.

Figure 4.5. Supporter Excerpt 1.

Supporter:	OK. You mentioned, um, several pictures [papers rustling]—I thought that was really important, too.
Writer:	It looked like a doodle he'd made on the phone. My vision was, like, to have it more based on pictures and have an explanation of the picture. Like, one—
Supporter:	That's a good idea.
Writer:	—one problem I had was with, uh, how he tossed all those temperatures into the, into the paragraph and you had to, like, you had to really think about what was going on in order to understand what these temperatures meant. And I thought if you had a drawing of each part of the system, like a drawing of the collector, and you could give the temperatures in, like, outline right on the drawing, and it would just—
Supporter:	Right.
Writer:	—make it so much more visual and easier to see what's going on.
Supporter:	Right. Or you could make, like, a little, like an outline of a house and put words to go with this building.
Writer:	Right.
Supporter:	Not just this thing in air floating somewhere.
Writer:	Right. More, well, less abstract than that, more like a real situation that someone would have.
Supporter:	Would you want, like, a little, like, paragraph applied next to the picture? explaining it? or, or totally everything in the text of the, of the, uh, brochure, you know, like, how with the illustrations, there'll be, like, a small paragraph explaining it?
Writer:	Yeah. I wanted to have, like, maybe have two columns, a column of graphics and a column of text explaining it. Have, you know, the picture right across from the explanation—
Supporter:	Ooh. So the whole thing would be made up of that?
Writer:	Yeah.
Supporter:	Aah.
Writer:	So that—well. OK.

Figure 4.6. Supporter Excerpt 2.

a willingness to conduct an inquiry project. The basic method for one of these inquiry projects is simple: You observe your students' planning sessions, listen to their reflections about the process, and then try it again—the sort of thing that creative teachers do all the time.

Inquiry projects require some commitment, but formal training in research methods is *not* necessary. Some of us in the Making Thinking Visible Project, mostly the university types, took on formal

Writer:	I would like to talk to my supervisor about this before I really write the memo. Just kind of informally, see if these things are possible before I go out on a limb.
Supporter:	Yeah. So would that talking with him, would that be the point of this memo?
Writer:	Well, not really—
Supporter:	You can't really—
Writer:	—because I want the memo to be seen by more than just the supervisor.
Supporter:	Like, you mean you're going to, you know, draft that? Talk to your supervisor?
Writer:	Well, gee, I don't know. I don't know if I should—If I can decide if this stuff is possible, I can write the memo. . . . What do you think?
Supporter:	Uh . . . I just thought that your memo would be pretty much the first communication and that maybe you're expected to be, like, a bit autonomous in this—
Writer:	Yeah. That's kind of a problem with my wanting to talk to him about this before I write anything.
Supporter:	It seems like he doesn't even want to deal with it.
Writer:	Yeah. That's a problem that I'm going to have to, uh, think about. . . . If I, if I should go out on a limb—
Supporter:	Yeah.
Writer:	—and hope that if my supervisor shouldn't like this one and snatched the memo out of circulation [laughter] and have me redo it right away, you know? [laughter] And I don't know that I can trust my supervisor to do that. Like, I feel that as a new employee in the company, I would want to, I'd want to show that I had potential, that I knew what I wanted to do and that I knew how to do it.
Supporter:	Right. Right.

Figure 4.7. Supporter Excerpt 3.

inquiry projects and worried about things like the reliability of our observations and the generalizability of our results (see Burnett, 1991; Norris, 1992; and Wallace, 1992, in the collaborative planning bibliography at the end of this book). However, the discovery memos in this book testify that informal inquiry done by teachers who are primarily concerned about the needs of the students that they know best—those they teach day in and day out—can yield exciting classroom discoveries and insights that other teachers can use. Moreover, these discoveries can talk back to more formal research, starting a dialogue that helps both kinds of inquiry. (See discovery memos by Flower, section 1, and Burnett, section 4, for examples.)

The way that an inquiry project unfolds depends on the teachers' goals, situational variables, and the amount of time and effort the teacher can squeeze out of a packed teaching schedule. Not surprisingly, the processes that teachers and students follow in inquiry projects vary quite a bit. The discovery memos and project papers in this book are the best description of how inquiry projects really work. There are, however, several common features that seem to define inquiry projects. First, the projects usually begin with the teacher's investigation of collaborative planning, the rationale and research that undergirds the technique. At this stage, teachers typically pose questions about how collaborative planning might help their students and how the technique will need to be adapted for their students' needs. As they investigate collaborative planning, teachers need to feel free to question and challenge the assumptions. For example, Andrea Martine wondered how valuable collaborative planning would be to her ninth-grade students if they did not take some kind of notes. Her experience suggested that her students might forget or ignore the ideas they came up with in planning sessions unless they had good notes to remind them as they wrote. The questions that teachers raise about how to interpret and apply research and the predictions that they make can be early indicators of the kinds of questions that they will want to investigate later.

The next stage in a making thinking visible project is to introduce collaborative planning to students and to observe them as they plan. Teachers are often surprised by what happens in the planning sessions. Frequently, some students have problems that the teacher did not anticipate, whereas other students have very successful sessions. Observing the planning sessions and discussing them with the students can help the teacher better structure the sessions for future assignments and may suggest a question or set of issues for further observation. Discussing problems that students perceive in their collaboration can become an important opportunity for the teacher to encourage students to take responsibility for the quality of their sessions. Like any instructional activity, the value of collaborative planning does not reside in the practice itself but in what writers make of it. By taking seriously students' reports of problems, the teacher is able to help students consider how they would redesign this process next time to make it work better for them. Also, by making reflection (and discussion of students' observations) a regular part of this process, the teacher can help to make the classroom a place for students to begin an inquiry into their strategies and choices. It is usually best to start slowly: Let your students become comfortable with collaborative planning before you put a tape recorder or a videotape camera in front of them. As Marlene Bowen's discovery memo (section 2) illustrates, simple procedural things, such as getting the cellophane wrapping off thirty cassette tapes, can make collecting observations a nightmare.

After these initial investigation and observation stages, the process of inquiry begins to vary greatly. Occasionally, teachers find and begin to investigate a well-formed question immediately. More typically, the teachers begin their next round of inquiry with a general question. Sometimes these questions are about how to help students have more productive sessions; for example, one of Jane Zachary Gargaro's early inquiry questions asked how collaborative planning might help students to understand genre elements such as dialogue and first-person narration and then to use these elements in a story they were writing.

Through various methods of observation (e.g., observing planning sessions, asking students to respond to their planning tapes, listening to students' planning tapes), teachers can often begin to answer their questions, or they may revise their question and set up a new situation for observation. Often what happens in the planning sessions is so surprising that the teacher abandons or greatly modifies his or her original question and takes on a new, more interesting issue. For example, Jean Aston's investigation of community college students' willingness to try new strategies for writing became much more complex when her students began to see the impact of academic tracking and banking theories of education on their own educational experiences.

A final note: It is possible to do an inquiry project alone, but working with a partner or a group of teachers can greatly enhance the inquiry process. The process is never solitary because teachers and students must share observations and insights, but sharing and comparing frustrations, insights, and breakthroughs with someone struggling with similar issues can help a teacher make sense of the inquiry process and make it much more interesting.

Note

1. Throughout the book, when students or teachers are referred to only by first names, those names are pseudonyms, unless the students or teachers preferred that we use their real names.

5 Interactions of Engaged Supporters

Rebecca E. Burnett
Iowa State University
Ames, Iowa

The origin of this paper can be traced back to the earliest months of the Making Thinking Visible Project's pilot year, when teachers worked to figure out why some collaborative planning sessions seemed so much more successful than others. In fact, a few collaborative planning sessions were dismal failures, and a few were successful beyond our expectations, but most were moderately successful, with a few unfortunate lows and a few welcome peaks. Curious as we project team members were about the reasons for the distinctions, we considered a number of possibilities: the ability of the students, their grade level, the courses, the assignments, the ways teachers introduced collaborative planning, the kinds of prompts or cue sheets students used (if any), the questioning strategies of the supporters. Although all of these possibilities seemed in some way important, we decided that two of them—the way teachers introduced collaborative planning (discussed by David Wallace in chapter 4) and the questioning strategies of the supporters—were particularly influential.

I decided to investigate the nature of supporters and their interactions with writers in order to learn more about what distinguishes effective supporters from weak ones. I hoped that knowing more about supporters would, ultimately, enable us to answer our questions about how to teach students to become better supporters. I began by sifting through lots of data during the pilot year (observing pairs and small groups of collaborators, viewing videotapes, listening to audiotapes, and reading transcripts of protocols)—data from students in my own classes as well as from students in classes of other teachers in the project. Then I read those data with a dual perspective, as an experienced teacher and as a project researcher. During the next two years, as I continued to collect and analyze data from a variety of high school and university classes, I decided that supporters can be distinguished by both their attitudes and their behaviors. I see attitude being displayed through a range of factors such as students' rhetorical awareness as well as their self-image, motivation, responsibility, and receptiveness to planning and collaboration. I see supporter behaviors being displayed through the collaborators' strategic use of what I call a "repertoire of verbal moves."[1] Both attitude (which I discuss briefly in this chapter) and behavior (which I discuss in more detail) work together to create *supporter engagement*.

Supporter Attitude

The issue of attitude calls attention to a range of factors such as students' awareness of their social and rhetorical contexts, or personal attitudes such as their self-image, motivation, responsibility, and receptiveness to planning and collaboration. Awareness of the complex social and rhetorical context, for example, can be encouraged by working with a supporter. Collaborative interaction with an engaged supporter reduces a sense of isolation and reinforces the idea that writers and writing are socially situated. Awareness of social context lets inexperienced writers know they are not alone in their frustration and insecurity, and that they can get help (which is not viewed as cheating; rather, it is encouraged), that the writing itself is influenced and shaped by context, and that their writing has an audience that will be affected and can respond. This attitude may lead to consensus between the collaborators, or it may "be a powerful instrument for students to generate differences, to identify the systems of authority that organize these differences, and to transform the relations of power that determine who may speak and what counts as a meaningful statement" (Trimbur, 1989, p. 603). In other words, awareness of social context can create a sense of community and support (Bruffee, 1984), but it can also provoke substantive conflict that may lead to a productive exploration of issues that would otherwise be ignored. An attitude that recognizes the importance of social context also provides an opportunity for inexperienced writers to define their task and exchange ideas, thus reducing problems that might not be managed so easily when working individually.

A number of attitude factors have been identified and explored by members of the Making Thinking Visible Project. Leslie Byrd Evans learned that ideas brought up by students during collaborative planning sessions were sometimes deleted in writers' final papers based as often on *supporters' or writers' poor self-image and lack of confidence* as on the inappropriateness of the ideas. For Leslie, "The process of recording pre-writing collaborations and comparing transcripts and final papers" led her to investigate, among other things, how she could "help students gain confidence, state their ideas and keep them" (see Leslie's discovery memo in section 1). Leslie recognized that students who believe they have little or nothing to contribute during a session make poor supporters, regardless of the potential value of their ideas.

A second critical attitude is the *collaborators' motivation*. Positive motivation is important because collaborators who are not motivated seldom have the involvement necessary for productive interaction. In fact, if either collaborator—writer or supporter—is unmotivated, the interaction is likely to be perfunctory, merely going through the motions. David Wallace demonstrates that such perfunctory planning by unmotivated collaborators results in a session in which students "were either unable or unwilling to use the session to explore and elaborate their ideas for writing" (see David's project paper in section 1).

Another critical attitude involves the *responsibility that students are willing to take during collaborative planning*. After analyzing students in two case studies, Jim Brozick suggests that "Those who take responsibility also become more positive in attitude; those who fail to take responsibility become more negative in attitude" (see Jim's discovery memo in section 2).

A fourth critical attitude deals with *receptivity to planning and collaboration*. Statements that Jane Zachary Gargaro collected from her students "seem to suggest that students will not benefit from collaboration when they are not open to the process." Jane suggests that this lack of openness seems to result from one of three dominant attitudes: (1) an inflexibility about their own ideas or established plan, (2) an unwillingness to improve process skills, or (3) an unwillingness to connect process to product" (see Jane's discovery memo in section 2).

These various aspects of supporters' attitudes play a critical role in the success or failure of collaborative planning. Lack of engagement showed up in a number of ways in the students I observed. Sometimes these unengaged supporters were not active participants in the planning. Some often did not listen carefully to writers, and they asked questions that were not tailored to the specific writer or task. Others did not seem to see themselves as collaborators who had an important role in helping writers shape their plan. As a result, they made few relevant or productive contributions and seldom probed or challenged the writers' inadequately developed ideas. A lack of self-confidence, motivation, responsibility, or receptiveness may stem from any number of sources—insecurity about collaborative interaction, unfamiliarity with the process, boredom with the task, minimal interest in the subject of the assignment—but these are not the only problems that can affect a supporter's engagement.

Sometimes, supporters met these critical preliminary conditions (that is, they were self-confident, motivated, responsible, and receptive), yet they were not completely engaged because they did not have the requisite strategic knowledge and moves. An example from the collaborative planning session of two twelfth-grade students illustrates this problem. Their teacher, Jane Zachary Gargaro, was pleased with the way that Juan, the supporter, listened to Aaron's ideas and asked questions that helped Aaron develop the key point for his narrative essay (Gargaro, 1991). However, part way through what began as a potentially productive collaborative planning session, Aaron and Juan seemed to hit an impasse. Juan's questions did not press Aaron to develop his ideas in more detail.

> *Juan:* So you want to use comparison?
>
> *Aaron:* Kind of, but not point by point, just we'll be comparing
> them because they each bring up a different quality.
>
> *Juan:* Yeah, that no two parents are really alike.

Here Juan asked a straightforward question about the way Aaron was planning to organize his essay, but he failed to make an important strategic move: asking a follow-up question. When given the opportunity, he failed to push Aaron to elaborate his plan to use comparison, to ask any number of possible follow-up questions: "Who will you compare?" "What qualities will you focus on?" "If you dont use a point-by-point comparison, how will you organize the information?" Instead, Aaron rejected Juan's attempt to provide an example or a possible point and, when asked, admitted that "I'm not totally sure what my point is."

> *Aaron:* Yeah, but that's not the point I'm really trying to make.
>
> *Juan:* What is your point?
>
> *Aaron:* I don't know, I just think, I'm not totally sure what my
> point is. I think I'm trying to bring out the good in family
> life. I'm going to show that, I'm going to try and show that
> it ends up working out for you usually and that it's important.
> I don't know, probably a positive view. I guess the adult will
> kind of be a mentor to the kid, I guess. He's learned over the
> years that it's not only easier, but [it's certainly nice?] to have
> people caring for you when you wake up in the morning and
> now he's having to wake up, you know.

Again, instead of following up, getting Aaron to narrow a point for his essay, Juan shifted to another topic and asked Aaron about the setting.

> *Juan:* Do you think that this has to take place in any particular setting to make it, do you think that in one special setting it could work better or not?

> *Aaron:* I'm not sure, but I think it'd be interesting if I put it in a hospital, like in *Dinner at the Homesick Restaurant,* when Ezra met that girl there, but I don't think I'm going to do that. I think that setting would be important, too, but I'm not sure what I'm going to do with that.

Rather than pursuing this point, Juan again shifted to another topic— this time asking Aaron about audience—missing the opportunity to ask follow-up questions that would have helped Aaron elaborate his plan.

> *Juan:* Any special audience?

> *Aaron:* I don't think so. I think it could be written for anybody, anybody who's got family, or a child. I don't know, nobody in particular though.

Juan and Aaron were clearly motivated; both were on task, and their discussion addressed several rhetorical elements. However, their discussion was limited in that Juan did not prompt Aaron to elaborate or justify his points, nor did he take the opportunity to challenge Aaron's statements to engender substantive conflict or offer direct advice.

Supporter Behavior

A positive attitude in its various guises is necessary, but, as the example with Aaron and Juan shows, is certainly not sufficient for full engagement. Collaboration will probably not have much chance of being successful—even with a self-confident, motivated, responsible, and receptive supporter working in a cooperative situation—if the supporter does not know what to do. In other words, supporters need to have a repertoire of strategic verbal moves they know when and how to use. Which moves a supporter chooses will depend on many factors, including the task, the supporter's experience, and the writer's needs— in other words, the complex context of the rhetorical situation.

Theresa Marshall had to confront such strategic knowledge and moves when one of her basic skills students said, "My supporter needed to ask me better questions. I mean she asked me questions and when I said the first thing that came to my mind she moved on. I mean really." Theresa's student isolated a critical strategic factor: It matters what supporters say, what they ask. Theresa responded to her students' requests to spend extra time helping them develop their questioning strategies, which they thought would help them both as supporters and as writers. The issue of supporters was placed on the agenda by Theresa's students: They recognized the value of having a strategy, of knowing how to ask appropriate questions at opportune moments (see Theresa's discovery memos in section 2). The importance of supporter questions has been pushed much further by Tom Hajduk, who recognized that access to assignment-specific sequences of questions can help student writers. Sometimes inexperienced student collaborators need some help, but one teacher cannot be everywhere at once to help individual students. Tom believed that the role of the supporter was so important that he developed computer software to act as a supporter scaffold. His Planner's Options© program enables teachers to model effective questioning strategies for a particular assignment while it provides structure for less experienced collaborators (see Tom's discovery memo in section 1).

Other critical aspects of supporters involve the roles supporters assume and the strategic choices they make. Len Donaldson not only recognized the value of supporters in successful collaborative planning, he identified their roles. Modifying a model of supporter roles that had been suggested in one of the monthly meetings, Len noted that students in his classes had an impact on writers in their roles as clarifying supporters, confirmational supporters, and problem-solving supporters (see Len's discovery memo in section 1). Turning the question about supporter impact in another direction, Linda Flower established that the strategic choices that writers make during their planning with supporters do influence the text they produce. In reviewing a recent study that she and her colleagues conducted with first-year college students, she explained that these freshmen writers responded to the constructive prompts of their supporters nearly ninety percent of the time, making critical changes to important parts of their texts. The effectiveness of collaborative planning "is determined by the strategic choices students make and their awareness of those choices" (see Linda's discovery memo in section 4).

Attempting to answer the questions that I started out with in this chapter—why some collaborative planning sessions are more successful than others and what students should learn about collaborative interaction that will help them become more engaged supporters—has led me to focus on verbal moves as one way to explain successful collaborative interaction and to help students learn to be engaged supporters.

Verbal Moves

As supporters, students provide each other with scaffolding, described by Bruner (1978) as a strategy in which capable peers help their classmates extend their zone of proximal development. Scaffolding is based on Vygotsky's notion that a supporter who provides assistance enables a person to complete tasks that would be too difficult to do individually (1986). The value of the engaged supporters I have observed seems to come not from their greater knowledge of content or tremendous skill in managing rhetorical elements, but from their strategic moves that encourage, reinforce, and challenge a writer.

Nevertheless, being an engaged supporter is difficult. In fact, many of the teachers in the Making Thinking Visible Project agree that becoming a good supporter is the single most difficult thing for students to learn as they work toward being effective collaborators. In the transcripts I have read and the audio- and videotapes I have studied, four categories of verbal moves showed up repeatedly; I have listed them here in increasing order of a supporter's assertiveness:

- prompting the writer
- contributing information to the writer
- challenging the writer
- directing the writer

These four categories of verbal moves are important for a number of reasons. Most immediately, they provide a framework for defining and teaching supporter behavior. Supporters can use this scaffolding to help writers bridge their zone of proximal development as they consider rhetorical elements. Being able to discuss these moves also enables supporters to analyze and then reflect on their own effectiveness. Equally important, the categories provide teachers and researchers with a way to analyze and evaluate collaborative interaction. Finally, these categories have parallels in the research about cognitive processes in composing, cooperative learning, decision theory, and collaborative writing.

Prompts, the first category of verbal moves, are a critical part of collaborative interaction, not only as cues that signal the listener's interest, but as neutral comments and acknowledgements, reinforcing comments and encouragement, reminders, and questions about rhetorical elements. Prompts used by supporters in this project urged clarification and elaboration, encouraging writers to say more, both about rhetorical plans and about actual text. Such simple prompts as "Tell me more" and "What else could you consider?" as well as "Yeah, I see" and "uh-huh" seemed to encourage writers to keep talking. Support for the value of prompts comes from composition research. For example, children who received "procedural facilitation" cards with planning cues (intended to stimulate new ideas, elaborations, improvements to existing plans, and synthesis of ideas) moved beyond the "what next" strategy to attempt sustained planning (Scardamalia & Bereiter, 1987; Scardamalia, Bereiter, & Steinbach, 1984). In a study with college students, the more specific and directive prompt, "Add things to improve your essay," resulted in better revised texts than the prompt, "Revise" (Matsuhashi & Gordon, 1985). Supporters can use the encouraging prompts of procedural facilitation as well as the more directive prompts in their attempt to stimulate more planning.

While prompts tend to be neutral, offering little in the way of specific information, supporters who *contributed* information provided writers with facts, observations, and suggestions. The information varied in form and content: a summary, synthesis, or a metacognitive reflection about the group, task, or text. Supporters contributed information for social as well as cognitive reasons, as suggested by Slavin (1990): "[A]ll cooperative learning shares the idea that students . . . are responsible for their teammates' learning as well as their own" (p. 3). He further noted that "encouraging contributions from all students reduces the likelihood of 'free-rider[s]'" (p. 16), which are a common frustration teachers encounter in their classes.

Challenging the writer is another highly productive supporter move that, for the students in this project, involved asking critical questions, suggesting alternatives, and arguing opposing views. A number of researchers have argued that challenges in various forms are productive. For example, Putnam (1986) explains that substantive conflict about the issues and ideas under consideration can be highly productive in decision making, while Slavin (1990) notes that the ability to take another perspective in a cooperative learning situation has benefits beyond the specific task; students generally demonstrate more positive social be-havior by being more cooperative or altruistic. In my own recent research, I have established a high correlation between coauthors who engage in a high percentage of substantive conflict about rhetorical elements and their production of high-quality documents (Burnett, 1991, 1992).

A fourth supporter behavior involves *directing the writer* to modify plans and/or text by adding, changing, or deleting. Research studies are divided in their opinion about the frequency and helpfulness of directive behavior in collaboration. Gere and Stevens (1985) have reported instances of writing students who are directive, sometimes politely and productively, but sometimes aggressively, even to the point of insult. However, Freedman (1987) reports that students avoid evaluating each other's writing, often negotiate conflicting answers on their writing activity sheets, and "rarely offer writers suggestions or advice" (p. 26), except in cases involving mechanics and form. In collaborative planning sessions I have observed, supporters were only occasionally directive.

These four verbal moves—prompting the writer, contributing information to the writer, challenging the writer, and directing the writer—normally appeared in combination in the planning session of the students I observed. During several conversational turns, a supporter might prompt the writer several times, offer a concrete suggestion, challenge the writer by disagreeing with him or her, and give the writer a specific change to make in the plan. Inexperienced supporters sometimes restricted themselves to using prompts, unless they had been taught the benefits of strategically using other types of verbal moves. More successful supporters typically used all four of these verbal moves, though not necessarily equally. The success of engaged supporters seemed to come not from the variety of verbal moves but from the strategic use of specific moves—being able, for example, to ask appropriate follow-up questions (unlike Juan, mentioned earlier in this chapter). Students can learn to identify the strategic use of these verbal moves in their own collaborative sessions. (Several teachers in this project—for example, Leslie Byrd Evans in section 1 and Jane Zachary Gargaro in section 2—talk about the value of having students examine the transcripts of their own planning sessions.)

Which behaviors a supporter chooses to emphasize depends on many factors in the context of the rhetorical situation, including the task, the supporter's experience, and the writer's needs. For some situations, minimal engagement, such as just offering prompts, is a good role for a supporter to play. Minimal engagement can be a good starting place for inexperienced collaborators because offering prompts is far easier than playing devil's advocate or making productive contributions. It can also be appropriate if the writer needs to maintain a sense of control and would feel intimidated by a supporter's more assertive role. However, effective supporters soon discover that writers sometimes get off task, lose sight of their objectives, or run out of steam; in such situations, writers generally respond positively and productively to a supporter's challenges or contributions. An effective supporter allows a writer to assume the authority of the session and set the agenda; within this agenda the supporter may raise challenges or suggest contributions.

Engaged Supporters

The examples in this section show how two different pairs of supporters use strategic verbal moves as scaffolding to help writers come up with ideas that they would have been unlikely to generate on their own (at least in the time available for the assignments). Both pairs of writers— Shauna and Lisa, then Ed and Anna—are self-confident, motivated, responsible, and receptive, demonstrating the positive attitude that is necessary but not sufficient for their successful interaction. The strategic verbal moves we can identify in their planning sessions can help answer the question, what makes a successful collaborative planning session, though they certainly do not identify all the possible successful approaches to supporting. This kind of analysis, with transcripts from other people's collaborative planning sessions as well as with transcripts from their own planning sessions, can help students learn more about the collaborative interaction of engaged supporters.

Lisa and Shauna were twelfth graders in an inner-city high school; they were in a college-bound class, working on the writer's plan for a paper defining a hero. As an engaged supporter, Lisa pushed Shauna, who was planning to focus her paper on Gandhi, to decide just who can be a hero and whether heroic actions must be unselfish. Lisa prompted Shauna to be decisive about her points. (The following excerpt has been edited to delete some detailed elaborations and off-topic comments.)

> *Shauna (writer):* I just think that if someone's a hero, they've made a good change for themselves and other people. I mean it doesn't have to be "and" other people because I think that everybody can be heroic.
>
> *Lisa (supporter):* You think that everybody can be heroic? Let's take a stand.

Clearly, Lisa was listening and thinking about Shauna's plan. Lisa's prompt was very assertive without, at this point, making a contribution to content: Lisa's question, which expected a thoughtful response, was followed by a directive, "Let's take a stand." When Shauna responded that heroes could "make a change for themselves," Lisa followed with a specific contribution.

> *Shauna:* Yeah, I think that everybody can be heroic, I mean if they make a change for themselves and it's for the better.
>
> *Lisa:* Yeah, you could fit that into your research, too, somehow. You could say, like—
>
> *Shauna:* Yeah, I could talk about how [Gandhi] changed, wanted it for himself, too. And that could be a hero.

Lisa was not just a perfunctory supporter. She not only contributed; she challenged and directed. She helped Shauna construct a plan. At one point, Shauna asked, "Why would being in jail make him [Gandhi] a hero?" to which Lisa shot right back, "Because he was in jail for what he believed in?" "Maybe you might want to include that." She was involved in helping Shauna develop a definition for "hero." In fact, even though Lisa was the supporter, she went so far as to contribute her own definition:

> *Lisa:* What makes a hero—I mean a hero is somebody who, of course, is brave. All right, my definition of a hero is somebody who is brave, does something to change for the better, okay? . . . That's what a hero is, what a hero does, makes something better.

Lisa helped Shauna think about the problem of whether heroic actions can help the hero as well as others and then suggested another way for Shauna to think about her definition. Not only did Lisa prompt Shauna to continue this line of thinking by acknowledging Shauna's point, but Lisa was directive in encouraging Shauna to include it and then contributed her own spin on the idea, which Shauna agreed with.

> *Lisa:* Yeah, that's right. You could include that, and maybe you could include toward the end that maybe anybody could be like Gandhi if they wanted to.
>
> *Shauna:* If they put their mind to it.

Lisa helped Shauna consolidate her plan, reminding her about a point she made earlier in the planning session about heroes acting unselfishly. She pushed Shauna to reconcile this point with the idea of doing something for themselves.

> *Lisa:* Wait, you said [earlier], he—when somebody is heroic, they are unselfish. They do it for themselves, but they are doing it for everybody.
>
> *Shauna:* Yeah, but they don't have to just do it for everybody.
>
> *Lisa:* They can do it for themselves, too, though?

> *Shauna:* If you're heroic and are making a change, yeah. I don't consider that being selfish, if you're making a change for everybody.

Sometimes Lisas questions were drawn from a schema, a well-learned pattern; although she did not shy away from asking generic questions from a list provided by her teacher, neither did she use these steps in a lockstep, question-answer sequence. Instead, she seemed to use these questions to establish the groundwork. Lisa asked this series of questions over several conversational turns to encourage Shauna to establish a position about factors such as reader reaction, definition of terms, and the paper's organization.

> What does the reader expect to learn?

> Well, I wanted to know... what do you really think a hero is? Do you have a clear-cut definition...? What exactly is your definition of a hero? I mean are there—do you think there are many definitions?

> Well, how are you going to set it [the paper] up? I mean, do you have any idea?

Then she used follow-up questions with which she pushed Shauna to explain, clarify, and elaborate. In fact, sometimes she seemed relentless in pursuing a point, which gave Shauna the scaffolding she needed to develop her ideas. Here are some of the questions she asked Shauna during an extended segment of their discussion when she tried to get Shauna to deal with why Gandhi starved himself as a form of political protest. This is no cookie-cutter series of questions, but rather a series that Lisa asked over several turns to help Shauna explore and elaborate her ideas.

> Okay, what I want to know is why did Gandhi, why did he starve himself?

> [H]ow did he think he would make a change? I mean the guys didn't care if he starved himself, did they?

> Do you think it's a good idea that he starved himself? I mean, would you have done it that way?

> Did you think it made them want to change?

Although engaged supporters like Lisa can help a writer by playing critic and devil's advocate, by prompting a writer to consider alternatives, by commenting on strengths and weaknesses, and by offering suggestions, inexperienced supporters are sometimes overbearing. Forgetting that the paper belongs to the writer, they may not only waste a writer's time, they may also alienate him or her by trying to take over. Their role as a supporter should be to balance prompts, contributions, challenges, and directions as a way to encourage the writer (even if the writer is a coauthor). A supporter who only criticizes the plan, provides most of the substantive ideas, or assumes ownership of the paper misunderstands a supporter's responsibilities.

While Lisa did a good job of prompting, contributing, challenging, and directing, the project provided examples of other approaches to supporting. A second pair of writers, Anna and Ed, were college juniors who were collaboratively planning a recommendation report they would coauthor. Their engagement included far more explicit, substantive conflict than we saw in the excerpts from Lisa and Shauna. Substantive conflict, which may be seen as a way to signal discrepant points of view, engages collaborators (whether a writer with a supporter or coauthors) in the examination of ideas critical to the task. Substantive conflict gives collaborators the opportunity to consider alternatives— for example, when one collaborator suggests "Let's do x," the other collaborator might respond, "Yes, x is a possibility, but let's consider y as another way to solve the problem." Substantive conflict also gives collaborators the opportunity to voice explicit disagreements, such as when one collaborator suggests "Let's do z," the other collaborator responds, "No" or "I disagree" or "I think that's wrong."

Anna and Ed were engaged in their collaborative planning session by actively listening to each other's ideas and providing the scaffolding that helped them build ideas they might not have thought of individually. They prompted each other (nearly always in the midst of an episode in which they were contributing an idea or challenging some point), and they did come close to what we could call directing the other. Though these directive statements were couched politely, their intent was clear. However, most of their interaction involved contributions and challenges; and since that is what most distinguishes them from Lisa and Shauna, that will be the focus of this discussion.

Their emphasis on contributions and challenges might be explained in part by their developmental and academic maturity (college juniors as compared to high school seniors); in part by the fact that they were coauthoring a document (and, thus, they were not only mutual supporters for each other, but they had a joint commitment to create an effective document); in part by the training they received in their business and technical communication class, which identified the benefits of substantive conflict in collaborative planning.

Ed and Anna discussed whether the cost of the solar heating system they were describing should be included in the product information sheet. In a clear-cut example of substantive conflict, Ed maintained that cost should not be included and contributed information to reinforce his position; Anna was not convinced.

> *Ed (coauthor):* I don't think it [the cost] should go in there, because it's so different between people. Like they see like—a system that costs them 8,000, all of a sudden we quote them some price of 20,000. I mean—I just—think we'd be better off keeping off, keeping out of there.
>
> *Anna (coauthor):* Okay, but they'll want to know.

Ed was upfront in his disagreement with Anna about including cost figures in their document. His comment led them to consider alternative ways of informing readers about cost. Here Ed prompted Anna to express her position. She began her challenge by providing her interpretation of the situation, but then she posed an alternative that opened the door for the two of them to solve the problem in a way that satisfied both of them.

> *Ed:* Well, I mean, I don't know, if you mean—we should, we should talk about it if you disagree.
>
> *Anna:* I kind of do, because, um, I mean if somebody says, "Can I have your information sheet," they're going to want to know about the price. They're going to want to have the price in front of them, especially if they're going to compare it to other systems. They're going to want to see the, the price, how much it's going to cost. Like let's face it, everybody's concerned about price. And I guess the sales people could have a different, a separate price sheet.

Exploring the reasons for their conflict is typical of good collaborators. Anna and Ed's next episode also shows how explicit disagreements can be managed; in this situation, their explicit disagreement led them to consider additional alternatives.

> *Ed:* We, we, I mean, I would say I probably consider it's in a low cost, it says, "Its low cost should convince you to install a Sundance system in your home or business."
>
> *Anna:* Even so, the range from 4 to 26 [$4,000 to $26,000] would at least give them a ballpark figure. Or we could find out a little bit more detail on the cost.
>
> *Ed:* Well, I thought we should put in a section like, depending on how big or how many you get, and just put all these

things in there. Maybe we could put it in the advantages thing, if it is a low cost.

Anna: Okay. Well, that's true. We could stick it in. Maybe we could stick it in and say, "Cost is one of the advantages" and put the price in there.

Ed: Yeah. I don't know. I just think it's going to be an information sheet. We don't, definitely in closing I don't think.

Anna: Okay.

As Ed and Anna explored alternatives, they often elaborated a variety of points and frequently expressed immediate agreements. When Anna finally said "Okay" at the end of this episode, she agreed with the alternative they had worked out. Their explicit disagreement followed by consideration of alternatives is a pattern typical of the successful collaborators I have observed.

Conclusion: Supporters as Context

This chapter started out to answer questions about why some collaborative planning sessions are more successful than others and what students should learn about collaborative interaction that will help them become more engaged supporters. I have suggested that both attitude and strategic behaviors work together to create supporter engagement. Attitude includes factors ranging from students' awareness of the complex social context in which they are writing to their own self-image, motivation, responsibility, and receptiveness to planning and collaboration. But a positive attitude is not enough if a person does not know what to do; to avoid contributing to perfunctory planning, a supporter needs a repertoire of strategic verbal moves.

There is more than one way to be a good supporter. Excerpts from the two collaborative planning sessions in this chapter demonstrate that supporters can be engaged in different ways; differences that can be explained by the assertiveness of the supporter as well as by the needs of the writer. For example, Lisa balances prompts, contributions, challenges, and occasional directives; in contrast, Anna and Ed spend more of their time making contributions and challenges. Lisa recognizes that Shauna is the author; although she is remarkably assertive, she does not assume ownership of the plan for the paper. Anna and Ed, on the other hand, may feel the necessity of making contributions and offering challenges because they are coauthors.

Focusing on the attitudes and strategic moves of supporters should go a long way in reducing teacher and student frustration when collaborating in writing. Students not only need to learn *about* these productive attitudes and strategic moves, they need to *engage* in them.

Note

1. I intend the term "repertoire of verbal moves" to convey a sense similar to the use of the term when a theater company refers to its "repertoire of plays": a collection of a few core or critical works (i.e., basic verbal moves) accompanied by several other works (i.e., additional verbal moves) that vary according to the skill of the acting company, the sophistication of the audience, the time available for the performance (i.e., collaborative session), and so on.

Part II Observations across Contexts

Section 1
Exploring the Beginnings

6 Transcripts as a Compass to Discovery

Leslie Byrd Evans
Steel Valley High School
Munhall, Pennsylvania

Leslie Byrd Evans teaches at Steel Valley High School in the Monongahela Valley on Pittsburgh's south side—where the mills and prosperity used *to be. As a writer, editor, and community activist herself, Leslie has helped document the labor union history that was made in this valley and has tried to bring her students into their past as well. But the biggest challenge now is making school seem relevant in an uncertain future. This series of discovery memos, taken from Leslie's first two years in the project, documents the necessary skepticism she brought to this project—"Would this really do anything for my students?" And it shows how a critical and experimental teaching style let her transform (and re-transform) collaborative planning to solve current problems in her classrooms. (In preparing this memo sequence, Leslie also includes a new set of notes to you, the reader.) Her series of discovery memos initiates the section on Exploring the Beginnings, which captures some of the questions, curiosities, uncertainties, and discoveries that marked both the beginning of the project and the initial experience each of us had in joining this collaborative group and using collaborative planning for the first time.*

A Discovery Memo

I had read about collaborative planning and was anxious to get some ideas about how to make it work—so anxious that I took a colleague with me to the October seminar of the Making Thinking Visible Project. Participants included teachers, professors, researchers, and community leaders, but it became painfully obvious to us outsiders that they had been working together for months, some for a year, comfortable in their vocabulary of "planners, supporters, and blackboard planners." My friend and I sat, panic-stricken, as a dozen people communicated freely in a language unlike any spoken in the teachers' lunchroom at my school. And at the end of the three-hour session, my friend made her decision about joining the project:

> I want something that I can take into my classroom and use.
> You can't use "conceptual planning" to keep kids from hitting
> each other over the head with their grammar books.

I credited her lack of enthusiasm to teacher trepidation of Something
New, but when I tried to talk to other teachers back in the all-brick,
windowless world of school, there were more bad vibes and "no"
votes:

> Collaborative planning? Whenever I use group work, there's
> always someone who sits there and lets all the other students
> do the work. Someone always gets a free ride. (English teacher)

> They don't really talk about the assignment; they talk about
> how many kegs they consumed over the weekend. (Social
> studies teacher)

Even when I mentioned to my classes that we would be trying some
new ways to plan writing, I got tepid responses.

> You're just making us do this for a class you're taking.
> University work is too hard.
> I'll be put with someone I despise.
> I'll be put with someone who despises me. (English students)

The cynics were in full battle array. No one wanted to try even
the generally accepted collaboration, much less the finer points of
collaborative planning; what once had sounded like a great idea now
sounded like too much work for too little reward. But Linda Norris,
the project's educational coordinator, had been so nice over the phone.
How could I call her back and say that because no one at my school
sounded enthusiastic, I wasn't interested? I could never get up enough
nerve to make the phone call.

I attended the monthly collaborative planning seminars, listened
to other teachers' experiments with the process, and got fired up
myself. In November, I introduced the collaborative planning process
with a vengeance into my writing assignments and, during the winter,
learned the process right along with the students. In my enthusiasm
to perfect the process, I tried collaborative planning with every essay,
paragraph, parody, and poem—documenting each attempt. I video-
taped it, audiotaped it, computered it, talked it, and abused it. My
students began to peek into my room before entering to see if the
room had been "bugged" for the proceedings that day. I knew I had
gone too far when I overheard them refer to me as Big Sister.

Note to readers: Once we got comfortable with collaborative
planning for writing, my students and I liked the process. An end-of-

year questionnaire produced such positive responses that I re-enlisted as a Making Thinking Visible groupie for the next school year. My first year in the project produced a box of audiotapes, a notebook of transcripts, two videotapes of nervous students, and a pile of my own seemingly unrelated discovery memos. What did all this data mean? I never had the time to reflect, but I had done one hell of a job recording the process! With the new school year, I hoped I could concentrate on *how* this process affects student thinking and writing.

During my second year in the project, a touch of discretion saved my students from collaborative planning burn-out. I made collaborative planning a special event or strategy, rather than using it for every writing assignment that came along. For example, I focused on using collaborative planning to solve a problem I was having in my Advanced Placement (AP) classes. Many of my in-class writing assignments are questions from past English AP Tests that I use throughout the school year to help students practice for the real thing in May. One problem in the resulting essays is that many students are not answering the question. In their anxiety and hurry to tackle the question, they write many paragraphs of specific references and examples to a question that is not precisely what is asked on the test paper. I thought collaborative planning before writing the timed essay in class might give them practice in figuring out what the question is really asking. Students interpreted what they thought the AP test question was asking and then compared it to their partners' interpretations. Two heads argued better than one; this paired exercise helped them develop their own critical inner voice. Students who were too accepting of any idea that came along began to reread and rethink the test question on their own. Students who were protective of their own ideas began to listen to peer suggestions, and included them in their final essays.

The second time I used this planning activity, each supporter and planner audiotaped the collaborative planning on one day. The next day, I had them transcribe a section of their taped conversation using the following instructions.

> *Assignment with Your Partner:* Transcribe (copy) a small section of your collaboration from yesterday's class period that you think is interesting.
>
> *Individual Assignment:* Reflect in writing on the conversation.
>
> *Step One:* Each collaborative pair should get a tape recorder and their tape. Play back the tape and listen to your conversation

from yesterday. Jot down some individual observations or re-actions to your conversation in your individual notebooks as you listen to the tape.

Step Two: Take a short section (one minute) of the tape and transcribe it (copy it). Select an interesting feature of the tape—possibly a section where collaboration seems very successful or a section where the thinking got muddled, but you tried to straighten things out. You may have your own reasons for selecting the section, which I'd like you to share with me at the end of the transcript. You can use your names or use "planner and supporter" as I did on the transcription that we read in class last week. If any of the transcripts are used for class, I will not use your names if you identify the speakers by planner and supporter. If you don't mind, use your own names.

Step Three: Using your individual notes and the transcript, write on a separate piece of paper any thoughts or reflections you have about the process that took place yesterday.

Step Four: Re-box and replace the tape recorders and tapes at the front of the room. Turn in your transcripts and reflections to me.

The first-day collaboration tapes were tedious listening, but the re-flections from Step Three read like true confessions:

I'll never use "ya know" again.

I never knew I completely dominated the conversation.

I let Jack do all the talking. Am I always that quiet around guys?

Playing back our conversation makes me realize that I wasn't listening to anything Lori was saying. And I don't think she was hearing me either.

I sound like I'm from la-la land. If I had been about 200% clearer, there might have been an outside chance that Melanie might have understood a sentence or two of what I said.

The communication and planning problems that students identified included jumping on the first idea that comes up because the planner and supporter feel pressured to talk rather than think; worrying that "my" idea is not as good as the "other" person's idea; being seduced by what seems to be the "easy" topic rather than the topic that would answer the question; one person doing all the talking; lacking good listening skills. I transcribed one of the planning dialogues that contained both strong and weak communication. We read and analyzed it aloud in class. (Liz, the planner, is writing about techniques that Shakespeare uses in Act III of *Macbeth*. Julie is her supporter.):

> *Liz (writer):* Is Lennox under Macduff or is he under Macbeth?
>
> *Julie (supporter):* Macduff.
>
> *Liz:* And the other ones don't have any idea that Macbeth has killed Banquo?
>
> *Julie:* Actually . . . by this time I think they know about Duncan, maybe not Banquo. (pause) Who are the "other ones"?
>
> *Liz:* Um . . . Lennox . . . um . . . Ross . . . Macduff . . . .
>
> *Julie:* You can't do all that. Isn't it too many for one essay?
>
> *Liz:* Why?
>
> *Julie:* Well, Macduff isn't even on Macbeth's side.
>
> *Liz:* Maybe I should go with the techniques . . . that would be like . . . symbols? . . . similes? . . . right?
>
> *Julie:* Yeah . . . but maybe, also tone . . . attitude . . . irony . . . .
>
> *Liz:* Irony, irony, like when it says, "A light! A light!" It's dark out, which is kind of strange.
>
> *Julie:* But what are you trying to show?
>
> *Liz:* How he used, like, darkness when something evil was supposed to happen. You know, like murder and then the ghost came. It was right after he just scorned Banquo. And that was irony there. So he says, "Pity him . . . what a shame." And I could do attitude. What would be, like, the attitude of their murderers? Whenever Macbeth was going to hire the murderers he, like, had to get them angry you know . . . and they didn't believe that Banquo was the enemy.
>
> *Julie:* Well, yeah, it sounds like irony, but how are you gonna connect these two? . . . the irony with the attitudes?
>
> *Liz:* This is gonna tie in, like, whenever he murdered them, when it was dark out . . . so that the murderers themselves didn't know what they did.
>
> *Julie:* So how are you gonna say that Shakespeare used these techniques to guide his audience?

Students read photocopied transcripts of the Julie-Liz collaboration and observed these positive results of the two students' collaboration:

1. There is clarification of original text.
2. The supporter extends ideas of the planner.
3. The supporter helps limit and focus content of paper.

4. Careful listening helps prevent mistakes and helps planner clarify so that misunderstanding won't take place.

Remember, I did not write these observations: Students read the transcripts and made these observations. Looking at a transcript and reading it aloud have the potential to teach on their own by letting students see and hear the actual words spoken during collaboration. Students discussed several questions: What makes a good supporter? What can a supporter say or ask that can help the planner? How did the planner and supporter differ in their approaches? From the transcripts, students make their own conclusions and meaning, which usually goes beyond my planned lesson and motivation.

Note to readers: Notice what is happening here. I began to share the transcripts with the students. They did not yawn; they were fascinated with their own conversations on paper. The first reaction was embarrassment, but once they realized that our purpose was to observe how the conversation helped them think of material for their writing, they took the discussion of the transcript very seriously. My subjective observation is that even the quality of the collaborations improved from that point on. They knew I was serious and interested enough to take the time to transcribe their collaborations. Analyzing the transcripts with my students created new questions for me as an instructor and opened up a whole new direction as a researcher by the end of the first semester of my second year in the project. Then, in January, I noticed that a few students were expressing dissatisfaction with using collaboration as a method for planning.

My AP students collaborate on college application essay questions, practice AP tests, skits, parodies, character portraits, and analytical essays, yet they are the most resistant to collaborative planning because they are not used to working with others; they are used to being wonderful students who think on their own and write on their own with fairly successful results, using grades rather than an audience for evaluation. Using collaborative planning with these groups led me to identify two new challenges: (1) helping students realize that two minds can be better and easier than one, and (2) experiencing active listening and supporting as skills that are as important as good writing itself. As I began to understand that even "good students" can be resistant to collaborative planning, a list of questions guided my further exploration:

Who are these reluctant collaborative planners?

Why are these individuals reluctant?

Where did the planner get his or her good ideas?

What made the planner back away from his or her original ideas?

Why does the planner use certain ideas and drop others?

Which part of the process worked for the planner?

Is there an intimidation factor that works against the planner (e.g., the supporter makes better grades, therefore has better ideas)?

How do I teach collaborative planning without competition?

I took this list of questions to a monthly meeting of the Making Thinking Visible Project and, after collaborating with two other members, devised a strategy for answering the questions and recording the students' responses.

I used an attitude survey (see David Wallace's discovery memo in section 2) to strain out my most reluctant collaborative planner, Scott, and decided to type and analyze two of his transcripts—one in which he was a planner and one, a supporter. This process led to a more focused study of Scott as well as insight into the reluctance toward the process that I was encountering with some students. Scott was an "A" student, but with an attitude. He liked to appear superior in class discussions. He had no time for slow thinkers, and his peers turned their backs to his argumentative approach to discussion. I enjoyed his aggressive contributions and frequently tried to soften his more critical comments and give credit for his insights. My theory was that he did not like collaborative planning because he refused to acknowledge that he could learn anything from talking with someone else. (See figure 6.1.)

In reading the collaboration between Scott and Sharon, I noticed some high-handed tactics on Scott's part.

> *Scott:* . . . that would be the end of Act IV and Act V. [directing Sharon as to which acts to discuss for her topic]
>
> *Scott:* . . . because he gets killed by Macduff. [telling Sharon what happened as if she did not know]
>
> *Scott:* You're gonna have to read Act V. [Sharon apparently had admitted off tape that she had not.]

Due to Scott's classroom reputation for acerbity, I decided not to read this transcript aloud in class but to show it to Sharon and Scott privately and separately. I asked Sharon to read the transcript of her collaboration with Scott, while I busied myself with another

Topic: What effect does Macbeth's reign have on Scotland?
Planner: Sharon
Supporter: Scott

Sharon: I guess I'm going to do what effect Macbeth's reign had on Scotland.

Scott: . . . and I guess that would be the end of Act IV and Act V.

Sharon: I'll talk about how everyone is against him now and wants him killed [stops tape]

Scott: . . . 'cause he is king throughout, well, pretty much from the banquet scene, Act III, scene iv, to the end of the play because he get killed by Macduff.

Sharon: Yeah, I knew that.

Scott: You're gonna have to read Act V.

Sharon: Act IV, though, they talk about how bad, how troubled, everybody is.

Scott: And probably the greatest effect is gonna be Malcolm and Macduff raising an army.

Sharon: Yeah.

Scott: That's going to be the greatest effect. There's going to be two factions. Actually Malcolm and Macduff are in England. Actually they're going to clash and Macduff and Macbeth are going to meet.

Sharon: Everybody doesn't trust anybody, do they?

Scott: No. That's why Macduff doesn't show up for the banquet. That's what I'm going to talk about.

Sharon: Come up with more. What else is bad?

Scott: Plus, he's not a good king. He's on the verge of a mental breakdown.

Sharon: Yeah.

Scott: Yeah, he's nuts.

Sharon: Yeah.

Scott: 'Cause how many people has he killed now? If not with his own hands but set up people's deaths.

Sharon: Yeah, that's true. He's mental. [pause] I can come up with something now. I don't know what I was doing when I wrote this.

Scott: Because he killed the king, two guards, had Banquo killed and tried to have Fleance killed, had Macduff's whole family killed.

Sharon: And his daughters . . . didn't he have two daughters . . . and a wife?

Scott: He had a son and his wife. [pause] I'm not sure what else though. [stops tape]

Scott: And you also end it with how his reign ends.

Sharon: That's good.

Scott: Give it a climactic ending . . . sort of pump up the scene between Macbeth and Macduff [pause] Oh my knee hurts.

In the play *Macbeth* by William Shakespeare, Macbeth's reign had a tremendous effect on Scotland.

Scotland changed from a prominent nation right after the successful war against Norway to a nation filled with turmoil under Macbeth's rule. The citizens of Scotland did not like the tyrannical ruler. After the deaths of Banquo and King Duncan, coupled with Macbeth's mental state, the people begin to distrust the King of Scotland. The people realized that Macbeth was behind all the problems of their land.

"It weeps, it bleeds, and each new day a gash is added to her wounds." Malcolm refers to the belief that each day seems to bring new terror to the already-troubled nation. Traitors are being named unfairly and hanged, fighting is taking place all over the country, and innocent people (Banquo and Macduff's family) are being hunted down and murdered. The people fear Macbeth; they do not want to become his next victim. Macbeth kills because he fears his evil doings will be revealed.

Macbeth's mental state also aids in the destruction of Scotland. Macbeth has an unstable state of mind. Macbeth visualizes Banquo's ghost at a banquet and begins screaming. Lady Macbeth hurriedly shuts him up, but the damage is done. Macbeth's people know something evil is weighing on his conscience. A leader of any nation cannot let his emotions and fears get the best of him. In Macbeth's case, he lets his emotions overcome him and his citizens lose all faith in him.

Malcolm and Macduff raise an army to defeat Macbeth. Malcolm and Macduff get aid from everyone, including Macbeth's army, to overthrow him.

In the climactic clash between Macbeth and Macduff, Macbeth is slain and the tyranny falls. Macduff proudly hoists Macbeth's head on a pole and exclaims, "The time is free!" Macduff refers to the horror being over; Scotland is once again a prominent nation. Malcolm is the new king.

Figure 6.1. Collaboration between Sharon and Scott.

task so that she would not feel pressured to read too quickly. I also got Sharon's permission to record part of our conversation. We were interrupted by a visitor, and after the door closed again, I forgot to turn the recorder back on; the final part of our discussion is from memory.

> *Leslie:* So what do you think? . . . Do you have any reaction to reading the transcript?
>
> *Sharon:* Scott really helped me a lot. I really didn't know what I was doing.
>
> *Leslie:* But I think you did know. You knew that you should be looking at Act IV to discuss Macbeth's effect on Scotland. Do you see where you say that?
>
> *Sharon:* Yeah.
>
> *Leslie:* Where does that idea appear in your written draft?
>
> *Sharon:* Here . . . [she points and then pauses as she keeps reading] . . . and all through here . . . [continues to point half-way down essay column]
>
> *Leslie:* Absolutely. That idea you had—to look at events and quotes in Act IV—ended up being half of your essay. [Sharon smiles broadly and looks at me with great relief. She took some time to reread her draft.]
>
> *Sharon:* Macbeth having mental problems . . . Malcolm and Mac-duff raising an army against Macbeth . . . and the climactic ending.
>
> *Leslie:* Yeah, you took just enough important ideas and let the rest go. A very good job of selection. And then you improve the ideas by elaborating with details and quotes. Nice job. [Sharon smiles again; she seldom smiles in class.]
>
> *Leslie:* Do you notice anything else about the transcript? any other observation you made or noticed about the transcript?
>
> *Sharon:* I let Scott talk a lot.
>
> *Leslie:* Yeah, I thought so, too. Do you remember why you let him talk so much?
>
> *Sharon:* [looks directly at me] Because he always knows so much. And I wasn't sure when I came to class . . . I wasn't sure about what to write.
>
> *Leslie:* But you did know that Act IV was the most important act to use?
>
> *Sharon:* Yeah, and then when I got my notes at home, everything fell together.
>
> *Leslie:* That's the way it should happen . . . .

Sharon: But Scott did help me a lot. [end of tape]

Sharon noticed that she asked most of the questions and that her comments were reduced to "Yeah." She apologetically said she really had not put much thought into her plans and, as a result, let Scott do most of the thinking and talking.

I pointed to her line, "Act IV, though, they talk about how bad, how troubled, everybody is." I asked her what her ideas were about Act IV. When she explained, I commented on what a wonderfully unified essay she could have had if she had focused on Scotland's troubles in Act IV. I also showed her where she let Scott bury her own good ideas.

"Yeah, you're right. I could have written the whole thing on that." She sounded pleased and annoyed with herself at the same time. I pretended to joke, "Don't let these men talk you into doing things you don't want to do!"

Scott was not apologetic and did not notice anything unusual about the discussion. I think he seemed a little embarrassed, however, when he pointed out that he asked only two questions that were even remotely rhetorical: "Cause how many people has he killed now? If not with his own hands but set up people's death?" Since we had discussed the role of a supporter and reviewed questions that supporters could ask, he started looking again to see if he could find any other questions in the transcript. He seemed fascinated with the transcript itself. I wondered what the other students would think about this transcript. I may use it next year, and change the names to protect the guilty. After a few minutes of searching, he admitted, "I should have asked her more questions."

To compare Scott's role of supporter to his role of planner, the next step was to analyze Scott's role as planner with a different student. With no malice intended on my part, Scott's partner, Desiree, was a bright low-achiever satisfied with Cs and Ds and the candidate for least likely to have read the assignment. As I heard their transcript, I quickly found what I had predicted: Scott did all the talking and Desiree did very little. I looked at the long sections of print where Scott talked and the one-liners by Desiree, but I decided to use the transcript as a point of discussion anyway. After having all that tape typed up, I wanted to use something!

Maybe I have just been lucky, but every time I use a typed transcript in class for discussion, I am surprised at the results. Perhaps the class took it upon itself to protect Desiree from Scott's superiority, but the observations during class discussion of the transcript were directed at the quality and appropriateness of Desiree's questions: "How do you *feel* . . . How are you going to *present* . . . *Why* were you gonna use cause and effect . . . . " I gained new respect for Desiree's question as the students gave as much credit to Desiree for eliciting the response as they gave to Scott for responding. Desiree had prevented their collaboration from becoming a "nod" session and demanded that Scott justify his content consideration, no doubt an unexpected activity for him.

The students' analysis of Desiree and Scott's transcript changed my opinion of Desiree's role of supporter so much that I decided to compare the transcript to the final paper, a frequent technique of collaborative planners. On the left side of the page is the transcript of Desiree and Scott's collaboration. On the right side is Scott's final essay after two revisions (see figure 6.2). I identified each separate idea mentioned by Scott with capital letters A through G. I then found and marked with corresponding letters each of these same ideas in the final paper and attempted to show the correlation with a lot of confusing hand-drawn arrows. The lines between the two columns trace where the ideas in the collaboration show up within the essay. I stole this cross-referencing idea from another participant in the Making Thinking Visible group.

Scott used not only his own responses to Desiree but also her suggestion: "Y'know the problem being him, you know, telling her what happened. The solution being him letting her keep that . . . ." Because Scott's response was rather tepid—"Yeah maybe . . ."—I never would have noticed that he actually used her idea in the final paper had I not drawn the cross-referencing. I wished I had thought of the cross-referencing before the classroom discussion. Better yet, why not let students do the cross-referencing as part of the analysis of the transcript? Again, the transcripts themselves become lessons and activities for students and teachers. As a result of the classroom discussion, I do think Scott became aware that Desiree's questions and suggestions led him to a better paper than he would have had without the collaboration. Now that I think of it, I never heard Scott complain about collaborative planning after that classroom discussion.

The drawback to using students' transcripts of collaborative planning is the time that it takes to transcribe tapes. Someday voice-activated computers will give us an immediate transcript of a collaboration. Think of what wonderful feedback that will be. Students can return to their own transcripts the next day, compare their notes to

Scott: Was it right for Marlow to be responsible ←→ **Topic Question**
for allowing Kurtz's fiancee to retain her
illusions about Kurtz?

Compassion is pity or sympathy. Marlow, the
main character of Joseph Conrad's *Heart of
Darkness* may be considered as one the most
compassionate heroes ever created. Leaving the
Intended's belief in Kurtz's love intact was
Marlow's greatest contribution to humanity.

Desiree: How do you feel about it?

Scott: Yeah, I think, I think it was right
because uhh, that was all she had to
cling to in the world, she didn't live, she

A [wasn't rich and she was obviously in
love with Kurtz and she had been in
mourning for a year and he was all that
she had to cling to. So believing that he

B [remembered her was y'know, the only
thing that she had to live for. So that's
what Marlow did.

C / **A** [The final meeting between the Intended, Mr.
Kurtz's fiancee, and Marlow, our merciful
protagonist, takes place about one year after the
death of the "great" Kurtz. At first, there was just
small talk, for the Intended had been in mourning
since the day that she received the news of her
fiance's death. Later, she wanted to know
everything that Marlow knew about him. Marlow
spoke highly of him, leaving out the fact that
Kurtz had murdered African natives to become
one of the most successful ivory traders in his
company. Listening to Marlow's every word, she
reinforced all he said. "It was impossible to know
him and not to love him."

Desiree: How are you going to present your
ideas?

Scott: **C** [Uhh, umm, I'm gonna to start out with
the scene between Marlow and the
Intended and I'm going to, y'know,
maybe get in some quotes. Of how the
Intended really felt about Kurtz and then

D [I'm gonna go back to the scene on the
boat between Kurtz and Marlow as
Kurtz was dying. And, umm, when,
when Kurtz is in the dark and even
before that when he gave Marlow all the
letters to give to his fiancee and then

E [I'm gonna close with just how Marlow
expresses compassion for human beings
in general with what he told the
Intended about Kurtz's final minutes and
Kurtz's life.

? Marlow admitted that he had heard Kurtz's last
words before he had died. Then Marlow faced the
biggest dilemma of his life when the Intended
confronted him with two simple words, "Repeat
them."

The two horns of the dilemma were the truth and
a lie. We are all taught that the truth is the right
thing to tell; Marlow opted for a lie. Marlow knew
the truth would have killed the young girl. Before

Desiree: OK, now why were you gonna use cause
and effect to tell the story?

Scott: **F** [Be . . . well the beginning and the middle
when I said I was gonna do the scene
between the Intended one and Marlow
and the flashback to the scene between
Kurtz and Marlow just gonna be real
short. Ummmm, the main body of the
paragraph is gonna be the thoughts on
Marlow's compassion and I was gonna
use cause and effect as ummm, if he

E [would've actually told her the truth
what the effect on her life would've
been. Even the effect on his life, y'know,
he wouldn't've been able to live with
himself. And now, ummm, that Kurtz
thought of his fiancee till the end. The

E [effect is y'know, gonna be that now
she'll be able to come out of mourning
and she'll be able to live with herself in
peace knowing that Kurtz loved her.

? **B** [Kurtz died, the Intended had two things for which
to live: (1) her fiance's return and (2) her fiance's
love. Now that his return was not imminent, the
only thought she could hold onto was that
Kurtz had died loving her. Marlow told the
Intended that Kurtz's last words were not "the
horror, the horror," but her name. With this

G [image, the Intended could go on with her life,
believing that the man she loved loved her in
return.

F [Marlow knew the consequences of both the truth
and the lie; he concluded that only he had to
know the truth. Hook the sin upon himself to
bring from inescapable depths a life that was
totally rejuvenated by his false confession. That is
true compassion for a human being.

Desiree: Did you read problem/solution?

Scott: Problems . . . who?

Desiree: **G** [Y'know the problem being him, you
know, telling her what happened. The
solution being him letting her keep
that . . .

Scott: Yeah, maybe.

Desiree: . . . in her head.

Scott: The problem would've been on whether
to tell her the truth or not.

Figure 6.2. Collaboration between Scott and Desiree.

their conversation, sort through and write, and still have time to analyze how the collaborative planning session went.

Note to readers: Looking back at my second year discovery memos makes me realize that this school year was truly the "mother of reflection." I scrutinized what was happening in the transcripts of collaboration between students. What I found were new insights not only into the process of thinking but also into the personalities of my students. One surprising revelation was that a recorded collaboration could differ significantly from the final paper. I began to ask students why certain ideas had been dropped or added. I heard similar doubts:

> I was afraid my idea wasn't good enough.
>
> I thought it would sound more important to talk about a celebrity's life than my own.
>
> I let him talk too much and gave up on my own idea.

These student reflections on their role as planners or supporters suggest poor self-image and lack of confidence. Comparing transcripts to the final papers showed that good ideas were getting dumped. My students were asking "Who has the better idea?" rather than "Who has some good ideas to trade?" The process of recording prewriting collaborations and comparing transcripts and final papers led me to other paths of discovery: Where do ideas come from? How are they transformed? Where do they go? How can I help students gain confidence, state their ideas and keep them?

Each September my senior students plan and write essays for actual college application questions. During my second year in the project, the University of Pittsburgh asked applicants to explain their choices of two famous people with whom they would spend an evening of conversation. I listened to the collaborations as I strolled the aisles and decided to compare Kristen and Melanie's taped collaboration to their final application essays. Kristen chickened out with one of her choices from the collaboration. Notice that Kristen's plan is to select Saddam Hussein and Princess Diana:

> *Kristen (writer):* dinner with **Saddam Hussein** and ask him **why is he doing this to the world** and ask him **why he wants to go to war** and **why he's in Kuwait.** And then I'm going to talk to Princess Diana and ask her what it's like to be a princess and what it feels to be in royalty and if she's treated differently than before.
>
> *Melanie (supporter):* Why would you choose Hussein? You said questions you'd ask him but why would you choose him?

Kristen: Because **I'm concerned about going to war** because I'm going to be eighteen and eighteen is the age to be drafted and **I don't want my close friend and relatives to go to war because of one crazy man.** I'd like to know what he thinks and what his thoughts are. Why is he doing this? **Is he happy with what he is doing or if he is just doing it to become powerful?**

Melanie: Why would you ask Princess Diana?

Kristen: I idolize her in a way. When I was little, I wished I could be a princess. What it would be like to live a life of royalty and talk with her about what her life was like and what it would be like to be in the spotlight and not to have privacy all the time just because you're royalty.

Kristen's final essay discussed Princess Diana and Sarah Ferguson (Fergie), a combination I had seen recently at the grocery check-out on the cover of the *National Enquirer.* I asked Kristen why she dropped Saddam Hussein. Kristen said that when she got home she did not have that much to ask Hussein. When we replayed the tape, I listed on the board all the questions she had asked during the collaboration (see the bold type in the preceding transcript). Kristen was surprised that she had more questions, feelings, and ideas prepared for Hussein than she did for Princess Diana. Then Kristen added that she would be uncomfortable asking Hussein controversial questions. The class responded with an interesting dilemma. Should they pick someone to whom they could direct challenging questions or someone to whom they could be complimentary and nice? We considered audience, tone, and text conventions in the discussion that followed. I encouraged students to stay with a good idea, have confidence in their own ideas and stick to them. I reviewed the advantages of taking careful notes from the collaboration tapes to use in their final papers, which may increase the confidence level for the final draft.

Lack of confidence limits student brainstorming, creativity, and performance. It leads to a "tell them what I think they'd like to hear" mentality. It prevents them from asking supporting questions that are not on the list which were intended as starting points, not as strait-jackets. My reflections about collaborative planning have provided new impetus in improving my students' confidence level.

Two processes continue in this third year of my participation in the project. In my own discovery memos I record experimentation and development of the collaborative planning process within my own classes. Each teacher in the research group shared his or her discovery memo each month. I am using two resources for discovery and refinement of this technique: my classroom and the classrooms of other teachers.

The collaborative planning seminars have enabled me to understand that an important part of collaborative planning is helping students to reflect on their roles of planner and supporter during collaboration. Each monthly seminar, package of discovery papers, members' presentations and comments gave me new angles and techniques for reflection and discovery. Feedback during my class time and private conversations with individual students led to some interesting observations about recognition of good ideas and confidence in keeping those ideas in the paper. The monthly seminars and the various methods of recording and reflecting helped me see how I could help students analyze their own process of thinking, sorting, keeping, and rejecting.

Note to readers: Ideas from our monthly meetings follow me home. Here are only a few from one session in March 1991.

> I see collaborative planning as a way of empowering students.—
> Pat McMahon

This slick piece of jargon actually makes sense; in collaborative planning, students assume responsibility for their thoughts. Pat knowingly brought up the flip side: Some students resist this responsibility. Her explanation for this resistance was intriguing: (a) some students doubt the value of their peers' contribution, and (b) it is difficult to change their idea of a teacher-centered classroom. How interesting that it is not only the teachers who are resistant to change.

> How do I do this on top of what I already do?—Jane Zachary
> Gargaro, quoting a teacher during in-service training of collaborative planning.

Jane precisely noted that a teacher might have this reaction when introduced to collaborative planning. She cited the skepticism that teachers had to the infamous Madeline Hunter series. Jane often asked other very good questions during the seminars:

> Should the blackboard planning metaphor be modified or simplified for younger students?

> Is there a way to present the concept of collaborative planning without jargon? With some consistency? . . . Some consistency in the way we speak about a writer's considerations may foster the development of mentally sound as opposed to schizophrenic students.
>
> —Jane Zachary Gargaro

Marlene Bowen suggested that the quality of the assignment relates directly to the quality of collaboration. Collaborative planning does not improve a weak assignment: "A good assignment for collaborative planning is some sort of controversy or writing from a particular point of view."

Karen Gist described a student whose collaboration partner was absent. Karen had noticed that the girl had been a good supporter and asked her to float around the room and sit in on various groups. The girl was so pleased with the reactions of the groups she worked with that she beamed. I used this same idea a week after Karen described it.

For each monthly meeting of the Making Thinking Visible seminars, teachers write a journal, double-entry diary, or discovery memo based on their use of collaborative planning in the classroom. From these reports I constantly plagiarize strategies and lessons. While students collaborate to plan their writing in my classes, I collaborate with colleagues. Do we let students choose their own partners or should teachers do the pairing? How do we categorize the responses from the supporters for analysis? How do we teach the roles of supporter and planner? How do we teach audience, topic, task definition, purpose, and text convention using collaborative planning? How do we use computers with this process? How do we extend collaborative planning to other projects within our schools?

My collaborative planning odyssey continues to be a wonderful adventure, and I hold the transcripts in my hand to guide the way to more discovery. It is a journey through patches of cynicism and confusion into practical applications. So far all paths have led to a better place for my students and me to learn.

7 Using Information for Rhetorical Purposes: Two Case Studies of Collaborative Planning

David L. Wallace
Iowa State University
Ames, Iowa

David L. Wallace, now an assistant professor of rhetoric and composition at Iowa State University, was part of the Carnegie Mellon team. Just as Leslie Evans's memos reveal some of the questions high school teachers brought to this collaboration, the project that David describes here was an attempt to document the group's initial plunge with high school teachers into the classroom experience of their students. This project paper comes from the pilot year of the project, a year before Leslie joined the group. The discoveries from this pilot effort were a valuable reality check that helped shape the group's sense of who we were as university and high school teachers and where this practice of collaborative planning might fit (and not fit) in the lives of our different classrooms. David's paper raised questions we continued to discuss: Is collaboration and/or planning only good for certain tasks, or are the assumptions teachers and students have about planning and collaboration the determining factor?

A Project Paper

Alicia, a tenth-grade high school student, is telling her friend Maria about her plans for the extended definition paper that their teacher recently assigned. This writing assignment asked Alicia and Maria to pick a phenomenon or abstract concept, to define it, and then to extend that definition based on their personal experience. Carol, their teacher, had them spend some time in class planning their papers together; their conversation gives us a glimpse of the kinds of plans that Alicia has for her paper. In the following excerpts, Alicia focuses on facts, on laying out the content that she has gathered from several sources.

In this first segment, she begins with a dictionary definition of a *nova*, the topic of her paper, and then explains her basic plan for writing the paper.

> *Maria (supporter):* What are you going to write about?
>
> *Alicia (writer):* A *nova*, that's when a star brightens intensely and then it gradually dims. It's more like an explosion of a star, like, of the sun. Okay, and other words . . . like a *supernova* is like a bigger explosion. Okay, and the sun and a star, you know, are like related. All right, and I'm gonna write the effects of it, so that's what it's really going to be about. That's the definition of a *nova* . . . and I just wrote some things down that are some effects that would happen, like hot summers, like really like a hundred and twenty degrees. . . .

As the session continues, Alicia moves from describing novas in general to describing in great detail what would happen to the earth if the sun were to become a supernova. As this excerpt illustrates, her plans are largely content based; she has collected a string of facts but has not yet considered how to use those facts.

> *Alicia:* Since the sun is going down, it's going to be cold all the time. Cold summers, like cold in August, and the same thing—the land will like get hard and dry and, of course, if it's frozen—everything—no plants will grow and no animals can eat the plants, and we can't eat the animals and all that. And it will freeze our rivers and stuff.
>
> *Maria:* So anyway we will die.
>
> *Alicia:* It will kill our fish. All in all the effect of it is, we'll like be gone, and plus since when the earth explodes, I mean, um, the sun explodes when it goes back down, it will lose some of its pull on the planet so we'll just be Venus, Jupiter, and Mars.
>
> *Maria:* Float off into space. . . .
>
> *Alicia:* We'll just be floating around in space and we'll just be floating around in space . . . and we'll just break up.

At this point, Alicia has amassed a great deal of information about novas and their possible impact on the earth. If her task were to write a report, she would simply need to find a way to organize this information. However, the extended definition assignment asks her to do more than find and arrange information in a skillful way.

In this paper, I look closely at what happened when Alicia and another tenth-grade student, Craig, were put in a situation that asked them to use information for specific purposes in writing an extended definition paper. Carol, my partner in this investigation, is a tenth-grade English teacher in a small Pittsburgh public school who had volunteered to try out collaborative planning with her classes. Our collaboration started when I visited several of Carol's classes; we had extensive discussions about implementing collaborative planning with her students. Our primary concerns were how to smoothly integrate collaborative planning into a packed curriculum and how to help her students understand and make use of concepts such as purpose, audience, and text conventions. We chose Alicia and Craig as our case study students because of their strong but very different writing styles and because Carol guessed that they would be willing to do interviews with me. Both proved to be excellent informants.

Carol and I decided to have students try collaborative planning with the extended definition assignment because it introduced them to a number of new text conventions. Guessing that the students might need some time to warm up to collaborative planning, we scheduled two planning sessions. What we learned from Craig and Alicia surprised us both.

Although Alicia and Craig had quite a bit of experience writing reports and short personal-response essays, the extended definition paper asked them to do more than recount their experiences or report facts—they needed to define a concept or physical phenomenon, explain that definition, and include some kind of personal experience or example. The writing task required them to use information for different purposes, and the collaborative planning sessions allowed Carol and me to observe the students, to see what happened when they were faced with a new kind of writing task.

Our decision to observe the students' planning for the extended definition assignment was informed by several research studies demonstrating that the ability to deal with content knowledge in terms of rhetorical concerns is a critical difference between experienced and inexperienced writers (Flower, Schriver, Carey, Haas, and Hayes, 1992). Inexperienced writers are often fairly good at creating what Flower and Hayes (1981) call *plans to say* (content generation and arrangement), but do not attempt or have difficulty with *plans to do* (rhetorical planning). For these writers, planning often means making a list of chunks of information to be included in a text, much as Alicia did in the earlier excerpt. Certainly, gathering and organizing information is an important part of the writing process. However, for many writing tasks, writers like Alicia need to learn to go beyond collecting and arranging information; they need to learn that their writing can do more than present information.

Given these and other studies that describe the difficulty students have using information for rhetorical purposes (see chapter 3), Carol and I guessed that Alicia, Craig, and their classmates were probably developmentally ready to take on the kinds of knowledge transformations that the extended definition paper required. We did not know if they would do it, or what kinds of help they might need. The extended definition did not fit neatly into the mold of the short argumentation or creative essays that they are familiar with, but we did not know if they would see the need for knowledge transformation—that the extended definition required them to use information in a way different from the knowledge telling they had done in reports.

In theory, collaborative planning is a good vehicle for investigating these questions because it cues students to pay attention to the relationship between topic knowledge and rhetorical concerns and provides a vocabulary for discussing rhetorical concerns. However, collaborative planning leaves control of the session in the hands of the students. Thus, although it opens a good window for observing how students are able to help each other, it does not guarantee that the students will embrace its goal, that they will try to do planning that considers rhetorical issues and transforms knowledge accordingly. Nor does it ensure that they will be able to make these transformations if they do see the need.

Session One: Perfunctory Planning

The first set of sessions illustrates a mismatch between Carol's and my instructional purpose for the planning sessions and the students' interpretation of that purpose. We intended the collaborative planning sessions to be an opportunity for these students to elaborate their plans for writing by developing their often skimpy sense of audience and rhetorical purpose and by considering alternative structures for their papers. However, Carol was also concerned that, as supporters, the students would have difficulty using the rhetorical prompts that collaborative planning suggested, that they would not be able to make the abstract rhetorical concerns of audience, purpose, and text conventions concrete in their planning sessions. To help them, she prepared a dittoed list of sample questions to illustrate the types of questions that the students might use as rhetorical prompts when serving as supporters. Carol intended these questions only as examples, but in the first set of planning sessions, both pairs of students used them as a checklist.

In terms of Carol's goal—that the students elaborate their plans and consider alternatives—the first planning session was not very productive for either pair of writers. Alicia and Maria did little to elaborate their plans for writing; instead, Alicia read questions from the dittoed sheet, and Maria responded perfunctorily to what she regarded as a checklist.

> *Alicia (supporter):* What is your audience?
>
> *Maria (writer):* Peers, I just told you that.
>
> *Alicia:* What kind of language is appropriate for this audience?
>
> *Maria:* Layman's terms.
>
> *Alicia:* Is there an appropriate introduction? What would the audience find interesting?
>
> *Maria:* The facts.
>
> *Alicia:* I got an X on almost everything [on the question sheet].
>
> *Maria:* How long did she say this is supposed to be?

Craig and Tony do much the same thing in their first session. Craig was writing a paper defining talent. This excerpt illustrates that Craig and Tony nominally played the game that they thought their teacher was asking them to play, but they were either unable or unwilling to use the session to explore and elaborate their ideas for writing.

> *Tony (supporter):* What points would you like to cover?
>
> *Craig (writer):* Um, that some have talent and that they're born with it.
>
> *Tony:* Just talent, all right. What's the reader going to remember from this paper?
>
> *Craig:* That some have talent. I have to work on this a lot . . . all the other points refer back to the main point [another of the dittoed questions]
>
> *Tony:* Do they?
>
> *Craig:* Yeah.
>
> *Tony:* Okay, what is your audience? Your peers or someone like yourself?
>
> *Craig:* That's what we're supposed to say, right?

For both pairs of writers, rhetorical concepts such as audience remain undeveloped. Maria responded with the single word "peers" when questioned about her audience, and Craig's response makes it clear that "peers or someone like yourself" was the answer that he presumed the teacher wanted. In these initial sessions the pairs of writers did little knowledge transformation or rhetorical planning. They reviewed their basic plans for content (knowledge telling) and used the rhetorical prompts in a perfunctory way. In short, they did a task for the teacher; however, their interpretation of the task was not what Carol intended, nor was it a particularly useful task.

Session Two: Using Texts in Planning

Unfortunately, these two perfunctory planning sessions are fairly representative of the sessions that most of the students had in Carol's class. It was clear that most of the students were not engaging in the substantive knowledge transformations that Carol and I had hoped to see. Not satisfied, Carol decided to try a second planning session after the students had written a first draft. Her reasoning was that the students might be more engaged when they had done some in-depth thinking about what they wanted to say in their papers.

Both pairs of writers brought drafts of their texts to their second planning sessions; however, they used those texts very differently. Alicia and Maria used their texts as a basis for discussion and further planning, while Craig and Tony subverted their planning session to a text-editing session—their texts became impediments to further planning. Craig and Tony read each other's text and made a limited number of suggestions. Given Tony's text to work on, Craig was able to point out a paragraph that really did not fit with the rest of the paper, and he helped Tony clean up a number of problems in grammar and punctuation, focusing largely on sentence-level issues. Tony, on the other hand, did not help Craig at all. In a later interview, Craig said that Tony could not find anything wrong with his paper. He said that Tony was "kind of wishy-washy"; he could not make any specific suggestions about Craig's paper.

Craig's draft indicated that he needed to address some larger issues in his paper; specifically, his development was shallow. The best part of the session, Craig reported in his follow-up interview, was when the teacher, who had noticed the trouble they were having, came back to read his paper with her "war paint on." She told him that he needed to narrow his paper down to one point instead of three and really develop that point. Thus, in this planning session, neither writer considered major changes for his text; as supporters, neither writer used the collaborative planning prompts to help the other weigh rhetorical issues or consider alternatives.

Alicia and Maria's second planning session is interesting because they were no longer dependent upon a checklist but were able to use rhetorical concepts, most notably text conventions, as means for selecting topic knowledge. In contrast to their first session, in which text conventions served as a static category provided by their teacher, Alicia and Maria showed remarkable flexibility in their application of text conventions to each other's plans for text. Maria used discourse terms that the teacher had introduced in class to help Alicia see how to use personal information to flesh out her extended definition, and Alicia addressed a genre-level problem in Maria's paper, distinguishing between an argumentation paper and an extended definition.

In the first part of this session, Maria interpreted the teacher's instruction about developing a general definition, using personal experience, to help Alicia see that she must do more than report the lists of information about *novas* that she had collected. Summarizing what she saw happening in Alicia's paper, Maria said, "You're speaking in general. I'm talking about you . . . how would *you* feel . . . . You personally, this is not talking about the world; this is talking about *you*." Alicia responded that she was not sure that she should spend much time in the paper talking about herself. Then, Maria, recalling the teacher's discussion about moving from generalizations to specific examples, advised Alicia, "Yeah, you can go from general to specific. Remember on the board you can go from a general writing to a specific." Eventually this discussion led Alicia to a new goal for revision, to make the general part smaller and then "get bigger on the specifics." Without directly referring to the concept of text conventions, Maria applied Carol's instruction to use specific, personal details as a means for Alicia to flesh out her definition.

Text conventions at the genre level were also the problem that Alicia pointed out in Maria's paper on the theory of evolution. As Maria discussed what she was planning to say, Alicia noticed that Maria was planning to turn her paper about evolution into an argument, while Maria maintained that she was still writing an extended definition. For example, Alicia said, "Oh, well, is this going to be like an argument? You're going to say . . . ." Maria interrupted, "It's still going to be the extended definition of evolution. And going along with the definition of evolution, going along with stating the other species are involved with the evolution theory."

As the session continued, it became clear to Alicia that Maria was missing the point of the assignment: Maria was writing an argumentation paper rather than an extended definition. Alicia stressed that Maria was trying to argue a point and that she would have to cite a great deal of evidence to make her point. Finally, Alicia suggested, "You know I think it would be, if you just write the standard definition of evolution . . . . It seems to me that would be like a whole different subject when you *argue* it." When Maria finally saw Alicia's point, the two continued by comparing their papers and found a way for Maria to restructure what she had already written.

In this session, Alicia and Maria were able to help each other turn the requirements of the assignment, and the instructions given by their teacher, into specific text convention concerns. They used these concerns to diagnose problems in the way that each of them was planning to further develop their drafts. Their experience illustrates that, as early as tenth grade, some students may be able to help each other identify rhetorical concerns that are specific enough to distinguish between appropriate and inappropriate global structures for a text and to serve as prompts for replacing broad generalizations with "specific, personal details."

Reflections on Observations

The most encouraging thing about these case studies was that, in their second planning session, Alicia and Maria were able to deal very effectively with rhetorical issues. Their success suggests that other students may be able to make the same kinds of rhetorical transformations. However, as Craig and Tony's sessions indicate, high school students do not necessarily begin to transform information for rhetorical purposes when asked to do so. Indeed, these case studies suggest three issues that may be important in helping high school students or any writers begin to use information for rhetorical purposes.

First, the most salient issue illustrated by these case studies is the need for students to understand the purpose of the planning sessions, as illustrated by the mismatch between Carol's instructional purpose for the collaborative planning sessions and the students' interpretation of it. In their first planning sessions, none of the students moved beyond the sample questions to make the generic concerns of audience, purpose, or text conventions specific to the task at hand: They treated collaborative planning much like a fill-in worksheet requiring the answers that they thought their teacher wanted to hear.

Thus, their experiences argue that students must take charge if instruction interventions such as collaborative planning are to lead to rhetorical planning and knowledge transformation. In Alicia and Maria's second session, *taking charge* meant two things: (1) seeing the sessions as something that could help them and not as something that the teacher wanted them to do, and (2) adapting the rhetorical prompts to the specific needs and situation of a writer. From an instructional perspective, these students might have benefited from some modeling of collaboration that showed them from the outset what Carol expected them to do and illustrated how to help their partners consider rhetorical issues (e.g., adapting the basic rhetorical prompts and questioning techniques for getting your partner to say more).

A second issue highlighted by these case studies is how differences in topic information may affect planning. One possible explanation of the students' initial difficulty in the planning sessions is that they had not yet thought enough about their topics to be able to do much rhetorical planning: They may have had difficulty transforming topic information because they did not yet have much to work with. Lack of preparation probably contributed to the difficulty that Craig and Tony had in their first session. Craig certainly had done very little thinking about his topic, although a more skillful supporter might have used the sessions as an opportunity to allow Craig to explore his topic.

At this point, I should note that it would be unwise to assign cause-and-effect relationships based on these two case studies. From these observations, there is no way to know if lack of topic knowledge, misinterpretation of the purpose for the collaborative planning sessions, a general resistance to school, or some combination of these issues was Craig and Tony's problem in their first session. In fact, identifying these issues as critical is really a speculation on my part. However, it is speculation informed by close observation. Given that caveat, I will risk one more speculation and raise a third issue, differences in writing styles, that I think explains some of the differences between Craig and Tony's second session and Alicia and Maria's second session.

The differences between the second two planning sessions are paralleled by striking differences in the way that Alicia and Craig typically used planning and drafts as they wrote and by the different levels of investment that each apparently brought to the planning sessions. Craig and Alicia make an interesting pair for comparison because of their different writing styles and experiences. Craig is a one-draft writer: Unless he is forced to do a preliminary draft for class, Craig's first draft is usually his last. He told me in his preliminary interview that his normal pattern for writing a school paper is to think a good deal. He focuses his early efforts on coming up with an original idea; then, he thinks of ways to develop those ideas while on the bus ride home from school or talking with his parents. He rarely talks to classmates about his ideas for writing. Alicia is quite different from Craig both in the sustained effort that she puts into drafting papers and in the great help she receives from her classmates. As soon as she has a topic for a paper, Alicia begins writing. She writes out a draft of everything that comes to her mind. Then she writes another, and a third, a fourth, and often a fifth. In short, Craig brings his writing ability but limited social interaction about writing, compared to Alicia's extensive interaction and willingness to revise in light of her interaction.

While Craig was probably the better of the two writers (Carol said that he was one of the best writers in her tenth-grade classes that year), Alicia and her partner proved much more skillful at helping each other elaborate their plans for writing and in focusing on rhetorical concerns. As the first set of planning sessions illustrate, both pairs of students needed to move beyond their checklist approach to see planning as something they could use for their own purposes. However, Craig and Tony had more difficulty doing so than Alicia and Mary. It seems that collaborative planning was a more natural addition to Alicia's writing process than it was for Craig, probably because talking about her writing and making new plans were a normal part of her writing process.

In summary, the process-tracing research cited earlier suggests that moving from "plans to say" to "plans to do" or from simple knowledge-telling strategies to knowledge-transforming ones may be an important developmental step for young writers as well as a continuing struggle for writers in new or difficult rhetorical situations. These case studies suggest that through collaborative planning, student writers may be able to help each other manage the interplay between arranging topic knowledge and addressing rhetorical concerns. However, they also illustrate that issues such as students' understanding of the purpose for planning sessions, their familiarity with their topics, and their typical writing styles may affect the extent to which techniques such as collaborative planning will help them to begin using information for rhetorical purposes in their writing.

8 Experiencing the Role of the Supporter for the First Time

Leonard R. Donaldson
Peabody High School
Pittsburgh, Pennsylvania

Leonard R. Donaldson has been teaching social studies at Pittsburgh's Peabody High School for 25 years. Although interested in writing across the curriculum, Len brought a refreshingly pragmatic perspective that was not concerned with writing in and of itself. He was not an English teacher. He asked if collaborative planning could help him teach the critical thinking skills that his history students needed—and could it do so within the demanding and structured syllabus of the city schools? For the first year, Len's memos recorded a series of "test drives" as he compared collaborative planning classes to his standard classes. When collaborative planning passed the test as a writing strategy, he began to turn it into a reading strategy, asking students (who had come to see themselves as writers with a point and a purpose) now to tackle original source texts (for example, to read the Declaration of Independence *and the* Communist Manifesto *rather than textbook accounts of them). Students interpreted these texts as planned, purposeful statements whose key points were directed to real audiences, motivated by the deeply held goals of people who were writers like themselves. In this discovery memo, Len describes how the mountains of data he collected in his second-year project began to make sense to him when he realized that he was not going to find what he was looking for in the tapes and focused instead on what use his students were making of their planning sessions.*

A Discovery Memo

Although accumulating vast amounts of data is an accepted necessity of research, placing the gathered information into a framework is another issue altogether. Following the completion of data collection for my research project, a veritable mountain of material had to be examined: student response memos written at the end of each collab-

orative planning session and a trilogy of content-related documents
(proposal, overview, and term paper). What evidence could be found
within these materials to verify that collaborative planning had improved my students' writing process and promoted their critical thinking?

Believing that there must be a relationship between the ideas
exchanged in the collaborative planning sessions and the students'
successes in the final paper, I sought confirmation in the audiotapes,
searching for clearly traceable concepts or procedures. This relationship
was difficult to prove. The evidence in the memos clearly indicated
that the collaborative sessions were useful, and the evidence of the
documents clearly indicated that students had become more skillful
in rational thought and argumentation. However, the tapes established
only an ambiguous relationship between the students' collaborative
planning sessions and specific patterns in their texts. Perhaps this is
due to the fact that a single collaborative session, although it provokes
thought, does not reflect the concept or issue discussed in its final
form. The sessions act as guideposts whereby one can clarify issues
and solve problems, but the actual writing process cannot be observed
on audiotape.

After examining the audiotapes and discovering that they did
not contain what I sought, it occurred to me that perhaps I was asking
the wrong question. I was looking for verification of my hypothesis
that the process of collaborative generation of ideas was traceable
from conversation to text. In the process, however, I had overlooked
the most significant question: For what purpose were the *students* using
the collaborative sessions? My reappraisal of the tapes and memos
based upon this question contains valuable insights into why collaborative planning works and why the response memos were so positive.

If collaborative planning is a tool used to improve thinking and
writing, then it must be examined from a utilitarian standpoint. Given
that the students were using the concepts of the Planner's Blackboard,
the more salient questions are these: For what purpose were the
students using these tools? What specific benefits were gleaned by the
individuals involved in these sessions? Why and/or how did this result
in improved understanding of the issues at hand?

My earlier observations had revealed that essential components
in my students' collaborative process were clarity of thought and
expression on the part of the planner and critical listening skills on
the part of the supporter. What the audiotapes revealed is that I had
previously overlooked a vital component to the success of the collab-

orative session: the intent of the planner upon entering the collaborative session. What was the planner seeking from this session, and how did the supporter provide it?

Approaching the audiotapes with this utilitarian question in mind opened a window on the dynamics of collaboration. Once students accepted that collaborative planning can be a beneficial process, they began to approach the sessions with very specific goals in mind. It was the fusion of the planner's objectives and the supporter's willingness to provide the necessary support that enabled a successful session.

Although each student had somewhat divergent goals in the sessions, a general pattern can be discerned from examining the tapes. Planners approached the sessions (in which they were developing their definitions of leadership) from one of three particular groups: those who believed they had a firm grasp of leadership and sought confirmation from a supporter for the validity of their argument, those who possessed a vague concept of leadership and who used the supporter as a means of clarifying their thoughts, and those who had very specific obstacles to overcome and sought specific advice from the supporter to overcome these obstacles. It might be said that the success of the sessions was dependent upon (1) the planner's clearly articulated goals, and (2) the supporter's capacity to provide what the planner required.

The role of the supporter becomes very distinct within this framework. Generally, the students assumed roles as clarifying supporters, confirmational supporters, and problem-solving supporters. By far the most evident types of supporters in the first collaborative session were the confirmational and clarifying supporters. Amy explained her concept of leadership to Brett and asked, "Does that sound clear to you?" The remainder of the conversation centered on clarifying and confirming her ideas, not in generating new concepts. In their planning session for the same assignment, Joan noted that her supporter "really didn't have to [ask questions] because I basically just used the session to express my thoughts on leadership." James noted that, "We were both pretty much set in how we were going to judge our individual leaders." Supporters in these situations simply assumed the role of eliciting the ideas of the planner and provoking him or her to articulate these ideas clearly. Little attempt was made to generate what could be considered new ideas.

In a subsequent session, when the students were struggling with the application of the criteria for effective leadership to specific individuals, the necessity for the supporter to assume a problem-solving role increased. Another pair expressed this concept in the following manner:

> *Ann (writer):* I'm uncertain . . .
>
> *Bill (supporter):* That's the key—the impact.
>
> *Ann:* Really?
>
> *Bill:* Yeah. Like, in their accomplishments. Did they accomplish what they wanted to. You got to, like, compare them to your criteria—like on leadership.
>
> *Ann:* Yeah? OK.
>
> *Bill:* You got to compare them direct—like on each aspect.
>
> *Ann:* Yeah? OK. Cool.

Although the dialogue may leave much to be desired, the importance of the insights gained by Ann cannot be discounted. (Indeed, this analytical approach is exactly the process Ann adopted in her paper.) Another student, Sam, noted that in their session his supporter asked questions that led him to discover deficiencies in his knowledge of the time periods with which he was dealing. He remarked, "I think a supporter who gives you ideas is more helpful because then you can better your report with things you hadn't thought of." Dan agreed when he observed, "I believe this session was helpful because it helped me to realize which areas of my project were weaker than others. [My supporter] helped me to find deficient areas."

The tapes and memos appear to suggest that the role of the supporter is critical to the outcome of collaborative planning, assuming success is based upon having one's ideas confirmed and problems solved (for that is how the students appeared to be using the sessions). We are once again drawn to the importance of the supporter as the dynamic link in the collaborative process.

9 Collaborative Planning and the Senior Research Paper: Text Conventions and Other Monsters

Karen W. Gist
Peabody High School
Pittsburgh, Pennsylvania

Karen W. Gist, who teaches English in grades 9–12, is a second member of the Peabody High School trio. A Western Pennsylvania Writing Fellow, she is a training program staff member who helps other teachers to use critical discussion in the classroom. She has served on the Pittsburgh Public Schools' curriculum writing committee and taught college courses in composition and in African American and women's literature. Her memo, written to us just before our final June meeting in the first year of the project, records another teacher's "first year" experiment with change. For Karen, the written reflections of her students played a large role in helping understand what happens when teachers try to open doors, but old habits and fears rise up to block the way.

A Discovery Memo

I decided to use collaborative planning to help my seniors at three stages in writing their research papers: selecting and limiting their topic, writing the thesis statement, and writing the outline for the body of their papers. Also, I decided to focus only on the assignment definition[1] and the purpose/keypoint portions of the Planner's Blackboard.

The Assignment

Throughout the year, we had been looking at heroes in various literary pieces. As a transition from the readings to their research work, we read and discussed an interview with Bill Moyers on heroes. Evolving from this, the students' research assignment was to construct a definition of a hero based on their concept of a hero and, then, to find an individual, literary or real, who fits their definition. They were to research this person and present him or her through their definition of a hero.

Collaborative Process

The students selected their own partners and tape-recorded their sessions. Some students also jotted notes during the planning sessions. I encouraged them to do some thinking about their definitions beforehand and to bring notes to the first session. From the outset, the students were enthusiastic. I took a class period to explain the Planner's Blackboard and the roles of the planner/supporter. One of the concerns that surfaced for the seniors in this college-bound class was that they felt uncomfortable questioning someone else's ideas. They felt they were expected to take over the teacher's role. "How do you know what to ask as a supporter?" "How do you start?" The following excerpts from their reflection journals exhibit common student reactions to being a supporter for the first time.

> When being a supporter I found difficulty in using dittos [sample generic questions] given us. Barry was a good supporter. He had fewer problems with the questions [generic samples] than I did. His questioning allowed me to solidify my ideas.—Dennis

> Being the supporter helped me think about points that were still unclear about my own definition of a hero. I think I could have used more feedback from my supporter. I'm not sure that I could bring my point across to him.—Jane

> I liked being a supporter for someone else except I felt I wasn't all that helpful due to the fact that he [partner] had no idea which direction he wanted to go.—Bart

> Collaborative planning helped me realize my definition of a hero was too super human. Noreen helped me figure out a realistic idea of a hero.—Karen

> Being a supporter is difficult. It is hard to start off with questions to ask the planner, but when you get those first couple out, it becomes very interesting.—Carla

I was feeling quite successful with this approach to getting students involved with their research papers, when things suddenly and unexpectedly became uprooted. Seemingly in unison, they were jolted into reality—they were doing "a research paper!" They were not supposed to be discussing their ideas and thoughts; they were supposed to be writing five, ten, how many pages? "Do we have to have note cards?" "How many footnotes?" "Does this have to be typed?" "When is this due?" "Will I survive to graduate?" Text conventions—like a huge, hungry monster—devoured the enlightenment, the calmness, and enjoyment of making decisions and planning with which the class had begun. It was as if the students had emerged from a dense fog and realized, "How could I have possibly conceived the idea that writing a research paper was not going to be stressful!" Using collaborative planning was unrealistic! Where was the stress? And so, I was coerced into providing limitations and restrictions that I did not want to. I constructed a calendar of due dates and deadlines; I provided them with a specific number of note cards and pages to be written. Barry, one of the students in this class, summarized my feelings within his own: ". . . I was in so much of a rush to get things (note cards, outline, rough draft) turned in within a reasonable time of the due date, I kind of lost the purpose of my paper."

I tried to have the students collaboratively plan the body of their paper through the development of an outline, but many of them were so consumed by text conventions that they became frustrated and irritable. I was also becoming frustrated because time was becoming a factor for me, too: I had a limited number of weeks to devote to this assignment. I battled the temptation to use the traditional approaches to teaching the research paper, allowing the students to research and write on their own—trusting that their planning sessions would help them focus their papers.

Final papers did evolve, and many of them did meet my objectives and expectations very well. However, I need to assess my approach and procedures and make some modifications before I attempt this again. I need to find a way to deal with the students' fear of the dreaded research paper. The students' candid comments in their final reflection papers reinforced for me both the need for and the value of collaborative planning in writing. For these reflection papers, the students responded to the following prompt: "Reflect on the benefits of planning with a supporter in a collaborative effort to write your paper. Focus on (1) at what point(s) in your writing process did you feel collaborative planning was or could've been most helpful to you? and (2) what effect did the collaborative planning process have on the final outcome of your paper?"

I really didn't know how to interpret my hero into my definition at first. But after the planning, I was able to get the feel of what I was doing. At that point was when the planning became the most helpful to me.—Lori

This collaborative planning didn't help me change my idea of what I wanted, but made it clearer so I really understood what I was doing.—Randy

I found it easy to plan my paper by talking about it. It helped me figure it out like a person goes to a psychologist to talk about problems he is having.—Barry

In the beginning I felt really good about the support groups. I feel that it could have been very beneficial to the outcome of my paper. It is important to get feedback from an observer. Maybe he/she can point out some critical points that might need to be reconsidered. Unfortunately, my experience with my partner did not turn out to be beneficial. I received hardly any feedback at all. The majority of responses I received was, "Yes, that's good." I wished my partner could have been a little more involved and had more suggestions. I totally encourage you to continue this exercise with your students for the next years to come.—Bart

I thought that having us talk on a tape was a good idea. Even though I had an idea of what I wanted to say about a hero, I still was a little fuzzy. Sharm did a good job of being a supporter. She kept asking me questions and making me think, really think of how I was going to organize my paper. She brought up some good points so I didn't end up with a 50-page paper.—Laurel

The collaborative planning helped me find my definition of a hero, but during the second planning session I found myself talking more about what I was planning to write about. Also, during the second session I got much more feedback from my partner and it was easier for me to ask him some questions and make suggestions.—Jane

For a first attempt, I was pleased with the effectiveness of the collaborative planning process and also with the outcome of that effort as shown in the students' writing. Through reflection, students were able to see their writing process: They were able to talk about what they did to reach their goals and assess the effectiveness of it. I underestimated the amount of time my students would need for the actual planning sessions, and I learned that they would need practice with the process to become really proficient. I intend to build more opportunities to use and practice collaborative planning into my future lessons.

Note

1. Editors' Note: The "assignment definition" element that Karen refers to appears in the version of the Planner's Blackboard that Tom Hajduk adapted for his Planner's Options computer program. See his discovery memo in this section.

10 Note Taking: An Important Support for Productive Collaborative Planning

Andrea S. Martine
Allderdice High School
Pittsburgh, Pennsylvania

Andrea S. Martine has taught high school English at Allderdice High School in Pittsburgh for the past 26 years. She has written curriculum for the Pittsburgh Gifted and Mainstream Scholars programs and has served as administrative assistant, instructional teacher leader, department chair, yearbook advisor, and gifted program facilitator. She also teaches part-time at the Community College of Allegheny County and won one of five HarperCollins Fellowships in 1990 for her college English curriculum "Pittsburgh, Our Classroom." Andrea was a finalist for the 1992 Pennsylvania Teacher of the Year. Her discovery memo explains how she integrated collaborative planning with other more familiar teaching techniques such as note taking to help her ninth graders to plan and write better comparison papers.

A Discovery Memo

For my first attempt using collaborative planning, I decided to work with an assignment that asked my ninth-grade students to respond to Jesse Stuart's "The Split Cherry Tree." Specifically, they were to contrast the views of David's parents in the story with the views of their own parents. When I think of all of the things that I was asking the class to do, I am amazed. First, I asked the students to take notes about the specific relationship of the views of the characters in the short story compared with their parents' views. Then, I asked them to learn the thesis-support essay format. This genre was new to them, and it involved learning to use an introductory paragraph, transition words, three elements of support, and a good conclusion. Finally, I asked them to learn the collaborative planning terminology and process. I discovered that these ninth graders were able, actually more than able, to follow these requests.

We began the assignment by reading the story and taking notes. Then we had a group brainstorming session about the differences and similarities between David's parents in the story and the students' own parents. Once again, the students took notes. At this point, I thought students were ready to try collaborative planning. After a class discussion about the Planner's Blackboard and a model planning session, in which I played supporter to a student's writer role, we spent the next class period on the planning sessions themselves.

During the students' planning sessions, I took notes about the social aspects of the process. I discovered that I was not even missed: They were so involved in what they were doing that they did not even realize how fast the process was happening. I did not use tape recorders for this first session, but the talk among the members of each group was active, on task, and challenging. It is not often that a ninth-grade class is so focused.

After the planning session, the students spent one class period writing the introductory paragraph and having it approved by me. Then the students wrote their rough drafts at home. The next class session, they prepared their final essays. I collected all of the notes, the rough draft, and the final essays. Of a class of 30 students, 22 successfully completed this assignment. Prior to this assignment, I was fortunate if I got papers from even half of the students. I began to wonder if the collaborative planning session was the reason for this high success rate. This suspicion prompted me to give the students a feedback form to see how they felt about the collaborative planning process. Their responses reflected two general themes.

1. *They used each other for reference points.* When one student did not know the spot in the story where specific information occurred, the other student did.

2. *They enjoyed having someone listen to their ideas.* I had asked the students to make a note of anything that the writer found acceptable during the collaborative planning sessions. This emphasis on what was good about their planning gave immediate positive feedback to both the writer and the supporter. The students enjoyed the fact that someone else liked what they were proposing.

Collaborative Planning and Note Taking

These first collaborative planning sessions made me wonder about the benefits of augmenting collaborative planning with good note taking. The note taking that these ninth graders did before the collaborative planning process helped them come to their planning sessions prepared to work. Students who came with notes were more clearly focused during the session; the notes that they had taken when they read the story became an integral part of each session. They constantly referred to their notes during the session, expanding, changing, and incorporating them into their dialogue about the assigned essay.

Another way that I asked my students to use notes was to jot down all the positive feedback that they got from their supporters. This note-taking process helped them to monitor and adjust their writing strategies; it reinforced good ideas as well as prompted the students to change or expand ideas as necessary. Also, these notes seemed to help the students understand their writing strategies. They asked themselves questions such as these: What is it that I do when I write a compare/contrast essay? Do I always tackle the essay the same way? Has the supporter helped me to change the same old approach I always use? What suggestions given by the supporter helped me to improve my approach? Will I remember and use these suggestions the next time that I write a compare/contrast essay?

The following excerpts from a planning session on a later assignment (to discuss the conflicting groups of people in *The Light in the Forest* by Conrad Richter) illustrate what can happen when one writer comes to a planning session prepared and the other does not. Eugene, the writer, brought good notes to the session; William, the supporter, was not as well prepared and had no notes to help him. Notice that the supporter is not able to move beyond generic questions because he does not really have control of the subject matter of the story.

> *William (supporter):* So what is the purpose of writing your story?
>
> *Eugene (writer):* So I can get a good grade. I'll write it to depict how the white man mistreated the Indians. Right, how the white man mistreated the Indians, and I'm gonna use my strategy by using step by step, fact after fact how the white man treated Indians.
>
> *William:* White man treated Indians, OK . . .
>
> *Eugene:* . . . And then, I don't have this written down, my purpose . . .

> *William:* Your purpose . . .
>
> *Eugene:* Yeah, to compare the different viewpoints of the two environments that they were raised in.
>
> *William:* So one's the savage, and one's tame.

So far, William has done no more than repeat Eugene's phrases. Then William elaborates on Eugene's point about the two environments. Eugene now makes what could be a productive move by disagreeing with his supporter, which leads him to explain his views a little.

> *Eugene:* But actually, I disagree. I'll say the Indians were more tame than the white men were.
>
> *William:* Because they have more prejudices . . .
>
> *Eugene:* Yeah . . . in some forms they did.
>
> *William:* There was no prejudices in any of the Indians. They just scalped people.
>
> *Eugene:* And I'm going to try to write this in the third person, all right, and use a lot of symbolism, and how do you say it [reading] . . . all right, dialogue. I'm not going to use much dialogue though . . . .

At this point, the discussion begins to heat up a little bit. Neither writer or supporter seem happy with the way that this session is going.

> *William:* You're not really explaining this to me. You've gotta um . . .
>
> *Eugene:* Ask more questions then.
>
> *William:* Oh, well, what are your main strategies in writing this story?
>
> *Eugene:* Like I said before, use step by step and describe most of the characters in the story, like their backgrounds and why they acted the way they did in the story, and to try to get Mrs. Martine to understand, you know, the basis of why they acted the way they did, why the Indians thought the white men were better, and why the white men thought they were better than the Indians.

In response to William's complaint that Eugene is "not really explaining this to me," Eugene reminds William that it is the role of a good supporter to ask questions that will challenge the writer to defend or change his or her point of view. Eugene's frustration as the writer is evident in his final comment—responding to William's generic question: "What are your main strategies in writing this story?" Eugene did the assignment and came to the planning session prepared, and he expected his classmate to do the same. When these expectations are not met by both parties, the strength of one student's efforts can still make the collaborative planning session worthwhile, but imagine how much more productive this session would have been if both parties would have been similarly prepared.

Reflection on Observations

My observations during my first year in the Making Thinking Visible Project convinced me that students who prepared more extensive notes for their collaborative planning sessions and took more detailed notes during the session produced better final essays. Does the assignment itself motivate these students' thinking process? Probably not. It is my belief, however, that these notes are key in spurring the thinking process that, in turn, ultimately directs the writing process. My contention is that students who took notes throughout their collaborative planning and reading seemed to be more focused on their thinking, reading, and writing. These students obviously followed each step in the overall process. As for the planning sessions themselves, bringing good notes helped the students become more organized and better prepared as both writers and supporters.

It is probably also important to note that I give a grade for the notes that students produce; thus, they get some feedback that enables them to feel more confident about being able to complete these tasks successfully. Also, they may see more value in the notes because I take the time to respond to them at each step of the process.

11 Exploring Planner's Options©: A Collaborative Tool for Inexperienced Writers

Thomas Hajduk
Carnegie Mellon University
Pittsburgh, Pennsylvania

Thomas Hajduk has taught college English since 1986 at Carnegie Mellon, the University of Pittsburgh, and Community College of Allegheny County. He is completing his doctorate in the rhetoric program at Carnegie Mellon and is currently a researcher with the Center for Educational Computing in English. Tom's interest in computers and writing was the catalyst for designing and implementing Planners' Options© *software, forthcoming from South-Western Publishing company, Cincinnati, OH (Stock No. EC10AH71). The program helps a writer and a supporter to plan their texts with the aid of the Planning Assistant. Here Tom explains how writers can do collaborative planning on the computer with as much or as little assistance as they choose from* Planners' Options©

A Discovery Memo

As writing instructors, we are sometimes challenged by helping inexperienced writers see writing as a complex process that begins with something that is inchoate and results in a tangible product—and we are not always successful when we try to illustrate this process for our students. For many students, what occurs between the inchoate and the tangible remains an enigma.

We can explain to students that there are various elements and dimensions to the writing process, including determining a workable topic, constructing a plan and shaping it through language, formulating and connecting ideas, deliberating audience perspectives, generating text, pondering rhetorical objectives, refining the topic(s), reshaping plans, revising text, and weighing genre and text conventions. However, many inexperienced writers are unaccustomed to thinking about writing in this mindful manner and attending to what often seems like an overwhelming number of time-consuming considerations (see "Snapshot 3" in chapter 3). An important question, then, is how does a writing instructor set about portraying the subtleties and nuances of planning a paper?

Although the student-teacher conference frequently occurs between drafts of a text, this same sort of collaborative arrangement could offer perhaps one of the most effective methods of providing an inexperienced writer with a fruitful planning session. After all, who better to collaborate with an inexperienced writer than an experienced writer who has a keen sense of the types of questions and concerns that need to be addressed? Yet, while this kind of dialectical interaction may be a successful way to help students understand some of the dimensions of the writing process in general and the planning process specifically, it represents an inefficient method of teaching students, given the large class sizes and heavy paper load that most writing instructors face.

An alternative to the student-teacher conference that preserves the interactive dialectic is peer collaboration, a label that represents an assortment of activities in various forms and generates a lot of discussion among people in the field of writing. Over the years, educators have looked at collaborative composing (Clifford, 1981), peer response groups (DiPardo & Freedman, 1988), and peer tutoring, to name a few. Inexperienced writers collaborating while they plan papers may present a viable approach to helping students with the planning process. However, inexperienced writers are often ill-equipped to step into the role of the supporter without guidance. Many first-time supporters do not ask relevant and attentive questions. Metaphors, such as the Planners Blackboard (see figure 4.1 in chapter 4) or the Writer's Maze (see figure 11.1) try to provide students with a functional way of structuring their planning session.

The Planner's Options© Program

As another way to help students understand the role of the supporter, I designed a planning tool for the Macintosh computer called Planner's Options, which runs in a Hypercard environment. Planner's Options provides sets of prompts, giving a pair of planners the opportunity to discuss possible responses, and then allowing students to record the gist of their responses via a computer keyboard. After students finish

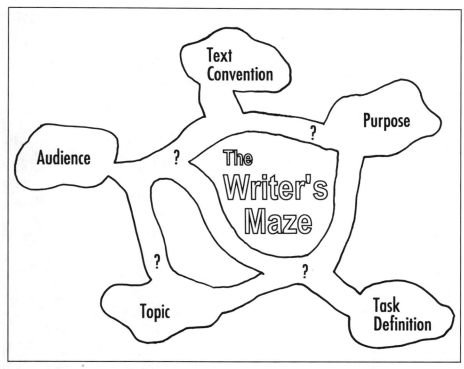

Figure 11.1. The Writer's Maze.

a collaborative planning session, they can save and subsequently print out a record of the ideas, goals, and text they generated.

The nucleus of the program is the Planning Assistant, which, in effect, becomes a second supporter providing an additional degree of structure for the collaborative planning session. The Planning Assistant offers either general or assignment-specific prompts and questions for the students to select, discuss, and respond to as they move through the different planning spaces contained in the program (see figure 11.2). Using the metaphor of The Writer's Maze, the software automatically and transparently invokes the conceptual framework that the planning spaces provide for the planners (i.e., the different planning spaces are present and available for the planners to use—and, therefore, students benefit from the structure of such a framework—but students are free to attend to the questions and prompts while the software sustains the conceptual framework).

While the program provides an easy method of delivering various prompts and questions for students, the Planning Assistant also models

Figure 11.2. The Planner's Options Map.

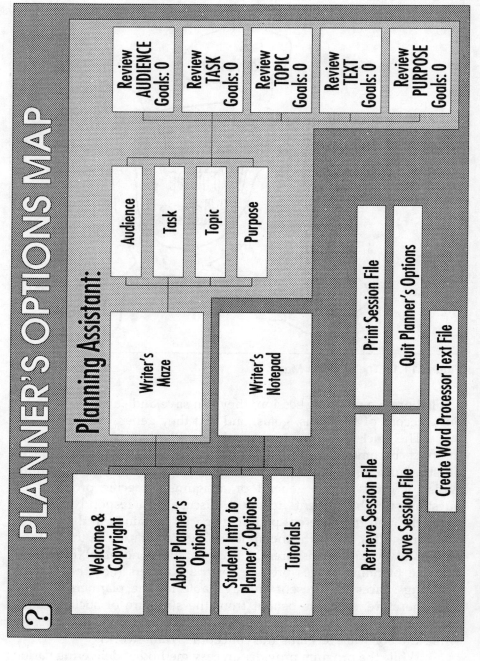

the type of serious and thoughtful questions an experienced supporter might ask of a writer. In this respect, the Planning Assistant is dynamic in that it allows teachers to use general questions and prompts supplied with the program and to enter and record assignment-specific questions or prompts. It also allows the student supporter to enter and record session-specific questions and prompts that arise while the students are actually planning and collaborating. In a very practical way, when a teacher creates a set of assignment-specific prompts using the teacher-authoring mode, Planner's Options allows the teacher to unobtrusively "join" each collaborative-planning triad, because he or she generates an original set of prompts and questions, which may be updated or modified as necessary.

Another potential benefit of Planner's Options is the ease with which students can create a written record as they plan (see figure 11.3). During a collaborative planning discussion, students may generate numerous useful ideas and plans: These oral planning sessions might be strengthened if students were encouraged to record the gist of their conversations as they respond to different prompts.

Although a benefit often cited for collaboration is that participants bring different knowledge, experiences, and perspectives to the writing task, paradoxically, this may also be a source of difficulty for the students. Two students operating with different knowledge, experiences, and perspectives may develop and take away from a collaborative planning session different understandings, plans, and goals. Further, because this collaborative interaction is usually verbal and ephemeral, it may be more difficult for the participants to compare and reflect on their interpretations of the interaction. Early exploratory research on between-draft collaboration suggests that writers collaborating face-to-face tend not to make notes of remarks with which they disagree, and they tend not to address those points in revisions of their drafts (Neuwirth, Palmquist, & Hajduk, 1990). Therefore, providing students with a simple way to represent externally the ideas and plans they have generated may furnish students with an easy way to review a "visible" record and engage in a more careful reflection of their plans. The Planning Assistant in the Planner's Options program also provides students with a Review Area that may encourage them to track their progress, review their planning goals, and reflect upon their statements and notes.

Of course, Planner's Options does not work magic. Students may find the accessibility of the questions, the ease of recording ideas, and novelty of working with a computer stimulating, but these features

Figure 11.3. Sample Question and Response Boxes.

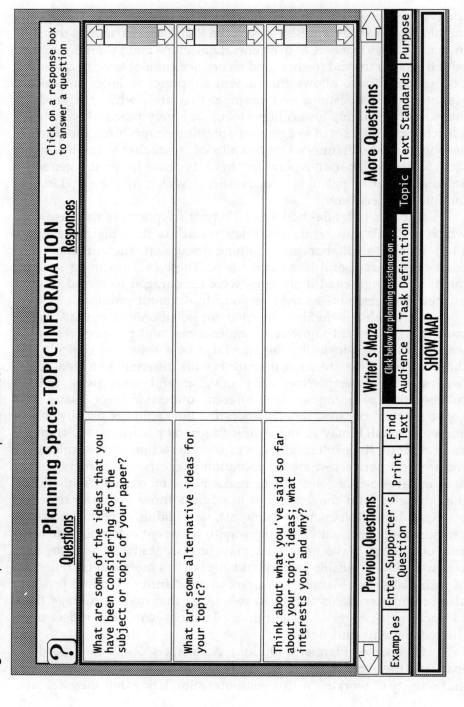

are aids, not guarantees of good planning or good writing. Therefore, students may need instruction about using the output from their planning sessions. Research demonstrates that writers have a difficult time developing a sense of the text whenever they read text on a smaller computer screen that shows less than full page, so students will need to print out computer logs of the details they have recorded. The program can also generate a computer file that students can access via any standard (ASCII) word processing program—allowing them to cut and paste text that they generate during the planning sessions. Finally, if a writer wishes, he or she can begin composing a draft of the paper using the Writer's Notepad area contained in the program; the text students enter here can also be printed out and used for reference during a first draft, or the student can retrieve the text from a computer file later so it might be cut and pasted into any word processing program.

12 Rewriting Collaborative Planning

Linda Flower
Carnegie Mellon University
Pittsburgh, Pennsylvania

*Linda Flower is a professor at Carnegie Mellon and co-director of the
National Center for the Study of Writing and Literacy at Berkeley and
Carnegie Mellon. As director of the Making Thinking Visible Project, Linda
knew she had a lot to learn, quickly. Teaching pilot classes at Pittsburgh's
High School for the Creative and Performing Arts was her first step (since
her own graduation) into a high school—much less into an energetic urban
classroom. Her memo reflects what we have learned as a group during the
pilot year, particularly the curiosity everyone shared—"What can I discover
about my own teaching by the chance to look closely at yours and to
understand your students?" And it suggests that problems that might seem
highly specific to one group of students can lead to solutions that cross the
boundaries of age, assignments, and institutions.*

A Discovery Memo

It has always seemed to me that one of the unsung songs of teacher
professionalism is the job of turning water to wine—of transforming
new ideas into practice. Thanks to the pilot year, we started the first
full-fledged year of the project with a pretty good 60-page introduction
to using collaborative planning. This statement of the philosophy, the
practice, and problems we had encountered at least gave us a common
starting point. However, I think the real story is in what each of us
did, trying to translate this shared image (of goals and techniques)
into a very distinct practice adapted to our students. I realize this
seems to fly in the face of some curriculum practices (whereby teachers
are supposed to use any given curriculum "by the rules"), but it seems
as though our success stories are stories of experimentation, adaptation,
and invention.

We have been hearing, for instance, how Len Donaldson was
so successful in teaching his Peabody social studies class to zero in on
purposes (their goals as writers, on the rhetorical goals of the famous

writers they studied) that his colleague, Jane Zachary Gargaro, had trouble the next semester. When she got Len's students in her English class and wanted them to use collaborative planning to read for the techniques and conventions of imagery and use them in their own autobiographies, she could not get them to stop talking about purposes.

For me, collaborative planning has become less a writing technique than a process that lets students record and observe themselves as thinkers—I wanted to turn it into a platform for reflection. Wittgenstein said that you could not define some concepts such as "game" by any set of necessary features, because they were really a *family* of related meanings (related versions of "game"). We seem to be creating a family of adaptive practices that go by the name collaborative planning.

But I keep wondering, what does it really mean to translate— to rewrite—an idea or practice, and still remain true to its vision and goals? For instance, when a teacher at a recent Conference on College Composition and Communication told me collaborative planning would only work with her students if she made them fill in answers on a checklist, my reply was, "if you take such authority away from the student as a planner, writer, and thinker, you are not doing what we mean by collaborative planning."

One form of translation we all experiment with is renaming the Planner's Blackboard concepts and, in many cases, replacing the blackboards themselves with an entirely different image or metaphor. It seems some folks love the blackboards; some folks hate them. Obviously, Dee Weaver (one of the pilot-year teachers) faced this problem when she decided to adapt the process for her fifth graders. (She was using a technique that was developed for college students with a "gifted" fifth-grade class.) Dee knew her version of collaborative planning would have to be concrete rather than abstract, but in a course focused on creativity and taking charge of one's own learning, she would never give her student writers a checklist of things to do. Dee's approach to the problem was interesting: She turned it over to the students. With 10-year-old exuberance, two girls decided to teach collaborative planning to the rest of the class by turning the static metaphor of planning blackboards into an action-packed tour through a Writing Theme Park, with stops at the Ink Fountain, the People's Paper Prairie, Home of Key Point, Writers' Block, the Gold Topic Room, and the Story Cinema. Later, to make the planning process itself more structured and manageable, Dee asked her students to turn the generic Planner's Blackboard prompts into specific questions a supporter could hold on to, look at, and ask. So, when students entered the NASA competition to name the new Orbiter, they decided the writer would need to be persuasive: The supporter should ask specific audience questions, such as, "Why will the judges like your name?" The questions were a sort of planning security blanket, but one the students themselves created.

What I learned from Dee is that an important part of being a teacher is treating translation as an open question—a good problem to be solved—and bringing students in on the process of interpreting, designing, and evaluating that instruction.

Part II Observations across Contexts

Section 2
Adapting Theory and Research in High School Settings

13 Measuring Students' Attitudes about Collaborative Planning

David L. Wallace
Iowa State University
Ames, Iowa

David L. Wallace (introduced earlier) worked with the Carnegie Mellon team to develop a questionnaire about planning and collaboration organized around what we saw as our key assumptions and values. Where would our students stand on these questions? Would any of their attitudes change over the course of a term, and would these questions themselves be a sensitive instrument for getting at their thinking? David (an enthusiast for interesting problems in statistical analysis) spent a large portion of one project year validating this questionnaire and refining its questions before he presented it to the group with this memo.

A Discovery Memo

Students' attitudes affect their learning—this is not news to those of us who teach writing. Identifying students' attitudes and making use of that information, however, is another matter. One of the things that we learned during the pilot year was that students' responses to collaborative planning could be influenced by any number of things. Of course, we were learning a great deal about how to present collaborative planning more effectively, but some things seemed out of our control. Some students did not like collaborative planning because they did not like writing or school in general. However, other students who were active classroom participants and seemed to like writing were initially cool and sometimes openly resistant to collaborative planning.

In addition to the many positive responses to collaborative planning that we observed during the pilot year, we also learned by paying attention to students who seemed uncomfortable with collaborative planning. Some students did not immediately see any value in planning before they wrote; they were single-draft writers or writers who preferred to write out their ideas in a draft before talking to anyone about them. Others were comfortable with the notion of planning before writing but felt that talking with their classmates was somehow cheating. For example, Craig (one of the case-study students in my project paper in section 1) reported that he nearly always talked over his ideas for his papers with his mother or father, but he was afraid that talking to another student might mean giving his good ideas away and making his paper look less distinctive.

We devoted several meetings of the Carnegie Mellon team to brainstorming about this problem and about ways that we could identify the attitudes that seemed to affect students' responses to collaborative planning. Our discussions resulted in four issues that we thought probably affected students' responses and a plan for me to develop a simple survey that would help teachers and students identify these attitudes so that they could deal more directly with them. The survey that I developed (with the help of Nancy Spivey, John R. Hayes, and numerous project members) appears as the appendix at the end of this memo.

Numerous *t*-tests and factor analyses led to the current version of the survey. The survey presented statements for which the students were to indicate Strongly Agree, Agree, Disagree, or Strongly Disagree. I have listed the statements by topic to make it easier to see how they address each issue. Also, I should note that even though there are no right or wrong responses, some of the statements are phrased positively and some are phrased negatively (denoted by plus and minus signs) in terms of how likely it is that someone would respond positively to collaborative planning. Thus, for the negative statements, the 4-point scale must be reversed for scoring.

Usefulness of Planning

Six of the survey statements focus on the writer's notion of planning: specifically, how useful a person thinks planning is and whether he or she has a rigid notion of planning (thinks that planning ends when drafting begins).

+ I am likely to come up with a clearer sense of what I want to accomplish in a piece of writing if I think about my ideas before I start to write.

− When I write something, I tend to jump right in and start writing the final draft.

+ I think it helps if I decide what my major points will be before I start to write a paper.

– Planning is something writers do only before they write, not after they start writing.

– When I have a writing assignment, I end up doing little planning because I don't have time for it.

– Writers should do all their planning before they start writing.

Considering Rhetorical Concerns

These five statements attempt to capture students' attitudes about the rhetorical concerns of audience, purpose, and text conventions. Some of these statements focus explicitly on these issues, and others try to discover whether students tend to focus more on content information— coming up with enough things to say.

– My major concern when I begin a paper is coming up with enough things to say.

+ I consider what I want to accomplish before I start writing a paper.

+ I test out my plan for a paper by thinking about my goals.

+ I often think about what my finished paper will look like before I write.

+ Thinking about my reader helps me decide what I am going to say in a paper.

Willingness to Collaborate

This set of seven questions asks how willing students are to involve others in early stages of their writing processes. Do they see writing as an essentially private, individual process, or do they see feedback from others as useful?

+ When I have a writing assignment, I like to talk to someone before I write.[*1]

+ When I have a problem writing, I like to bounce ideas off other people.[*]

+ Telling a friend about my ideas for writing helps me write better.[*]

– It's a waste of time to talk with other students about my writing.[*]

+ People can give me useful advice about what I'm going to write.*

− Writing should be a very private process.

− I like to wait until I've finished a paper before I tell people about my writing.

Sense of Control about Writing

The final set of thirteen questions parallels one of the emphases in the Daly/Miller Writing Apprehension Survey (Daly & Miller, 1975), the extent to which students feel in control of writing. These questions contrast trusting to luck with having strategies to use.

− My major concern when I begin a paper is coming up with enough things to say.*

− When I start writing an assignment, I have no idea if I will succeed in saying what I mean.*

− I waste a lot of time when I write because I don't know what I want to say.*

− When I write, I never know if what I write says what I mean.*

− I know writing techniques that I can adapt for different kinds of assignments.

+ When I get stuck writing, I come up with other strategies to try.

− The thing which determines how well I do in writing is luck.

+ I know when I have a good idea for something that I'm writing.

− I think the ability to write well is an art: either you can do it, or you can't.

− No matter how much time and effort I devote to my papers, they all seem to turn out about the same, as far as quality goes.

− A writing strategy that I use in one class is useless in another class.

+ Even when writing is hard, I have confidence in my own abilities to solve problems.

+ The thing which determines how well I do in writing is how hard I try.

Using the Writing Attitude Survey

The survey can be used for a number of purposes. First, you might use it as an opportunity for students to reflect on their attitudes after they have tried one or two collaborative planning sessions. Score the survey with them, explaining that there are no right or wrong answers, and ask them to talk or write about how their scores relate to what they experienced in their planning sessions. Questions that you might consider or ask your students to consider include: Did their overall scores or their sub-scores for any of the four categories predict that they would like collaborative planning or that they might feel uncomfortable with it? and Did their attitudes change because of the sessions?

Another way to use the survey is to get a baseline measure of students' attitudes before they try collaborative planning. You might use students' initial scores to choose case-study students (e.g., those who score higher or lower than their classmates) as Leslie Evans did (see her discovery memo in section 1). Students who score high or low or who seem particularly resistant to collaboration are likely to provide interesting comparisons that are worth following up in some detail.

Finally, you might use the survey to assess change in students' attitudes, comparing pre- and posttest scores for individuals or an entire class. When I use the surveys with my classes, I pretest early in the semester. At the end of the semester, we do the posttest and score it together in class. As a final writing assignment, I ask the students to write about how their attitude changed, comparing the total pre- and posttest scores as well as the scores for collaboration and sense of control. I explain that a higher score is not necessarily good or bad and that no measure is perfect. Thus, they should not feel bad if their score stayed the same or decreased, and they should feel free to disagree with what the survey results say. Whether they agree or disagree, however, I ask them to give specific examples of things that happened in the class that they think affected their attitudes. Even when the class as a whole has a statistically significant gain in their attitude scores, I discover a great deal about what that overall change meant by reading what individual students have to say about how their attitudes changed.

Let me end with an admonition to use the results of this survey *descriptively* rather than *prescriptively* for two reasons. First, the survey is descriptive in terms of design. I have not correlated the results with any other kinds of measures, so the results based on the overall scores have to be interpreted in light of other data. Also, any differences in pretest and posttest scores may or may not be due to collaborative planning. Unless you use a control group for comparison, there is really no way to know what caused a change in attitude. Second, the four categories of statements represent key goals of collaborative planning, but the groupings are not set in stone—some of the statements might work equally well in another category. Thus, the categories reflect my intention in designing the survey and are not guarantees that the constructs they attempt to measure exist in real life. I can be more positive about two of the categories: *willingness to collaborate* and *sense of control* about writing. A factor analysis identified and confirmed the questions that I marked with asterisks in each of these categories as "factors," indicating that students tend to respond to these questions consistently. Thus, you can feel fairly comfortable using these two sets of questions as representative of the constructs suggested in the category titles.

Note

1. The questions marked with an asterisk in each category are those that a factor analysis found to be consistently related. Thus, these questions can be seen as measuring the same factor (e.g., willingness to collaborate or sense of control about writing).

Appendix

Name: _____

Writing Attitude Survey

Different people bring very different attitudes to their writing in school. This survey will help you define your attitudes toward writing. Respond to the following statements about writing by circling the appropriate letter(s) to indicate how strongly you agree or disagree that the statement applies to you. There are no right or wrong answers; answer honestly in terms of your own writing experiences in school.

SA=Strongly Agree, A=Agree, D=Disagree, SD=Strongly Disagree

1. SA A D SD   When I have a writing assignment, I like to talk to someone about it before I write.

2. SA A D SD   I know writing techniques that I can adapt for different kinds of assignments.

3. SA A D SD   My major concern when I begin a paper is coming up with enough things to say.

4. SA A D SD   When I get stuck writing, I come up with other strategies to try.

5. SA A D SD   I am likely to come up with a clearer sense of what I want to accomplish in a piece of writing if I think about my ideas before I start to write.

6. SA A D SD   Writing should be a very private process.

7. SA A D SD   When I write something, I tend to jump right in and start writing the final draft.

8. SA A D SD   I think it helps if I decide what my major points will be before I start to write a paper.

9. SA A D SD   The thing which determines how well I do in writing is luck.

10. SA A D SD   I consider what I want to accomplish before I start writing a paper.

11. SA A D SD   I like to wait until I've finished a paper before I tell people about my writing.

12. SA A D SD — Planning is something writers do only before they write, not after they start writing.

13. SA A D SD — I know when I have a good idea for something that I'm writing.

14. SA A D SD — When I have a writing assignment, I end up doing little planning because I don't have time for it.

15. SA A D SD — I think the ability to write well is an art: either you can do it, or you can't.

16. SA A D SD — When I start writing an assignment, I have no idea if I will succeed in saying what I mean.

17. SA A D SD — I test out my plan for a paper by thinking about my goals.

18. SA A D SD — People can give me useful advice about what I'm going to write.

19. SA A D SD — I waste a lot of time when I write because I don't know what I want to say.

20. SA A D SD — No matter how much time and effort I devote to my papers, they all seem to turn out about the same, as far as quality goes.

21. SA A D SD — When I have a problem writing, I like to bounce ideas off other people.

22. SA A D SD — I often think about what my finished paper will look like before I write.

23. SA A D SD — A writing strategy that I use in one class is useless in another class.

24. SA A D SD — Telling a friend about my ideas for writing helps me write better.

25. SA A D SD — Writers should do all their planning before they start writing.

26. SA A D SD — Even when writing is hard, I have confidence in my own abilities to solve problems.

27. SA A D SD — When I write, I never know if what I write says what I mean.

28. SA A D SD — Thinking about my reader helps me decide what I am going to say in a paper.

29. SA A D SD — The thing which determines how well I do in writing is how hard I try.

30. SA A D SD — It's a waste of time to talk with other students about my writing.

14 Using the Writing Attitude Survey

James R. Brozick
North Hills High School
Pittsburgh, Pennsylvania

James R. Brozick has been a teacher for 27 years at North Hills High School where he is currently department chair. In 1976, his dissertation on the composing process won the NCTE Promising Researcher Award. Jim joined the project informally in year one. His hunch from the experimenting that he did that first year was that students' attitudes were not only an important part of learning, but were changing in important ways around collaborative planning. In year two, he designed a way to compare the pre- and post-instruction results of the survey, but as these two memos show, he found that the real story was not in the group scores, but in what changes could reveal about the strategic thinking and responses of individual students.

Two Discovery Memos

Memo #1: Abandoning Statistics

At the first meeting of the Making Thinking Visible Project this year, I listened to David Wallace talk about the use of the Writing Attitude Survey. As David spoke, I became increasingly interested in the use of that survey. Several years ago, I used the Thematic Apperception Test and the Meyers-Briggs Personality Inventory to identify particular "types" of learners and to track four twelfth-grade students in a series of writing assignments. I wanted to see if four different personality types wrote in substantially different ways when given structured and non-structured writing assignments. It was on this basis that the Writing Attitude Survey intrigued me. It seemed to me valuable for teachers to have insight into students' writing attitudes. Knowing what the students thought about writing could very well be a window into describing some of the problems they must overcome in writing; subsequently, it might prove valuable in learning how to teach students.

Over the years, I have dealt with students' reluctance toward writing. Particularly at the beginning of a term, it seemed that when I asked them to write, they groaned, and when I asked some students why they did not write a particular paper, they said "I'd fail it anyway."

This reminded me of Daly and Miller's research about writing apprehension (e.g., Daly & Miller, 1975). Daly argues, "Qualitatively, the messages written by high apprehensives are evaluated as being significantly lower in quality than those written by low apprehensives" (1979, p. 38). What we may theorize from this information is that writers who fear writing may avoid writing and not develop the requisite strategies. A fundamental question associated with writing apprehension is, do we look at apprehension as a cause or an effect? Are there cognitive limitations and boundaries, such as rigid composing rules, that inhibit the writer and cause him or her to become more apprehensive? Typically, students' interest in writing falls off in the upper elementary schools when detailed criticism of writing begins, although there is no clear cause of the problem. Some researchers have even suggested that we need to decrease the mystery surrounding writing. This problem of why student interest in writing decreases concerns the teacher as well, because the teacher is a major force in the classroom, either proactive or reactive, creating the classroom environment that either fosters or deters writing.

As I looked over my basic composition class this year, I saw more than just a wide range of abilities; I saw some students who expressed an overt dislike for writing and other students who were not the least bit shy about the fact that they hated to write and were capable of hating me if I forced them to write. Some, more covert, communicated by their body movements—turning their bodies away, dropping their eyes as if to say, "If you don't bother me, I won't bother you." Still other students were alert and willing. They obviously had internalized an idea that learning to write was a "necessary evil" or that a "spoonful of sugar will win the teacher over." Attitude, yes. The question is, what do those attitudes mean in terms of my responsibility as a writing teacher? Do I turn away from those who do not want to be bothered, and do I give my attention to the students who are willing to learn? How do I effect changes in the classroom that will help students become better writers and not turn them off to writing? I thought that the Writing Attitude Survey was a good way of identifying students more carefully and that insights into their writing attitudes might serve as a means for introducing a new technique into the classroom.

David Wallace and I discussed how we might use the Writing Attitude Survey. I thought I might use it as a means of measuring the students' pre- and posttest attitudes to show if there were an improvement in their writing attitudes when collaborative planning was used as the primary method of instruction. We talked about Daly's conclusions about apprehension and thought that collaborative planning might be a way of assuaging my students' negative attitudes. I thought it would be fantastic if we could show that collaborative planning had a positive effect on students' attitudes toward writing and we could demonstrate that those attitudes did, indeed, change. So, over the course of the semester, I used collaborative planning and audiotaped four pairs of students planning collaboratively at the beginning, middle, and end of the course in basic composition. The four pairs of students volunteered to follow through on the project for the semester.

I administered the survey at the beginning and at the end of the course and calculated the pre- and posttest totals for each student as well as the sub-totals for each of the individual constructs (usefulness of planning, consideration of rhetorical concerns, willingness to collaborate, and sense of control about writing). The overall results were rather dismal: The general attitude of the students rose 1.65 points, which is not statistically significant. At first I was disappointed in the results, but after talking to David Wallace and Linda Flower, I noticed that there was an intriguing range of changes in the students' attitudes. One student's attitude increased from 82 to 96 points, an improvement of 14 points, while another student's attitude went from 85 to 60, a decrease of 15 points. Looking at the statistics of the change from pre- to posttest proved to be of little merit, but looking at the range on the attitude survey proved to be helpful in identifying particular students who changed both positively and negatively. The question that immediately rose in my mind was, "When the students had the same teacher, assignments, and method of instruction, why did one student move positively while the other negatively?" Fortunately, I recorded the planning sessions and interviews for the student (Kate) whose attitude increased most positively. Although I do not have the interviews and rough drafts on the student who decreased the most, I do have interviews on a student (Dave) whose attitude decreased substantially. I abandoned my statistical approach in favor of looking at Kate and Dave and reporting on some intriguing classroom dynamics.

Memo #2: Case Studies

Over the course of a semester, I gathered quite a bit of information about Kate and Dave: pre- and posttest results of the Writing Attitude Survey, pre- and posttest results on an essay entitled "How I Write," audiotapes of their collaborative planning sessions at four points during the semester, as well as observations and examples of their writing. By examining these data, I was able to draw profiles of Kate and Dave that proved to be valuable in terms of describing some of the dynamics of classroom interactions.

Case Study: Dave

Dave's score on the survey, 87 at the beginning, cannot be considered good (some students had much higher scores); neither can it be considered negative (many students also had lower scores). Yet during the course of the semester, with instruction in writing and emphasis on collaborative planning strategies, his attitude toward writing became less positive (81). I had no preliminary planning session with Dave because he did not agree to become a case-study subject until after the first week of school and only after I assured him that he would be given special consideration for being part of this study.

Background Information. In general, Dave is a rather private person, at least about his writing; he's somewhat ritualistic in the performance of tasks and does not consider alternative ways of doing things even when he thinks of them. When I asked Dave in an interview how he writes, he said, "I write in many different ways. When I'm mad, I write faster and have more mistakes. If I am in a good mood, I can think of better ideas." Apparently, his attitude affects his writing; when he does not see the point of an assignment, he does not put forth much effort. For example, when given a freewriting assignment that stipulated that he write for 15 minutes on any subject, Dave strictly timed himself: He wrote for 15 minutes; when his alarm sounded at the end of the time limit, he quit writing. There is evidence here to suggest that Dave knows what is expected of him but does not always put into practice what he knows he should; the assignment seems to set absolute boundaries for his participation. It is a curious paradox in Dave that he seems to know what to do but does only enough to get by.

I also observed that Dave became visibly frustrated at times, which I perceived to be about his inability to adapt to new situations. He had a short fuse; I could see him become angry when his ideas did not work out as he expected. One day I saw him working at a computer terminal, unable to get the machine to do what he wanted it to do, and trying various procedures on a random basis to get the computer to respond. When he had worked for most of the period, I asked him how he was doing. "Do we have to type this on the computer?" he asked. "Yes," I responded. "Well then, I'm not going to write it." I offered to help him, and he reluctantly accepted.

Collaborative Planning Sessions. Dave's difficulty with new situations and his minimal approach to writing assignments that he did not like were overt in his attitudes toward collaborative planning. He appeared not to appreciate the help and advice from his peers; he seemed willing to accept advice only from me—the person who controlled his grade. He was more at ease talking about his writing to me as teacher and observer than he was with his collaborative planning partner.

His comments from the first planning session after instruction in collaborative planning demonstrate not only an attitude of disdain for his partner (an attitude that becomes increasingly negative throughout the semester) but also a knowledge of what is to be done, even though he chooses not to do it. In the excerpt below, he dismisses Larry's possible challenge and Larry's misreading of his text and directs Larry about what to do as a supporter.

> *Larry (supporter):* "Your yellow chrome and silver machine?"
>
> *Dave (writer):* Well, if you think about it. I just turned sixteen this year so what could it possibly be?
>
> *Larry:* I guess your bike, right?
>
> *Dave:* Correct. You are correct. Yes, I did bail out if you read the story right. How could I stop? I didn't have any brakes. If you read the story, you can interpret it; you didn't interpret it. It's one of them thinking stories. Now an acknowledgment; tell me how awesome it was.

Dave seems to have internalized part of what the teacher's expectations for collaborative planning were—ask questions and then acknowledge the writer at the end. However, he feels compelled to tell his partner how to do it. In essence, he goes through the motions without grasping the impact of what should happen in the planning session; the session demonstrates a knowledge of collaborative planning, but it does little if anything to expand Dave's thinking on the subject. He seems to have already decided that Larry's advice is of no value and that he is wasting his time with Larry.

Dave's final collaborative planning session presents the same kind of dominance of Dave over Larry. Dave begins the session by telling Larry what the paper was about, the main point, the purpose of persuasion and the overall construction, and point-by-point solutions to the problem. As this excerpt illustrates, Dave leads Larry to ask the questions, and he reveals only as much as is necessary for him to get the job over and done.

> *Dave (writer):* Title of my paper is, uhh, students should be allowed to go out and eat for lunch and, uhh, I'm gonna start if off as a bunch of questions, as if it was a petition to, uhh, persuade and get them involved into my paper. And then I will talk and points, the good points and the bad points of this paper and then I would present possible solutions to this paper.
>
> *Larry (supporter):* OK, what are the good points on your paper?
>
> *Dave:* Well, see, some students don't like to eat what they like to call school food, and it's resulting in malnutrition, and it's pretty expensive for the junk food there. You know, and they have cars, uhh, they could go out to McDonald's or something.
>
> *Larry:* Umm, you think you really have a chance of this ever coming true?
>
> *Dave:* Well, there are many people in this pressure group called "Students for Lunch" and, uhh, I don't know, there's been, uhh, demonstrations, advertisements for this. They're doing everything to try to get this to be a law or force the school lunch. There are bad points though, cause anyone could just go out to lunch and just not come back to school, in their car, and I can see where that would be a problem. But, there can be compromises.
>
> *Larry:* I was thinking, uhh, you could just shut down the school lunches altogether and open up some sort of food court, like in Ross Park Mall, inside a school. Would that be an idea? Maybe you could use that in your paper or something.
>
> *Dave:* That's true. I don't know, I don't think the school makes any money off them lunches, or maybe they do, I don't know. But schools aren't supposed to make a profit, they're just here to teach kids so, I don't know. I guess it would save 'em money.
>
> *Larry:* Yeah.
>
> *Dave:* Well, it's been fun, Larry.

Larry's idea in the last session is a rather good one, a food court in the school; it opens other areas of thinking that are otherwise lost in Dave's paper. He also challenges Dave's idea. However, Dave deals with the profit issue and ignores the creative part of Larry's idea; Larry doesn't have the strength of his convictions to pull the idea together for Dave and, thus, the idea is lost. There is an intellectual constraint on Dave's thinking, perhaps tied to his original idea that Larry is incapable of generating a good idea.

In Dave's written essay, he does indeed begin with questions, "Would one like to have the choice of what one likes to eat and drink? Would one like to eat at a peaceful environment? If one said "yes" to both questions, one would see that students are not allowed to do this." The final draft of the essay addresses issues that he already has in mind—junk food, restrictions on the food service by the school board. Essentially, the organization of the ideas that Dave has in the draft are not furthered through his discussion with his supporter. Dave was the controlling force in the dialogues; he had already made up his mind what he would write about, and maintained a rather inflexible attitude. The reformulation of his text is bounded by his inability to alter his perception of Larry.

Dave seems to have come to the writing task with an opinion that the teacher was in charge, and he could not accept the notion of a student collaborator. When I took the role of collaborative planner with Dave (early in the course before the university intern took responsibility for teaching the course), his attitude was more positive and he accomplished a great deal. Dave is not a fool or a slacker; he did as much as was necessary to get by. He learned the system and controlled it to his advantage. His perception of his collaborator, his perception of the teacher, and his notions of the purpose and task would not allow him to engage in collaborative planning as a means to discovery.

In talking about Dave's collaborative planning, I must say something about his partner, Larry. Larry never seemed to have reached an understanding of purpose in writing, audience, and the relationship of text conventions to the writing. He was laid-back and just did what was required. His concerns typically seemed to be on a cursory level: understanding what happened and checking punctuation errors. To Larry, writing was not a means to a better life, but a course required for graduation. I believe that, had Dave faced a challenge by a student who was knowledgeable about writing, his attitude would have become positive rather than negative. Dave had a meta-awareness of the process but failed to profit from the experience.

Case Study: Kate

Kate began the semester with a survey score of 82 and increased to a score of 96, a positive change of 14. One may have been able to predict this change through her general behaviors: increasing in-class participation, spending morning free time in the computer laboratory, cooperating in class, and participating as editor of the class magazine.

Background Information. In her initial responses to the "How I Write" assignment, Kate said that she found her past writing assignments to be difficult primarily because she was not permitted much "freedom in her writing." She said that she did not have much trouble finding an idea to write about, but frequently got bogged down with the rewriting. According to Kate, "I like to take most of my writing serious because I usually base it on a real person or story."

Her unstructured collaborative planning session (before any instruction) illustrates how willing Kate was to engage in exploration about her ideas for writing. This session came after the students had written a draft of their assignment. After her partner had read Kate's paper, Kate said, "Go ahead and tell me what you thought of it." Her partner commented that Kate's writing was more descriptive, and "When you get more descriptive you get more personal." Together they ended up talking about words and dictionary definitions, expanding on sentences, using "big words," and combining sentences. Kate's willingness to accept criticism and consider changes even after she had produced a draft stands in stark contrast to Dave's perfunctory use of his planning sessions.

Collaborative Planning Sessions. Kate's general level of engagement in her planning sessions was very high. One of Kate's more interesting writings was "Burning Dreams," a story about an event that took place when she was seven. For the planning session on this assignment, the university intern who was teaching the class at that point asked the students to divide into groups of three—a planner, a collaborator, and an observer. Each took a turn as observer who was to take notes about the collaborative planning session while the other two worked as writer and supporter. Not surprisingly, Kate took the most extensive notes when it was her turn to be the observer; also, the notes that she took when she was the writer were also much more extensive than those of the observers. In the session, Kate addressed many important issues: her purpose, her audience, and text conventions. It was not, as had been the case with Dave, a cursory discussion of the editing of the story. Kate seemed to have absorbed much of what collaborative planning is about in a few lessons, and, apparently conscious of the fundamental issues of collaborative planning, she was able to reflect upon her role as writer.

Similar things happened in her next recorded collaborative planning session. In response to an assignment to write a story with a moral, Kate planned to write a story that involved rabbits. When her collaborative planning partner asked why she was writing about bunny rabbits, Kate's reply, "Because it is for children and they can relate to them," suggested that she had done some thinking about her audience. In the course of the conversation, they addressed the idea of believability and audience appropriateness.

At this point, a comparison between Dave and Kate might seem unfair; despite Kate's obvious engagement in the planning sessions, part of her success might be attributed to having better supporters than Dave had. However, Kate's final collaborative planning effort illustrates that even a negative supporter, whose advice tends to sidetrack discussion of rhetorical concerns, could not keep Kate from getting something out of a planning session. In this session, Kate began by explaining her proposal to deal with the problematic issue of whether or not students should be required to watch the daily broadcast of the Whittle Network (a commercial television broadcast for high school students) in her problem/solution paper. Initially, her supporter got involved in the issue of Kate's approach to the problem of getting rid of the network, but then the supporter sidetracked the issue and told her that not all of the homerooms have the network. Her partner became increasingly negative throughout the session, pursuing other problems rather than focusing on how to deal with the immediate issue of writing about Kate's chosen subject. Despite little help from her partner, Kate managed to write the paper, and, as it turned out, she wrote about her original idea.

The negativism on the part of Kate's partner ("I don't think that is a good topic to write about" and "If you really want to write about this, go ahead") certainly must be addressed. Sarah (Kate's supporter) exercised a bit of control over the planning session; she tended to usurp authority in their session. Kate acquiesced but went on to write about her original idea. Despite the lack of help by her supporter, Kate produced reasonably good pieces of writing, became co-editor of the class magazine, and worked diligently in the morning on her writing assignments.

Some Thoughts on the Case Studies

The Writing Attitude Survey worked well for identifying students to look at in case studies. It served to open the door to classroom inquiry. While my first thoughts when entering this classroom investigation were to prove the success of collaborative planning as a tool, I found that collaborative planning is only one of the many dynamic structures working in the writing classroom. Through collaborative planning, many students expanded their ideas and developed a better understanding of the conventions of writing.

Collaborative planning depends, at least in part, on the students' willingness to create a shared experience. The problem arises when students are not willing to engage in that process. Some writers view writing as a private experience. Some students seem unable to detach themselves emotionally from the process and product. For others, writing is much less private; they are more inclined to share their experiences.

Students' willingness to engage in collaborative planning may also interact with the ability of their supporters. In these case studies, both students had weak supporters, yet each student responded differently to the supporter. Because of the personality and attitude that he brought to the class, Dave shied away from sharing his writing with his supporter; he went through the motions of adhering to a process because he was expected to do so. His responses were mechanical and ritualistic but indicate some misdirected interpersonal skills in the way that he dominated his supporter through intimidation. In short, he had learned the collaborative planning process on a procedural level, but he had not internalized the attitude of receptiveness that is an integral part of the process. Dave's attitudes toward sharing his writing did not improve as a result of his experiences with collaborative planning. If anything, his experiences seem to have increased his animosity toward sharing experiences, which he views as a violation of his personal thoughts. His pre-judgment that a peer supporter could not help him, coupled with Larry's passivity, precluded Dave from getting any benefit from a collaborative planning effort.

Like Dave, Kate had a poor supporter for one of her planning sessions—a disruptive supporter who was negative and tended to derail the collaborative writing experience for Kate. Despite this, Kate's attitude improved, and the writing experiences were positive for her. She was able to produce good pieces of writing despite the interference of her partner. It appears that Kate internalized not only the process but also the attitude of receptiveness to grow, not only in her writing, but also in her attitude toward writing, the class, and the teacher.

The primary difference in the two case studies is that Dave failed to profit from the collaborative planning experience because he preferred to take ultimate responsibility for his own writing. For Dave, writing is a private rather than shared experience. Dave ventured nothing and profited nothing through the experience. Kate, on the other hand, took responsibility for writing well and saw collaboration as a method of doing this. She gleaned whatever information that she could from her supporter but enlarged the support system to encompass other students in the class as well as the teacher. Ultimately, Kate became stronger in her ability to cooperate, more adept at writing, and more positive in her attitude.

These case studies seem to argue for taking responsibility for learning to write and for understanding the dynamics of both the writing process and the classroom. New techniques have different levels of acceptance in the classroom that are negotiated through a complicated web of intellectual and emotional criteria that may or may not be logical. The point of view that a student takes toward this responsibility seems to make a difference in the way he or she approaches the writing task. When we perceive writing as private and personal, we tend to wrap ourselves up in the personal and emotional expressions of the process; when we perceive the responsibility for writing well for audiences, we tend to unfurl our ideas and emotions and reach out to others for help and support for communicating for a particular purpose and for a particular audience.

Attitude may be a function of the amount of responsibility that one exercises for his or her own work. Those who take responsibility also become more positive in attitude; those who fail to take responsibility become more negative in attitude. There are many variables in operation in the writing classroom, issues such as success in writing and lack of success in writing; attitude toward the subject, supporter, and technology; and attitude toward change itself. There are personal, social, and political agendas that must be negotiated to produce a text; assumptions about writing, the task, the purpose, and artistic and personal criteria to manage. There is also the issue of knowledge base and reward system; students' attitudes toward the teacher may also influence their attitude toward the process that the teacher is using.

Teachers must be knowledgeable of the plethora of influences brought to bear on the writing process and the ways these pressures interact in the classroom. They must know how different writers write and be able to accommodate the various students' styles and needs. Collaborative planning shows promise in that it helps to frame the process of writing for students, allows individual differences to occur, and encourages students to come to grips with the process of collaboration and, ultimately, to take the responsibility for their own writing.

15 Questioning Strategies and Students Reflecting on Planning Tapes

Theresa Marshall
Iroquois High School
Erie, Pennsylvania

*Theresa Marshall has taught at Iroquois High school in Erie,
Pennsylvania, for the past 19 years. She has served on the
Pennsylvania Writing Advisory Committee since its inception and is
a judge for the NCTE Program to Recognize Excellence in Student
Literary Magazines. Every month Theresa and Marlene Bowen made
the two-hour drive from Erie for the Making Thinking Visible Project
seminars. Although they work as a team, teaching reading and
writing for ninth-grade basic writers, they described this trip as one
of the few times they really had for sustained talk about their
teaching and plans. Theresa's two discovery memos examine the role
of the supporter as the asker of questions in the collaborative
planning process. The first memo chronicles her discovery of the
problem and subsequent action plan several months after she joined
the Making Thinking Visible Project in year two. Her second memo,
written one month later, reports what happened when she asked her
students to listen to their planning tapes.*

For nine years we've answered questions and now you want us
to ask questions. Well, we just don't really know how. We can
ask simple ones, but you don't want simple ones. You're just
gonna have to do something.

—Monica

Two Discovery Memos

Memo #1: Questioning Strategies—You're Just Gonna Have to Do Something!

Monica's candid remarks in a teacher-student conference challenged
me. As I plowed through reams of notes, folders of transcripts, and

stacks of tapes searching for the perfect focus for my collaborative planning inquiry project, she found it for me. Because effective questioning skills are integral to collaborative planning and because my initial discoveries revealed mutual supporter and writer frustration with questioning strategies, I decided to redirect my focus (1) to identify the features of questions and responses most beneficial to the writer and (2) to initiate strategies that would help students incorporate effective questioning into their collaborative planning session.

To help me formulate an action plan, I asked my students to write reflection memos responding to the following questions:

1. What supporter questions helped you most with your text?
2. If questions were asked encouraging you and the supporter to consider alternatives, what impact did they have on your text?
3. If you could have changed places with your supporter, what would you have done differently?
4. List the information and skills you want included in the questioning workshop.

After reviewing the students' reflection memos, my class notes, and notes from student-teacher conferences, I saw that my students had problems asking good questions during their collaborative planning sessions. The following excerpts typify the responses I received during student-teacher conferences and in the reflection memos that I asked students to write about their planning sessions. Notice the frustration both supporters and writers experienced as inadequate questioning skills impeded their progress.

We need better questions [a reference to the list of generic questions I gave them as an aid].

—Mary

I need to think of better questions to ask the writer. But I can't. I really tried.

—Betsy

My supporter needed to ask me better questions. I mean, she asked me questions and when I said the first thing that came to my mind she moved on. I mean really!

—Nina

Do something to make me think more. Lousy questions.

—Jason

Using the information collected from the responses to the above reflection memos, I designed the following action plan to address their major concerns. Students suggested the analysis of tapes, transcripts, and role playing situations. I now had to make a big decision. Should I adjust my original time schedule just a little and allow one extra day to follow one of their suggestions, or should I "take the plunge" and do all three? I decided to do all three. What I witnessed was a real ownership of their learning. *They told me* what they needed and what they wanted. I felt compelled to oblige.

Action Plan

1. Share with the students a summary of the discovery memos. Use one class period to discuss aspects of questioning from the wording of a question to the diverse responses inherent in different types of questions.

2. Use two class periods to listen to tapes and read transcripts of the two previous collaborative planning sessions, keying in on questioning problems and solutions.

3. Use one class period to role play collaborative planning sessions. Ask students to analyze the multi-purposes of the supporter's questions and to evaluate the responses encouraged by different types of questions.

4. Look for any research linking good questions to good text.

Are four class periods excessive to devote to developing better questioning skills? It seems so when I consider how much longer everything is taking me. How will they respond to these lessons? Will subsequent collaborative planning sessions be more successful? Will supporter and planner frustration decrease? Will I observe more analytical, evaluative considerations in future sessions? Remember Monica? She challenged me to "do something."

Memo #2: Student Reflections on Planning Tapes—Doing Something

I've made great discoveries since our last meeting. Even though some of them do not focus on my study, I feel compelled to share them.

I discovered that I cannot type a bullet on the Apple II GS.

I discovered that I cannot organize the Staff Lottery Club, a 600 participant bike race, the district Team Fitness Run and

Quad teams at the same time I'm directing three plays, drowning in paperwork, and still do windows.

I discovered that I have no *Me-time* at school. Every study hall, computer lab period, and prep is occupied by students who drop by to chat about their latest papers.

I discovered that collaborative planning has turned many students onto writing. Proud, yet insecure about their accomplishments, they require much nourishment.

What have I really discovered since the last Pittsburgh trek? A lot. Since then I have implemented my action plan. The students were enthusiastically engaged in each class session. When I asked why, many claimed ownership of the lessons, since their concerns and frustrations shaped them. We enjoyed ourselves in the role-playing session. I played the supporter once, and they analyzed the type of questions I asked and evaluated the quality of my responses and follow-up questions. When they replayed sections of their November tapes, lively interaction ensued as to the usefulness of specific questions and responses. Thinking was visible. The following excerpt is from the tape of the collaborative planning session that Nina and Jeremy analyzed.

Leah (supporter): Who did you say this was for?

Nina (writer): The class.

Leah: How long do you plan to make it?

Nina: I really haven't figured it out. It will probably take a couple of pages. Maybe more.

Leah: Do you have a title?

Nina: Do we need a title?

Leah: I don't know but I like it when essays have titles. How about *Romeo and Juliet:* a Tragedy of Accidents?

Nina: I like that. Thanks.

Nina was the planner who previously wrote, "My supporter needed to ask me better questions. I mean, she asked me questions and when I said the first thing that came to my mind she moved on. I mean, really!" As you can see from the excerpt, Nina was not exaggerating about lack of substantive engagement in this planning session. I wanted Leah and Nina to analyze Nina's tape, but Leah was absent so Nina worked with Jeremy; an excerpt of their analysis tape follows.

Jeremy: It's hysterical. The only good thing I see is the suggestion of a title. I understand why you thought it didn't go too well.

Nina: That was the only thing I got out of it. I used that title.

Jeremy: When you answered "the class" for audience, she should have asked you something to make you consider um, um, what you should include, you know what they need to know or expect to know, something like that.

Nina: That was definitely a problem. I could have said that most kids will disagree with my position so I'll have to put in lots of reasons to persuade them.

Jeremy: You know what would have been good? If you guys would have discussed audience more, you, um, could have thrashed out what the arguments against your position could be and, what's the word that means to cancel out?

Nina: Negate?

Jeremy: You could have discussed the other side and in your paper negate their reasons.

In this situation, Jeremy quickly addressed the issue of audience. As Nina and he discussed alternative questions that Leah could have asked, the vague concept of audience was replaced with a rhetorical connection to task information. Later in their interaction, Nina wished for a chance to redo the assignment. Their reflections revealed the problems with Leah and Nina's session and suggested viable alternatives—genuine problem solving and critical thinking occurred.

Our next taped collaborative planning session is at the end of this week. Did they internalize some, all, none of the questioning skills we have been practicing? Had frustration been reduced? What questions and responses did the planner find most beneficial? What was transferred to text?

16 Initial Expectations, Problems, and What Is Success?

Marlene W. Bowen
Iroquois High School
Erie, Pennsylvania

Marlene W. Bowen, a reading specialist with the Iroquois School District in Erie, Pennsylvania, team teaches a ninth-grade English course for basic students with her colleague, Theresa (Teri) Marshall, another member of the Making Thinking Visible Project. A member of the International Reading Association, the Keystone State Reading Association, and the Association of Supervision and Curriculum Development, Marlene has presented workshops to teacher groups on cooperative learning and teaching remedial readers. In addition to full-time teaching, she is completing her Ed.D. at the University of Pittsburgh. In this series of three memos, written in year two of the Making Thinking Visible Project, Marlene recounts the unexpected problems she and Teri encountered using collaborative planning with their ninth-grade remedial readers and the slowly emerging sense of accomplishment and self-esteem they saw in these students who often think of themselves as unsuccessful in school.

Three Discovery Memos

Memo #1: Initial Expectations and Problems

After the September meeting (my first), I was very eager to begin collaborative planning with my students. I was looking forward to the enthusiasm I thought they would share in becoming a part of the project, and I was excited about the potential of being able to view my students' thinking processes. Perhaps then I could get a better handle on what I could do to help them become better readers and writers.

When I came back to the classroom, I looked at my students in terms of collaborative planning and was surprised at the number of concerns that surfaced. For example, in one class the disparity among the students' performance on reading and writing tasks seemed to prohibit collaboration. How could students still trying to master the art of writing a sentence be paired with students who were writing senior research papers? Also, there were social barriers to overcome. Some members of the class were not only new to the school but had been mainstreamed from special education classes. How would collaboration work in this situation? Could these obstacles be overcome in such a way that collaborative planning would be beneficial to all of the students involved?

The other group with which I would use collaborative planning is team taught by Teri and me. From past experiences with this class, I have noticed several recurring problems. First, students' lack of background knowledge hampers their ability to succeed. These are students whom E. D. Hirsch would term the "culturally illiterate." Second, and of most significance to me personally, is that although students eventually master the structure of a particular piece of writing, they have difficulty extracting from texts relevant information to use in their papers. Isolated bits of topic information are chosen by these students, with no idea of how this information fits into their papers.

When I ask these students what makes it difficult for them to read a piece of text and what strategies they could use to improve their understanding, their responses indicated an apparent inability to be reflective and a lack of terminology to discuss their reflections. They are, for the most part, passive rather than intentional learners.

In view of the literature on the efficacy of cooperative learning, the social construction of knowledge, and the importance of metacognition in the development of strategic readers, collaborative planning seems to offer a methodology that will aid my students in becoming more reflective, provide them with a language for discussing a piece of text, and give me a way to gain insight into their thinking processes.

Memo #2: Problems with Implementation . . . One Month Later

By the time you read this memo, some of you will have already heard this story; my frustration level is high and I know will not have been able to refrain from telling this tale of woe. It begins thus.

Since collaborative planning (CP) was a new approach for me as well as my students, I spent a good deal of time preparing my presentation of it. After years of working with remedial students, "academically disadvantaged," "at-risk," or whatever description you choose, I knew that confusion at the outset would sabotage my best efforts, so I labored to avoid that confusion. I prepared overheads and sample transcriptions and used discussion techniques, handouts, and role playing. Teri and I even modeled a collaborative planning session for the students. In short, I used every teaching strategy I knew to make CP palatable, understandable, and usable for these students. To say I felt like a dismal failure would be an understatement. I was not prepared for the utter chaos that followed. To illustrate:

My first setback came when Teri came to model a CP session with me. The students had been reading about a rock group scheduled to perform in Erie and about the possibility of the city censoring the performance. This sparked much discussion among the students, and many had additional information about other music groups who had been censored. I decided that this would be the perfect opportunity to use CP, and so, suggested that the students write a letter to the editor expressing their opinions. They eagerly brought in articles from other sources, which I photocopied for them to read. They asked me my opinion about censorship of music, and I told them I was against it, although I might find some things personally objectionable. They told me I would hate Two Live Crew and their music. I was not convinced, so one of the students pulled a tape out of his Walkman and played it for me. I later told other teachers about the tape and my "poker face," but in reality I was in shock. (Those of you who are familiar with this group and their music will probably understand this; for those of you who are not . . . it is a whole other story!)

I did a 180 as far as my opinion about censorship went. I told Teri in our planning session that I wanted to write an article for a magazine that parents were likely to read. Since she had not heard the tape and was of the same opinion that I held originally, we talked at great length about including lyrics in my article. After all, parents were always objecting to the music their kids were listening to, so how was this different? I was not sure that would be effective because frankly I did not see how anyone would print the lyrics even if I did include them. We were really into our CP session at this point, and the students were intrigued (more by our differing points of view than anything else). Imagine my surprise when Teri pointed out to me that one of the students had fallen asleep. I called his name, but no response. He had not just nodded off, *he was out cold.* It should have been an omen. I could feel the tension building.

The next day, the students had a CP session. Their first problems concerned the operation of the tape recorders. They acted like they had never seen such devices in their lives, when in fact, most owned Walkman versions, and all had frequent access to stereo equipment at home. I was on the brink.

They were not sure what questions to ask (mind you, the model questions were in front of them), they thought it was unfair that the supporter did not have to write a paper (where that came from is still a mystery), and they were hesitant to talk with a tape recorder in front of them, or kept pausing it until they thought they had something important to say. Postcards from the edge.

The icing on the cake came the following day when I collected their tapes after they had listened to them again at home. I noticed that one student's tape looked different from the others, and since they had all spent the same amount of time doing CP, I questioned him about it. He informed me that the CP session was not on the tape anymore because he had recorded the Two Live Crew tape over it so he would have some of the lyrics to use in his paper in case he wanted to prove a point.

I have never felt so frustrated as a teacher. I was so angry with them I could have done bodily harm. Thankfully, I refrained and am back to the drawing board to rethink CP, my students, their reactions, and my entire career.

Memo #3: What Is Success? . . . Six Months Later

Because our students have been traditionally labeled as unsuccessful, the issue of what constitutes success has become very important to us. Over the past several months, Teri and I have labored over this question. Collaborative planning was taking a lot of time, and we wondered whether a direct instruction model of the process and types of writing would be just as effective. Many times, we questioned the practicality of using collaborative planning with our marginal students. There was no question that it was working well with other types of students, but was it worth the effort and time for these kids? Luckily, we were in a team-teaching situation, and although we had our doubts, they rarely occurred at the same times. Besides, the two-hour ride to Pittsburgh gave us a chance to talk without interruption about what was going on in the classroom, and the opportunity to share with other members of the project boosted our morale.

One of the first decisions we made was to modify our teaching of collaborative planning. The terms of the Planner's Blackboards and the generic questions from the handbook on collaborative planning were just not enough. We had to get students' reactions and reflections from listening to and looking at transcripts of their own tapes and incorporate what we learned into our teaching. We spent many hours transcribing sessions and photocopying the transcripts for students. Our students needed lots of practice looking at pieces of writing and transcriptions before they could understand what the areas of the Planner's Blackboard meant and how they were interrelated. We placed sections of their transcripts on an overhead projector and talked a lot about the planner/supporter relationship and how the session contributed to the actual writing of the papers. It was effort well spent. Let me share with you some of the highlights:

1. After talking about questions and their importance in the collaborative planning process, one of our students looked at us and said, "We just don't get these questions. Teach us more about questions!" I think this represented a milestone. We showed them their transcripts, talked about the kinds of questions they were asking one another, and introduced new questions that would help them become better questioners and responders to other students' writing. We practiced together by asking students questions such as "What area of the planner are you dealing with?" or "Who is this for?" or "What are you really asking?" to get them to begin to internalize the planning process. By seeing how certain questions and responses challenged planners and allowed them to elaborate their plans, they began to build a sense of engagement with another person's text and with their own texts. For perhaps the first time in their lives as students, these kids were taking control of their education. This was a first step in becoming an intentional learner.

2. The visual metaphor of the Planner's Blackboard empowered the students with a common language. Whether they came to ask us or each other for help, they were better able to discuss a piece of text knowing what our comments meant.

3. After transcribing a tape of a CP session that Teri and I had done for our research paper, I was dumbstruck by the discovery that *we* were not always on task. I have come to realize that while time on task is an important component in the educational process, learning is not dictated by it. I still monitor students during their sessions, but I am more inclined to let diversions occur. After all, if we digressed and still produced, why couldn't they?

4. Because students are taking more ownership for their work, they are spending more time with their writing and ultimately creating better products. Teri created a bulletin board for

these writers to show how their planning sessions pay off by having their writing displayed for a real audience to read and enjoy. This sense of ownership has not only affected their achievement, but given them a sense of accomplishment in their work. For the first time, these students are working on making their writing better; they are willing to rewrite, they take pride in their work, and they feel good about sharing their ideas with one another. This nurturing of self-esteem has created a cycle. One student recently told me, "I've really got to do something about my spelling. What can I do to get better?"

I do not want to leave the impression that all students are making strides like these all the time. But it is happening with enough regularity to make me feel that my students are benefiting from collaborative planning in ways I would not have anticipated. Perhaps more important, I am evolving as a teacher. This process of making thinking visible has given me the opportunity to help my students make decisions to help themselves become successful learners. And after all, isn't that what teaching is all about?

17 Transferring Talk to Text

Jane Zachary Gargaro
Peabody High School
Pittsburgh, Pennsylvania

*Jane Zachary Gargaro has taught English in Pittsburgh Public
Schools for 24 years, 14 of which she spent as the Instructional
Teacher Leader at Peabody High School. The third member of the
informal Peabody team, Jane has also been a Fellow of the Western
Pennsylvania Writing Project and has served as a curriculum editor
and coordinator of the Partnerships in Education program for
Peabody teachers. As a result, in part, of her active role in the
Making Thinking Visible Project, the Pittsburgh Public Schools
invited her to spend a year as one of four curriculum practitioners
writing a curriculum that would eventually make collaborative
planning a part of the new systemwide ninth-grade curriculum unit.
In this professional writing process with other teachers (described in*
Discoveries and Dialogues, *Norris, Brozik, & Gargaro, 1992),
collaborative planning moved out of the classroom to become a fluid,
and politically charged, process of persuasion and problem solving.
Jane wrote the memo presented here at the end of a two-semester
inquiry into the ways students move from talk to text. In this year-
end retrospection, she draws together a series of discoveries made by
comparing students' transcripts to the texts they actually wrote.*

A Discovery Memo

As a member of this project, I have come to appreciate the importance
of both planning talk and the use of the Planner's Blackboard for
establishing a plan for writing. Being a classroom teacher, however,
has made me realize that a collaborative planning session does not
always lead to improved text. As a teacher-researcher and an advocate
of the writing process, I am intrigued by the transfer, or lack of
transfer, between planning and text. Therefore, my classroom research
this year has centered around the following questions, relating planning
to text:

- How did writers actually incorporate the questions or comments of the supporter into the text?
- What questions/comments did writers tend to ignore?

- What elements of the planning session enabled the writers to utilize effective writing strategies in the text?
- What writing strategies did students develop (what learning took place) as a result of collaborative planning, as evidenced by the text?

I worked with eighteen students enrolled in two classes for eleventh-grade gifted students. I used audiotapes and transcriptions of the students' planning sessions as well as their texts and the reflection papers. I reviewed both the audiotapes of their collaborative planning sessions and their written essays in order to assess the value of collaborative planning to their writing progress.

In this memo, I present snapshots of student collaboration and text production to see what learning actually took place as the students worked on their assignment: "plan and write a character sketch in which you convey a dominant impression of the character." Following these snapshots, I include my observations, gleaned from the students' reflection papers about the connection between their collaborative process and their product.

The first two excerpts are from a planning session in which a student attempts to establish a setting for a character sketch in relation to a key point or dominant impression of her chosen character. In much of the collaborative planning session, the writer attempts to identify a dominant impression. Her planning gives evidence of confusion about her chosen character, her exchange-student "sister," Malacho. In the excerpt that I have quoted here, the writer, working with two supporters (we had an uneven number in class that day), leads her supporters into a discussion about the setting of her character sketch. Notice, however, that she does not defend her initial decision to use the Colombian setting when challenged by Supporter 1. She does, however, express surprise at the question. Note also that at the end of this excerpt, a new text convention is introduced by Supporter 1; he suggests a "looking back," although he does not specify what form this looking back could take.

> *Supporter 1:* Are you going to have a conversation between you and her [your character], or between your parents and her or a couple of conversations, or . . . ?
>
> *Writer:* I hadn't really thought of that. Um, I don't know where I want to set this—at my house in reference to when I was in Colombia or to set it in Colombia. Maybe I should just have it there.

> *Supporter 1:* Maybe you should just set it at your house and
> nothing at all about—
>
> *Writer:* Nothing at all about there?
>
> *Supporter 2:* But you wouldn't know—
>
> *Supporter 1:* I guess it is an exchange though.
>
> *Supporter 2:* She was so adaptable—
>
> *Writer:* —adaptable—
>
> *Supporter 2:* If you hadn't gone to Colombia—
>
> *Writer:* Right. Maybe I should just set it in South America.
>
> *Supporter 1:* Yeah, well, set it down there and talk about how
> much you had to change, and look back and say how much
> she must have had to.

In evaluating the success of her collaborations in a reflection
paper, the writer points out that there is the possibility that "I ignore
the questions I am not prepared to answer." Note, for example, that
the writer ignores the comment in this excerpt about including conversations and moves to a discussion of setting. She says that she
does not know where to set the piece, but when the suggestion is
made that the setting should be her house in the United States, the
writer objects. She receives the encouragement she is looking for from
Supporter 2 (Supporter 2 seems to be encouraging the writer's own
intentions) and quickly determines to set the piece in Colombia.
Supporter 1's "looking back" suggestion surfaces in the following
excerpt with the suggestion by Supporter 2 to use "flashback." Also
in this excerpt, Supporter 1 challenges the writer to think further about
the text conventions she will use to create the character for her
audience. Both excerpts reveal a writer who at this point is not really
open to challenging or extending her thinking in relation to her chosen
setting or other text conventions.

> *Supporter 1:* Okay. Are you going to write a story about her, or
> use dialogue, or quotes?
>
> *Writer:* Yeah, I . . . um . . . see if I put it—I want to use dialogue
> because that was—I liked the way she phrased things. I
> liked her English. I mean her foreign accent in English, but
> do I write it in the way she would actually have pronounced
> things, or do I just write it?
>
> *Supporter 2:* I think so. 'Cause did you read in the book where
> a young girl was writing about her father in Germany, and
> she just felt it how he said it. So I think that would be a

good idea and that would help to get your dominant impression across.

Supporter 1: So, your dominant impression, how's that going to come out in your conversations, or are you going to make them up?

Writer: Well, I'm certainly not going to remember them word for word.

Supporter 1: Well, I know, but are you going to, do you remember specific conversations that have to do with—

Writer: Well, I think so. I remember conversations with her, with her family, with friends about the drug situation, and I always used to ask her when we were at my house looking around for something to do, "Well, what would you be doing at your house right now?" And we'd always have conversations about that.

Supporter 2: Well, maybe if you could do a sort of flashback to your house from Colombia.

Writer: Yeah, I don't know. It just impressed me that she fit in my family so well without losing her identity. She was definitely South American the whole time. She just adapted.

The suggestion to use a flashback could have enabled the writer to expand her piece and reveal Malacho's adaptability. The writer, however, dismisses this strategy, with "Um-hmm" and "Yeah, I don't know . . . she just adapted," in favor of restating her key point. The dialogue (conversations), which she discusses at length, are not used in the paper either. They are obliquely included as "I know from past conversations that. . . ." (See the character sketch in figure 17.1.)

The writer of this character sketch is a young woman with strong opinions, one of these being a firm belief in feminism. The writer's entire planning session gives evidence of confusion about the dominant impression (key point) she will give of her chosen subject. She marvels at Malacho's adaptability to a culture other than her own; moreover, she expresses confusion over Malacho's ability to accept her own society's cultural expectations of her as a woman. *Adaptability* and *liberation* were both considered as possible key points. One of the supporters, in a part of the session not quoted here, suggested that perhaps the two were related. The writer accepted this suggestion. In her own words, this is how she incorporated her supporter's advice: "My final draft of the essay included them both, making the point that despite the restrictions Colombian society had placed on her, Malacho maintained her own identity while adapting to the ways of

> "Las medias, por favor." Rodrigo holds his feet out for Malacho to remove his socks. She puts down her hair brush and does this immediately. Things of this nature are a frequent occurrence in the Llano family and in all of Colombia, as well, I imagine. The father comes home from work and the wife and daughters are expected to do everything for him. Despite that, all requests are made with "pleases" and "thank you's" and everything is done good naturedly. I dislike this practice. I am, of course, surprised to see Malacho take her father's socks off for him without protest or hesitation. In my mind she is a feminist: a young woman in complete control of her life, with a sincere interest in succeeding. I know from past conversations that she is a firm believer in the "women can do anything men can do" theory, and yet she jumps at her father's every command. However, as I watch this process many times in various circumstances, I notice that Malacho does what is demanded of her without ever compromising herself or losing her identity. She goes along with the South American chauvinist conventions because they are a strong part of her, a major shaping force in her life. They are a driving portion of her culture. She has set tight boundaries for herself within which an amazing amount of freedom is possible. She maintains the inner strength, ambition, and constant desire for self-improvement I associate with a truly liberated woman. Whether or not she goes along with her society's demands or lack of opportunity for women is superficial; she will always strive for achieving her personal best.

Figure 17.1. The Character Sketch.

her non-feminist oriented country." In her reflection paper, the writer credits collaborative planning with helping her sort out her confusion about her chosen subject.

The key point of the essay is clear, but Malacho's character seems to have gotten lost in the writer's struggle to state a key point directly rather than establish a dominant impression of the character. The writer ignores the supporters' suggestions that would have enabled her to show us a character rather than utilize her subject to make a point. As Flower and Hayes (1980) argue,

> An audience and exigency can jolt a writer into action, but the force which drives composing is the writer's own set of goals, purposes or intentions. A major part of defining the rhetorical problem then is representing one's own goals. As we might predict from the way writers progressively fill in their image of audience, writers also build a progressive representation of their goals as they write. (p. 27)

The writer's goal seems to be something like *I am going to make some sense out of this character who seems to have feminist views similar to mine but whose actions within the boundaries of her own culture, in my opinion, contradict those views.*

Why, then, did the writer incorporate so few of the textual strategies suggested by her supporters? Her planning transcript seems to indicate that she was not yet ready to *show* the reader a character (as the assignment requested) because she was still confused about the character she chose to depict. Her immediate intentions were to come to some understanding of Malacho's character and actions. If a writer is not clear about his or her key point, a discussion of textual strategies may not be directly transferable to a first draft of the assignment. A collaborative planning session on these strategies (text conventions) might have been more helpful to the writer after this draft had been written. Another session might also have enabled the writer to redefine her rhetorical problem and set a new goal that, hypothetically, could be stated something like this: *How do I show the complexity of Malacho's thoroughly Colombian but independent character?* I now think that asking students to restate the assignment in the form of a question before they begin their collaborative planning may assist both the teacher and the student in this learning/teaching situation, enabling the teacher to understand how students are defining the assignment for themselves and enabling the student to focus more clearly on the problem that the assignment presents.

Connecting Process to Product

I have observed that students do not always use the comments of their supporters in producing text; however, many times they do. As learners, students in any given class exist on a developmental continuum—intellectually, emotionally, experientially, psychologically. Generally, I find that students easily incorporate ideas that are perceived as consistent with and as enhancing their own intentions. They readily incorporate ideas or strategies with which they are familiar and that do not involve much risk. Other students, however, challenge themselves to understand a strategy in relation to overall purpose or to relate overall purpose in a strategically unique way. These latter writers have begun to use collaborative planning for their advantage. They have begun to see the importance of reviewing and consolidating a plan via the decisions encouraged by the Planner's Blackboard.

In addition to learning from the collaborative planning transcripts, the students' texts, and the students' reflection papers central to this study, I gained a great deal of insight regarding the relationship between collaborative planning and text from the reflection papers of other students in my class. These quotations from my students' reflection papers suggest some of the reasons that students do not incorporate the comments/questions of their supporters into their text:

> I reject ideas when they challenge my preparation and I think I am anchored with a good idea.

> When the questions became too difficult, I would shy away and not answer them.

> Sometimes I answered too many questions and said too much instead of really listening to what the supporter was trying to emphasize to me.

> I must listen to my supporter's comments.

> I did not ignore my supporter's questions/comments, but when actually writing my essay, I did not incorporate them.

> I tended to ignore questions that involved experimenting and changing my plan in a big way. I think that this is done out of fear.

> I need to be more careful about passing over the things that don't strike my fancy at the moment.

> The questions I tended to ignore were those that involved the revamping of my entire paper.

All of these comments seem to suggest that students will not benefit from collaboration when they are not open to the process. This lack of openness seems to result from one of three dominant attitudes: (1) an inflexibility with regard to their own ideas or established plan, (2) a lack of willingness to improve process skills, or (3) a lack of willingness to connect process to product. These three attitudes are further illustrated by the following students' comments:

■ *Inflexibility/not willing to question one's own ideas or plan*

> I ignored my supporter's comments because I usually have thought it (the plan) over enough so that I don't like switching for any reason. . . . A portrait of myself as a writer would be a reckless writer, who dives into an ocean of ideas with no life jacket of planning. I wade through ideas with only a vague sense of what direction I'm proceeding in. . . . Collaborative planning was not entirely helpful to me only because of my hard-headedness. It was helpful to me when I allowed myself to be open to it. If someone asked me whether or not they should use CP as a writing technique, I would definitely recommend an attempt at using it. Whether or not it works, it is up to them.

- *Going through the motions/not using the process to advantage*

  Throughout the three collaborative planning sessions, many plans and questions were thrown around. As I would learn as the year went on, paying attention to the questions posed by my partner was the single most important thing that I could do as a planner. Unfortunately, I didn't always do this, and I think my essays reflect it.

- *Utilizing process for the sake of process/no connection between process and product*

  I always seem to deviate from my original plan. I didn't ignore any questions the supporter asked. I answered all the questions and took all the comments into consideration. I had an answer for *every* question and/or comment that was made. . . . I always thought about what I would say in response to a supporter's question, but I never once said, "Oh, yes, that's an excellent point." I never thought about it or perceived it in that way. . . . It is much easier for me to write from the heart and let my ideas flow. That's why I love poetry.

In assessing the benefit of collaborative planning for their development as writers, these students show their own complex response to this process. The first two students are fully aware that they did not use the process to its full advantage. The third, however, believes she took advantage of the process. But if we look further, we see that even she recognizes that she never said, "That's an excellent point." Such a comment on the writer's part, I believe, would indicate recognition that the supporter has made a significant statement that will enable the writer to develop her plan more fully. This writer, by her own tacit admission, however, is resistant. She is not willing to revise her plan. (This lack of willingness to revise was evident in successive written drafts of an assignment as well.) In fact, it is questionable whether she puts any plan into action. As she says, "It's much easier for me to write from the heart and let my ideas flow." Her comments lead me to believe that she enjoys writing from inspiration; she does not accept the value of making connections orally, of thinking a plan through and getting reactions to it. Many times during the year, she expressed resistance to any new type of thinking she was asked to do. Asked to think about how a particular author made meaning in a piece, for example, she indicated that she had difficulty answering because she "doesn't think that way." She often commented that she is more of a "science/math" person than an

"English" person. This defensiveness did not allow her to use collaborative planning to her advantage.

Developing Planning and Writing Strategies

The students' planning transcriptions, texts, and comments give evidence of growth in planning and talking strategies which include:

- Developing listening skills
- Asking pertinent questions of oneself and of one's partner
- Answering rather than ignoring questions that are asked
- Connecting areas of the Planner's Blackboard (purpose, audience, text conventions)

Their texts and reflection papers suggest that these students are now more conscious of using the following writing strategies in text production:

- Using planning decisions in the actual text
- Limiting information
- Organizing information in relation to purpose
- Considering alternative structures
- Using specific detail and example

Collaborative planning enables students to guide their own cognition and enhance metacognitive awareness. Looking through the lens of meaning making, these snapshots reveal students' efforts to ask and answer questions, making their thinking more visible to themselves. The snapshots also reveal a process that is language based. Students learn by using talking strategies and by making connections between oral and written language. They learn the significance of communicating for a purpose. Also, the collaborative process allows students who are open to it the opportunity to use their prior knowledge and beliefs (individual aspect) and interact with a community of learners (social aspect) to further develop their knowledge and skills.

When teaching and writing curricula, therefore, we should consider not only the "what" but also the "how." As educators, we have a goal to develop independent thinkers and learners. We cannot accomplish this goal unless we pay attention to process as well as to educational materials and specific content knowledge that we as a society deem necessary for our children to have.

Observation of what transpires in a collaborative planning session gives teachers as well as students a valuable assessment tool, helping both to answer the question, "Where do I go from here?" Self-analysis of collaborative planning sessions and the resultant texts enables the students to assess their progress as writers. These self-assessments, in turn, provide the teacher with valuable information on the progress of both a class of students and individual students within the class. Collaborative planning is one method that, paradoxically, enables students to engage each other for the purpose of becoming independent thinkers and writers.

Part II Observations across Contexts

Section 3
Adapting Theory and Research in Community College Settings

18 Collaborative Planning and the Classroom Context: Tracking, Banking, and Transformations

Jean A. Aston
Community College of Allegheny County
Pittsburgh, Pennsylvania

Jean A. Aston is professor of English at the Community College of Allegheny County (CCAC), where for six years she chaired the English department of this large city campus. Recently, Jean took on a special projects assignment in the CCAC administration, helping support new initiatives and coordinating the system's reaccreditation process. And at the Community Literacy Center, located near CCAC on Pittsburgh's north side, she is helping to create some bridges between high school and college for urban teenagers. Earlier, Jean's dissertation had given her an inside look at the logic behind some of the errors that typify basic writers. She showed how the personal essay, assigned as a non-intimidating invitation to write and develop detail about one's neighborhood, elicited strategic evasion and abstract prose from students who did not wish to be identified with the places they and their family (who also read these texts) were forced to live. Collaborative planning gave Jean a new way not only to explore the decision making teachers may never see, but to make this reflective process a part of her students' learning as well. The paper that follows comes out of an extended project, tracking students' changing understandings of what is expected of a college writer.

A Project Paper

When I was in high school, I was a low-track student. I was never taught to compose an essay (like this one), never taught to think for myself, or do scientific work. I was taught how to do my taxes, fill out job applications, and sit quietly without asking questions. I would go from class to class like a zombie for eight hours. Each class was different; one class I was learning, one I was sleeping. When I was in eleventh grade, I slept every day in class and the teacher would always read his newspaper. At the end of the year, much to my surprise, I passed with a B+.[1]

—Cathy, a community college student

After two semesters of working with collaborative planning, I learned from students like Cathy that the way students conceptualize and act on the principle of "authority belong[ing] to the writer as planner and thinker" is linked to strategies, rules, and attitudes shaped and reinforced by their past (and present) classroom experiences. For most of my students, who, like Cathy, had been shaped by a banking pedagogy in a low track in secondary school, both my problem-solving pedagogy and the use of collaborative planning within that framework demanded a restructuring of their concepts of themselves as learners reading, writing, and thinking if they were to succeed. Specifically, the restructuring depended on their ability to know when to use, adapt, or abandon old strategies and to learn new strategies to meet new demands.

The intricacy of this process I saw only in retrospect as I analyzed all of the data I collected for this study. But it is the intricacy of the transformation that I want to focus on in the three parts of this paper by presenting the following:

1. A contextual framework, a description of my two semesters of using collaborative planning in a community college developmental course and the consequent evolution of a research strategy and a theory about change indicators;

2. Cases of five students who represent a developmental continuum illustrating barriers to and strategies for students' negotiating transformations in their learning;

3. A discussion of the patterns illustrated by the five students in relationship to the class as a whole and the implications for the use of collaborative planning in classrooms.

The Classroom Context: Two Semesters of Collaborative Planning

The study was conducted in Eng-100, Basic Principles of Composition, a second-level developmental writing course for students at the Community College of Allegheny County who have either tested in through the placement process or who have passed the preceding lower-level developmental course. The course objective is to help students who have basic control over writing conventions learn to write short, analytical essays in response to reading-based topics. *Rereading America: Cultural Contexts for Critical Thinking and Writing,* a thematic reader exploring contemporary issues through a variety of discourse types, is the primary text in this reading-based writing course.

A problem-solving pedagogy framed both semesters. The students and I would review the text topics and pick the themes that they wanted to read and write about. The fifteen fall-semester students chose *work,* reflecting their multiple work experiences; the nineteen spring semester students chose *education,* a choice triggered by an analysis of their recent high school experience. Students worked in small groups to discuss readings and then shared analyses and questions with the entire class. The groups also responded to drafts at various points in the writing process.

Observing students using collaborative planning in the fall class, I saw a distinction that was to be the center of my spring inquiry, the difference between rigid and adaptable planners. Denise illustrated the former. Depending on well-learned formulas acquired in high school such as the five-paragraph essay, she would transform all assignments to fit her formulas rather than use the rhetorical guides of the Planner's Blackboard to plan her work. She applied her formulas like the rules of an algorithm, always generating a response, albeit a weak one that left her peers puzzled over the meaning of her generalizations. In contrast, Donna worked with the rhetorical guides of the Planner's Blackboard to shape each assignment. The collaborative planning session helped her to test ideas, and to modify, adapt, and negotiate meanings with her supporter.

The contrast between and the consequences of these rigid and adaptable planning styles were illustrated in the class's analysis of the papers Denise and Donna wrote for an assignment asking them to examine the work environments and attitudes of two workers from Studs Terkel's *Working* and to draw conclusions about the relationship between the two variables. Denise's general, unfocused essay asserted only that the workers were different, using a methodical, point-by-point list of the differences. In contrast, Donna tied the differences between the workers to a concept, alienation, that she had written about in a prior assignment. The class, in examining the two papers for revision, asked the writers to explain how they had defined the writing task, the purpose, and the audience.

Their respective responses to the questions revealed the differences in their planning. Denise's purpose was simply to compare and contrast, a constraint that lead to sparse details. She imposed a high-school-learned schema that she generalized to all writing assignments, one that always guaranteed her a five-paragraph essay: "Just state a subject, then compare and contrast, and then summarize it."

In contrast, purpose to Donna was assignment specific and meant articulating a theory about how attitudes are shaped by environments in work places and carefully choosing details to make her argument credible. She transformed knowledge to fit her goal, a flexibility that made her a strong writer.

I began the spring term hoping to learn more about what caused the two kinds of behaviors I had observed in Donna and Denise, but my inquiry expanded and became more complex because of the initial resistance from a majority of the spring students to both the problem-solving pedagogy and collaborative planning. Because most did not want the responsibility of discussing readings, they demanded that I should lecture and tell them "what things meant" so that their papers would contain "what I wanted." The idea that authority should rest with the writer was a very foreign and frightening notion.

Two of the readings in a unit on education—one on tracking and one on Paulo Freire's concept of banking education—revealed to the students and to me the sources of their resistance to and fear of the shift in authority and responsibility posed by the problem-solving pedagogy and collaborative planning. The students saw in the readings that expectations for high-track students centered on thinking critically and independently, whereas expectations for low-track students centered on following directions. Students erupted with anger and surprise that *tracking* was an intentional action on the part of educators. Although every student in the class had been tracked into a low track in high school, none knew of the term *tracking*; all spoke of the consequences of being tracked.

Cathy's description, quoted at the beginning of this paper, typified the experiences many recounted in their papers. Many noted that their experience had not prepared them for the literacy demands in their present assignments. They also connected Freire's description of banking education to the passivity inherent in their wish for lectures that would tell them "what things meant." A student expressed the consensus when she said, "I find it easier to listen to a teacher lecture and memorize one right answer." Their new conceptual awareness of the implications of their past education, and the challenge posed by the pedagogy of their present class, marked a turning point for a number of the students who then began to do the hard work demanded by a problem-solving pedagogy.

A rough chart I drew helped me to see the conflict between the demands of my class and the behaviors learned in low-track classes modeled on a banking pedagogy that did not demand use of higher level cognitive skills. Students were well practiced in listening rather than discussing and questioning, in responding to recall and recognition tests rather than to essay exams or paper assignments, in reading for information rather than for analysis, and viewing the teacher as the authority. To succeed in my classroom, students had to move from the secure and rewarded role of a passive learner to the risky, unknown role of an active learner.

Prompted by what was evolving in the class, I reread parts of Freire's *The Pedagogy of the Oppressed,* but with new questions prompted by Linda Flower in a collaborative planning session I had with her over this paper. "Is it enough," she asked, "to make students conscious of the banking model? Will just the critique liberate? How do you get from banking to problem solving? What must students learn to do?"

To answer the questions she and I generated, I had to look beyond the surface behaviors I had noted in the rigid and flexible planners during the first semester. I had to find out more about the students' histories, attitudes, and strategies that had shaped their learning behaviors and seemed to conflict with the assumptions of my classroom pedagogy and of collaborative planning. The effects of tracking suggested only one source of difficulty. If I could gain a deeper understanding of the problem, then I might better define and trace the kinds of transformations students needed to make if they were to improve their role as learner and I might gain some insight into the barriers to change. My gradual understanding of the conflict between past and present learning behaviors and demands shaped and reshaped the research strategies I used during the term.

To gain a beginning understanding of the variables affecting whether and how students move from passive to active learning, I decided to gather data on factors that could be indicators of the movement students made in the transformation. These factors included the following:

- Prior attitudes and knowledge about writing
- Changes in reading strategies and attitudes during the semester
- Attitudes about and changes in classroom discussion behaviors

- Pedagogy used in prior classes and in current college classes
- Attitudes about and changes in collaborative planning behaviors
- Perceptions of differences between home and school environments in terms of the freedom to discuss or debate ideas, or the receptiveness toward debating ideas
- The image the students held of themselves as thinkers
- Time demands from jobs, credit loads, and families

Because of time constraints, I used questionnaires rather than interviews to assess these factors. Listed below are brief descriptions of the questionnaires that yielded the context for the discussion in the next two sections of this paper:

1. *Prior Composition Knowledge (given in February)* This questionnaire asked students about their writing process, their prior writing experience, attitudes toward writing, and their understanding of terms often used by writing teachers. Questions were structured to find out what formulas or rules students had for writing.

2. *Reflections on Reading, Writing, and Thinking (given in early April)* On this open-ended questionnaire distributed after the discussion on tracking and banking education, I asked students to reflect—through a variety of prompts—on the classroom pedagogy, on their reading behaviors, on the writing assignments, on collaborative planning, on thinking and on any differences between the kind of critical thinking and reflection they were asked to do in class and what was valued at home. (An essay by Richard Rodriguez gave them a framework for the latter question.)

3. *Reflections on Attitudes and Learning Behaviors (given the last week of class in May)* This questionnaire was more structured than the April questionnaire. The students were asked to reflect on their behaviors as readers, writers, collaborative planners, thinkers, and class participants both at the beginning and the end of the class and to identify and discuss any changes in behaviors that they had made.

The data from these questionnaires allowed me to form a picture of the class as a whole as well as portraits of individual students. In addition to the questions, I had the students tape two collaborative planning sessions and, after they used the tapes for their papers, I transcribed them to see if there were any relationships between the behaviors in the collaborative planning sessions and the background information I had from the questionnaires. As the next section will show, there were strong connections between the factors I had structured into the questionnaires and the thinking exhibited in the collaborative planning sessions. All of this, plus notes from my classroom observations, formed the basis for my discussion in the next section about the five individual students and their relationship to the general patterns discussed in the conclusion.

Individual Collaborative Planning Portraits: A Continuum

The following five portraits present a continuum of behaviors, from Doug and Kara, who operate in a rigid model with behaviors influenced heavily by a past history of banking classrooms, to Suzette, who struggles to shift from her past history of banking behaviors to a problem-solving pedagogy, and finally to Janet and Valerie, who represent a flexible model, who can accept their own authority as writers and learners. In the following discussions, the questionnaire and observational data document the classroom behaviors and attitudes through which students construct a learning environment in which each embeds collaborative planning.

Doug: Rigidity and Rules in a Banking Environment. For Doug, collaborative planning was embedded in a framework of banking behaviors constructed from his high school courses and his prior college developmental English class (Eng-089). A 1989 graduate, he attributed most of his knowledge about writing and reading to his prior developmental English and reading classes. Although he could define terms such as *thesis statement* and *topic sentence*, his papers showed that in practice he did not know how to generate these structures. He had learned and was successful (earning B's) with the five-paragraph essay in high school and in college. As his collaborative planning excerpt shows, this is the formula he imposed on writing assignments. Outlining was what he had been taught to do to plan, but he never came to a collaborative planning session with an outline. The kinds of papers he had written prior to Eng-100 included narratives, comparison-contrast "where you discuss one thing and then another," and cause-effect. He defined revision as "to correct mistakes."

In the first reflection questionnaire, he observed that "the work demands in this class has changed alot from 089. We have alot more papers and it is alot harder to write these papers because they consist of other people's feelings and not my own. My expectations were set high in this class because I did good in 089 but now I just want to pass." He elaborated further on his frustrations over his reading-based writing:

> My attitude has changed [toward writing], I feel for the worst.
> In 089 I liked to write and I put alot of time in to my writting
> Now I just put the best writting I can down the first time and
> I don't change it cause it never really mad sense to me. I
> wouldn't know if I was making the right changes.

In his May analysis, Doug indicated that he had not changed his single-draft strategy. When asked to reflect on critical thinking, he wrote, "I did not think of myself as a critical thinker in 089 because I had lived all of my writtings and know I have to think about the writtings."

Collaborative planning he viewed as "good cause I can hear my views and explain them which helps me understand them and then I can hear others views on the readings." On the May questionnaire, he indicated that he spent most of his time in his collaborative planning session discussing purpose, audience, text information, and text conventions. Yet, both the sessions I observed and the taped dialogue revealed that he dealt with text information only in the form of knowledge telling. He wrote that he disliked taping sessions because he did not like to hear his own voice and because he "did not feel right about using it."

His need to discuss the readings came from the difficulties he was having with the assigned essays:

> I try to pay alot more attention to the readings know and my
> reading class has helped me in some cases. I don't take reading
> notes the first time through but I reread the material and then
> take notes. I did not like the readings in this class, I found
> them very hard to relate to one another and I never realized
> when to use my words or the books words. The readings in
> this class has made me learn to sit and read even the most
> boring ones.

In his final assessment of changes in reading strategies, he indicated that, in the first months, he would read an essay about three times, would highlight and take some notes, but by the end of the term he added two additional strategies: writing in the margins "to better understand the paragraph" and writing a summary "to see if I understand the whole writing."

Doug's participation in class discussions was minimal, a behavior that he acknowledged in his response to a question about talking in class: "I am not a talker. I like to listen and when something reall controversal comes up then I like to talk." Although he claimed that he listed questions on difficult readings and perceived himself as asking questions, he did so only a few times. His general silence might perhaps be explained by his need "to feel more comfortable with my peers." Although he described his home environment as one where he could talk freely about ideas, such discussions at home did not take place. Home "was a quiet place to study." His comments and his behavior suggested that he had not had much practice in using talk to explore ideas.

Three factors are reflected in the following excerpt from Doug's collaborative planning session on an essay for a PTA newsletter.[2] First, his five-paragraph formula offers him a sure answer in the midst of all the confusion he reveals about writing and reading. Second, he uses the collaborative planning session as he indicated in his questionnaire, to hear his views and explanations so that he can better understand himself, the evolution of writer-centered prose. This purpose shapes the collaborative planning session into what Barnes (1990, p. 50) calls "presentational talk" in classroom dialogues between teacher and student where there is seldom risk taking or exploration and where there is a presumed "right answer." Doug's supporter reinforces this style in taking the teacher's inquiry role and asking for more topic information, but he never challenges Doug's thinking even when Doug gives evidence of a serious misreading. The third factor, Doug's not discussing the task assignment, was consistent with his tendency to reduce all of the assignments to a five-paragraph essay whether or not they fit that formula.

> *Jerry (supporter):* How do you plan on starting your paper off?
>
> *Doug (writer):* I plan on bringing an opening paragraph . . . on saying how Asians are different from American students and how they excel faster than American students. And then I plan on going into an outline type paper from the rest of the first page to the second where Asians do good and Americans do bad for such and such reasons. The rest of my second page two paragraphs and on to a third page, maybe three paragraphs in all and the end. And this is why and compare.
>
> *Jerry:* You mentioned they excel better and faster. How do they excel better and faster?
>
> *Doug:* Well, their parents teach them from very little they need the schooling. They're not going to do anything without

education. While the United States parents don't give that into their heads. They don't put that in American kids' heads.

Neither Doug nor the supporter discusses Doug's purpose or the audience beyond what parents should be told, so Doug never connects the text information to any rhetorical components. He reveals a kind of Calvinistic attitude about the ability to change attitudes and behaviors toward learning when he discusses the feasibility of his solution to better education, giving kids more free time in school. When his supporter asks him whether kids would waste it, he agrees that kids from seventh grade on would abuse the freedom, but that younger kids would not, but "you've got to install it now so that generation isn't lost." His rigidity about older students changing reflected his own tendency to cling to behaviors that were well practiced even though they were no longer working for him.

Time was perhaps one reason why Doug did not alter his one-draft five-paragraph strategy. He was working twenty-five hours a week and taking sixteen credits. Experimentation and multiple drafts would have taken time that he did not perceive himself as having.

Kara: Getting By in the Banking Model. Kara, even more than Doug, operated in a banking milieu, as the following discussion will show, but was far less reflective than Doug. For her, the road to success, as an excerpt from a collaborative planning session will illustrate, lay in applying what she perceived to be a rule to please the teacher and to get a good grade. The goal was the grade, not a conceptual understanding of what she was doing.

A 1989 high school graduate, Kara had taken Eng-089. Although she never filled out the first questionnaire, she indicated in a conference that she "had no writing" in high school, that she "wasn't asked to do much of anything" in her four years. Throughout the term, she returned again and again to this theme of lack of preparation. Reflecting on the demands of her present class, she wrote, "When I was in high school the work demands and responsibilities were a lot different than college. When your in college everything is up to you. If you don't care or try to pass, you will fail. High school was not like that." In an exchange in a collaborative planning session where Suzette, her partner, was the planner, she said:

> *Kara (writer):* If you think about it here, all through school, I never really worked hard on anything.
>
> *Suzette (supporter):* Neither did I.

> *Kara:* I never had to and if you don't have to, then you're not
> going to do it.

Her minimalist attitude characterized her approach to writing and preparation for collaborative planning. Only in reading strategies did she make any change, and that only in the last month of the course. About writing papers, she wrote, "I read the assignment and tried to see what it was saying. I took notes on it then I look at what assignment was and wrote my paper. I spent about 2 or 3 hours on a paper." Like Doug, she wrote only one draft and generally avoided any kind of planning. In collaborative planning sessions, she acted always as a supporter because she never came prepared to be a planner. Only in reading did she change strategies. In the first months of the course, she read an essay once, highlighted and took notes. Her change consisted of reading an essay twice and, in addition to her other strategies, writing a summary to "understand more." She was silent during class discussions because, as she wrote, "I basicaly listen to everyone else." At home, she felt free to discuss ideas, but she seldom did. She, like Doug, had little practice in using talk to do more than recite knowledge, a functional strategy in banking education, yet one that would not help her transform or restructure knowledge.

In her role as supporter to Suzette, she repeatedly offered one strategy, no matter what Suzette was attempting to do as planner. As the following excerpt illustrates, Kara's comments reveal that she lacks a conceptual understanding of the function of examples in exposition and seizes on the idea of adding examples as a remedy for failing papers. Consistent with her behavior was the emphasis on an extrinsic goal—in this case, a grade pay-off. It is Suzette, later in the planning session, who tries to tie her comments to audience and purpose.

> *Suzette (writer):* Cause I'm writing on behalf of the PTA and . . .
>
> *Kara (supporter):* Go ahead.
>
> *Suzette:* um, about the American children.
>
> *Kara:* Compared to what? Give examples.
>
> *Suzette:* Students in local communities, ideas on enriching school-
> ing, parents need to motivate children to work hard—
> improve performance. Compare Asian American students
> against American students, difference in study time.
>
> *Kara:* How do you know that?
>
> *Suzette:* I read it.
>
> *Kara:* You have to give me an example.

> *Suzette:* Asian American children are not interested in social life and American kids are.
>
> *Kara:* Do you actually give a reason why you know that?
>
> *Suzette:* Asian American parents accept A's and B's as opposed to American parents who accept C's and D's.
>
> *Kara:* You have to find something to support that, too. Summarize. Just say what it has in it. Differences in school. Make sure, like I told you that you have something to back it up. That's why we're getting F's on our papers. Cause if we just say something we have to have something to support it. That's why our papers are always F's. We need something to support it. . . . It's probably in the reading. Give examples and back up your examples. And that way we'll get a good grade on our paper.

Later in the session, Suzette recognizes that Kara has no understanding of the function of examples and tells Kara that her examples are coming from the readings. Only then does Kara reveal that she has not read the essay Suzette is working with.

Kara is similar to Doug in several ways. She, too, holds a fatalistic attitude about the ability of learners to change behavior after a certain age, arguing "they have to start [a change in attitude] at a young age. 'Cause there's no way if you start in high school they're going to be that way." She also has a passive model of learning, but she invests far less time and work than Doug does. (She, too, had a job working thirteen hours a week while taking twelve credits.) For both, collaborative planning must operate in an environment that the two have erected from the banking model where each operates either with a strategy that paid off before (Doug) or with one that she hopes will pay off (Kara). For all assignments, purpose is part of an extrinsic reward system—do it right and get a good grade.

Suzette: Risking Change from Banking to Problem-Solving. Suzette, Kara's collaborative planning partner, was also a 1989 graduate, but she was admitted in the class based on her placement scores. When she received comments on her first essay asking her to expand her ideas, she demanded of me after class, "Tell me what you want me to say in this." The idea that *she* was to determine the content was one she resisted until mid-term. The reason seemed to lie in her past experience in high school writing classes. She wrote the following: "This class is very different from my other English writing classes. My past classes helped me alot because the teachers I've had helped people individually. And told us exactly what we were doing wrong and how to correct it. . . . I need to know exactly what is expected and what will help me." A discussion with her revealed that right and wrong referred to errors, that her teachers would correct all of her errors and she would copy the corrections to get a good grade. She wrote, "I was always told my writing was very good. When I entered this class I was totally lost and confused on your feelings about my writings." New to her was the focus on the content of her work and the idea of communicating to an audience. With a D at mid-term, Suzette began to make specific changes in reading and writing behaviors and in her approach to collaborative planning. Her strategies for reading had been to read once or twice, highlight and take notes, but after the mid-term, she increased the number of strategies she was using to include underlining, writing in the margins, writing summaries, and answering questions at the end of the essay even if they were not assigned. She also began to take a second set of notes structured around her analysis of the writing task, something she had never done before. As she said, "I use more strategies and found new ones that helped me alot more." These new strategies moved her from simply processing knowledge like Kara and Doug to restructuring knowledge.

She made similar shifts in her writing process. She described what she did prior to mid-term in the following way: "At the beginning, I would get the assignment, wait till last minute, read it, and write my rough draft, the way I did in high school. I hardly used any notes." Of her revised procedure, she said, "I have changed my writing alot. When I get the assignment I start right away by reading it. I read the essay, take notes, reading it again and take more notes. I take alot more time on my papers." Her collaborative planning session revealed that she also was using an outline for focusing ideas, another new strategy. Asked to advise students to help them become more effective planners, she cautioned them to do what she had not done in the beginning, to have notes with questions and ideas, "so you can ask questions and get a good point of view."

Suzette was shifting away from the presentational talk that had characterized her initial collaborative planning sessions and was moving toward the kind of exploratory talk that would allow her to shape ideas. But questioning behavior did not come easily to Suzette. Like Doug and Kara, she labeled herself as a listener and expressed discomfort at what she regarded as "controversial" topics, "like sexism and racism" discussed in class. She feared asking questions or voicing an opinion because she did not want to sound stupid. She came to value the collaborative planning sessions because they provided her with a response that she could not obtain elsewhere. As she said, "I don't have anyone to give ideas to at home. By the time I get home from work, nobody's awake. And I know my friends won't tell me the truth. They will just tell me it's good."

The excerpt from the collaborative planning session in the prior discussion on Kara, Suzette's supporter, shows Suzette at the beginning of the session trying to describe the information she wants in the paper, but the session is derailed by Kara's confusion over examples and her attempt to convince Suzette that the key to good papers lies in examples. I entered this session to provide another supporter for Suzette when I observed Kara's counterproductive behavior. This taped session occurred about the time that Suzette was initiating changes in her behaviors, and the following excerpt illustrates, on one hand, her tentative move toward an exploratory questioning using pieces of the Planner's Blackboard and, on the other, her pull toward the old behaviors when she casts me as the dictating teacher in the banking model.

> *Suzette (writer):* OK. I'm doing an outline 'cause I used to do them in school and I did really good on the . . . . Do we have to write stuff from all the essays?
>
> *Jean (supporter):* What are the points that you want to make in the paper to the parents?
>
> *Suzette:* Oh, yeah, my purpose. I want to show them why American education should change, so I give examples and my own experience.
>
> *Jean:* This little outline—have you had time . . .
>
> *Suzette:* What *all* should be in there?
>
> *Jean:* Again, what are the points that you want to make to the parents?

In the next class, Suzette returned to show me a detailed informal outline that listed all of the key points that she wanted to make along with relevant points from one of the essays. When she showed it to me, she said, "This is what I want to say," a marked shift away from her prior pleas for me to tell her what to say.

Suzette differed from Kara and Doug in two critical ways. First, she modified and changed her approaches to reading and writing, adding strategies to her reading, such as answering questions and summarizing, that allowed her to restructure the meaning. Regarding her writing, she added task analysis, tried to focus on purpose, and spent time developing a detailed plan that she wrote down. By her estimate, she doubled the time she was spending on her papers, from the three-and-a-half hours Doug and Kara spent to seven or eight. Like the others, she was working twenty-five to thirty hours a week and taking thirteen credits, so the additional allocation of time meant a sacrifice: She cut back on work hours. This willingness to commit additional time was the second difference between her and Kara and Doug. A comment she made on the May questionnaire to a question about what she had learned that would be useful in other classes marked her progress: "I have learned to think on my own, to express my own opinions." Her change was not easy and demanded her giving up old attitudes, learning new strategies, investing limited time, and risking questioning.

Valerie and Janet: Flexibility in Problem-Solving Pedagogy. I write about these students as a symbiotic pair because from the first week of the course, they collaborated beyond the class, calling one another to discuss readings and drafts. They had much in common: Valerie had graduated in 1975; Janet had earned her G.E.D. in 1976. Both had long histories of factory work, but had lost jobs because of takeovers and were retraining through a federal program. Work continued at home for Valerie with preschool children and for Janet with elderly, ill parents. Both took an active part in class discussions, often initiating inquiry. They had neither the self-consciousness of the younger students nor the fear that others would view them as stupid. As Valerie said, "I wasn't concerned what others thought." In response to a question about what prompted participation in class discussions, both focused on the need to know. As Janet said, "I needed to understand."

For both, the classroom was the only place where this verbal exploration could occur because neither came from homes where this kind of discourse took place, as the following excerpts from their questionnaires indicate:

> I really have no one at home to bounce opinions with, but I have classmates and parents which support and help keep me on the right base. I act as a mentor occasionally to my parents. I feel free in class to discuss issues of the readings. I enjoy when there is a response, to tell me if I'm on good thought processes or not.
>
> —Janet

> College has opened my eyes to different views, good and bad, that I might not have thought about before coming back to

school. The only drawback when writing any papers is that I
don't have anyone at home to read and discuss my ideas with.

—Valerie

Although the collaborative planning sessions provided the interchange each sought, both approached collaborative planning with
caution in the initial sessions—Janet, because of unproductive sessions
working with a peer on revision in her prior 089 class, and Valerie,
because of the initial difficulty of "having someone question my paper
and of taking advice." Yet, each overcame her skepticism and came
to view the sessions positively—Janet, because she "began working
with someone prepared with more material written down . . ." and
Valerie, because she "realized they were being helpful, not criticizing
my work and because I learned that there could be different versions
of the same reading."

Both began the class with knowledge about composition acquired
from either high school (Valerie) or college (Janet in Eng-089). Valerie
had been taught the five-paragraph essay and the point-by-point
formula for writing comparison-contrast papers that Denise had operated with in the first semester. For writing *rules*, she listed "never
use I" and "always write four paragraphs." But what separated her
from students like Doug and Denise, who refused to go beyond their
well-practiced schema, was her willingness to use the rhetorical
components of the Planner's Blackboard to shape her papers. As she
said, she learned early in the term to analyze the task before she
planned her paper. The plan she brought to collaborative planning
sessions was a detailed informal outline with bits of the essay written
out. She dropped her prescription about numbers of paragraphs and
made paragraphing part of revision: "I start writing, see how it sounds,
then divide into appropriate paragraphs . . . I read what's written,
move sentences or paragraphs around where needed, go back and
change or add whatever is necessary." For Valerie, writing meant
multiple drafts.

All of Janet's prior writing experience came from her Eng-089
course, which had stressed descriptive, narrative, and process writing.
Because the focus in that course had been control over error, Janet
entered Eng-100 believing that revision was proofreading. It was the
combination of reading the writing process chapters in her handbook
and her work with Valerie that led her to reconstruct her view of
revision from error correction to clarifying and expanding content: "I
have to expound on points that I make to make my writing clearer to

the reader (understandable)." Her concern with audience evolved from Valerie's sensitive responses to her work, as the excerpt from a collaborative planning session will show.

Both Janet and Valerie expanded their reading strategies in response to the complexity of the readings and the demands of the writing assignments; both added the kinds of strategies that allowed them, like Suzette, to restructure the text. Both began with the strategies that characterized nearly all of the students in the class—read once and highlight or underline. But from the beginning, both already showed themselves to be more active readers, with Valerie writing summaries and Janet writing marginal notes and questions. What each added were notetaking and answering textbook questions. As Janet said, "At the end of the semester, I began to read the questions at the end of the readings first, to try to evaluate what I was to focus on." She was using the questions like advance organizers to give herself purposes in her reading.

This examination of Janet and Valerie's evolving strategies revealed to me the complexity underlying the adaptability Donna exhibited in the fall semester. I observed only her adaptability in her planning strategies. Through Janet and Valerie, I saw the shifts in strategies and attitudes each had to make that were the underpinning for their behavior in the collaborative planning sessions. Perhaps one reason for their willingness to change was the intrinsic reward each experienced: Both wrote of their growing confidence in themselves as thinkers and writers.

The following excerpt from a collaborative planning session with Janet as the writer and Valerie as the supporter illustrates how the two went beyond the concern with topic information that characterized the sessions of Doug and Kara and emphasized the interrelationship between audience, purpose, and text conventions. (Janet's plan consisted of a partial outline and drafts of parts of the paper.) The interaction between the two has a plasticity that is missing in the excerpts quoted from the other students.

> *Valerie (supporter):* I wanted to ask you about what you were writing. Sometimes I know that you like new words. Talking to . . . teachers would understand it, but ordinary people like parents at home, like housewives wouldn't. A lot of the words are good, but I don't think . . . like that one. I don't know how to say it. . . .
>
> *Janet (planner):* Compendium. I know.

Valerie: They aren't going to understand it. But I like some of the ideas that you have in there. I didn't see a lot of, like, quotes from anyone in particular.

Janet: Yeah.

Valerie: I wondered if you were going to add something like that. What actually do you want to say in the paper?

Janet: I'm more or less going with the ideas of suggesting things that can be done, slight descriptions of the research that's been done on it. But I guess where I'm really . . . OK. I understand what you're saying about the . . .

Valerie: Support. Yeah, you do say in here, cited by Butterfield. Do you want to put any quotes or statistics in here?

Janet: Not really. But statistics might be a good idea, could be very, very good.

Valerie: Are you going to rewrite this?

Janet: What I'm going to do, I'm going to outline it if you think it shows good pattern. So some of the words won't be there that are in there now. I'm sure they won't be.

Valerie: [Refers to a strategy that Janet had used on an initial paper that produced a weak essay, an incident that had become a source of humor between the two] Oh, that means you're not going to copy this again. [laughter]

Janet: No, I'm going to outline it and just go from a new outline. So I'm trying to decipher if you think the content is . . .

Valerie: OK. You talk about interactive pedagogy. See, I don't know if you really explain . . . [reads] "this constructs a coherent vocabulary for interaction" . . . that sounds a little bit too wordy . . . OK, you're not really saying . . . . It's more or less telling students ask questions and get involved . . . or come and do what I learned to do. Why don't you just say that this example *is* interactive pedagogy?

Janet: Right. OK.

Valerie: It's a suggestion.

Janet: No, I hear you.

Valerie: If I were reading this, I'd think it was really wordy.

Janet: It's 700 words, babe. Alright it's got to be a little wordy.

Valerie: No, it's just that a lot of them I didn't understand.

Janet: They threw you?

Valerie: So, I would just Suzette it and miss something I was supposed to understand.

Janet: Well, that's why I wonder if my suggestions seem if they stand out enough. Do you think when you get to the part where it suggests things that the parent can do at home that you would remember any of that?

Valerie: Maybe put your suggestions at the end.

The excerpt illustrates the level of trust between Janet and Valerie. Valerie, from reading Janet's prior work, knows that she is fascinated with new words and that she has become addicted to a thesaurus. But as Janet experiments, she often uses words that are inappropriate for reasons of register or semantics. Valerie, who has discussed this with her in prior sessions, illustrates in this session the impact the diction would have on the behavior of a reader. This vivid instantiation of the concept of audience worked for Janet, who was gradually learning how to balance her drive to expand her vocabulary against the needs of an audience reading her paper.

In contrast to the presentational talk of Doug, Kara, and Suzette, Janet and Valerie's talk illustrates Barnes' concept of exploratory talk. Each took care in the role of the supporter to recognize the authority of the other as writer; comments like Valerie's "it's just a suggestion," typified this sensitivity. The emphasis each put on purpose and audience in the collaborative planning sessions resulted in essays that went beyond the schema- and knowledge-driven papers of Doug and Kara. Each attributed her improved attitude about writing to the influence of the other, and each gradually increased the time she spent preparing for the planning sessions.

Patterns and Implications

In designing the questionnaires, I incorporated eight factors that I theorized would be indicators of change in the students' learning behaviors. The patterns that emerged in the case studies revealed not so much the dominance of one factor over another but the interrelationship of factors affecting the student's willingness to alter and adapt learning behaviors. In addition to the factors that I began with, the collaborative planning sessions revealed factors that I had not anticipated, namely the student's attitude toward the possibility of altering behavior and the importance of the style of talk used.

All of the students shared a common background of low-track classes in high school in which the goals, expectations, and behaviors were the same as those underpinning banking education. But this fact did not predict that all would continue to operate out of this model.

Those that either made the transformation from passive to active learning, like Valerie and Janet, or attempted to change, like Suzette, did so because they were willing to alter both attitudes and behaviors and to invest the time demanded by new behaviors. For these students, reading, writing, talking, and collaborative planning strategies changed. In reading, this meant altering reading strategies from the passive behaviors of underlining and highlighting to the transforming strategies such as summarizing, notetaking, and answering text questions. In writing, students moved from the one-draft strategy to multiple drafts and invested more time in the planning process. They abandoned well-practiced and rewarded schema such as the five-paragraph essay and learned to use the planning blackboard. The changes demanded a redefining of concepts such as revision with consequent alterations in behavior; for example, Janet learned that revision did not mean error correction.

The change in classroom talk with its consequent effect on collaborative planning was, perhaps, one of the more critical and more difficult shifts students had to make. Except for Valerie and Janet, all of the class preferred to listen rather than talk, citing reasons that included self-consciousness in talking in front of strangers, fear of sounding stupid, anxiety over possibly being wrong, uncertainty over how to phrase ideas, and tension over discussing issues where there could be disagreement. The preference for listening and the reasons given for the reluctance to engage in discussion underscore the effects of the banking pedagogy and the experience of low-track classes. Another reason students gave for not discussing was that they were not good thinkers. Freire argues that this self-deprecating image is, in banking education, a consequence of being told "they are good for nothing, know nothing and are incapable of learning anything" (1970, p. 49).

Both the educational histories and responses to the query on talk in their homes underscored that most of the students had little or no practice in or models for the kind of exploratory talk needed for both the classroom discussions and the collaborative planning sessions. A majority described home environments where there was no one to share ideas with or where doing so risked hostile behavior. Willa, a black woman from a low-income neighborhood who spent her summers cleaning houses to earn her fall tuition, wrote,

> At home I can't discuss ideas that I may have because just the
> fact that I am in college is not acceptable to everyone around

me. Some see me as trying to be something they can't be . . . .
They feel I am trying to be better than them. I may speak of
situations at school such as descriptions of attitudes and characters, but not issues or what I read because education is still
frowned on for women. When I speak on issues that I may
read I am told I am flaunting my education and it doesn't look
or sound attractive. So I keep my ideas to myself.

For students like Willa to risk breaking their silence takes more than
courage. As those who moved from silence to talking in class said,
they had to feel that they could trust their peers and that they would
not be humiliated for a wrong answer. They learned to accept criticism
of their thinking if it came in the form of questions to help clarify or
to point to other evidence, but what they were frightened of was what
they had experienced in prior classes, an attack on their intelligence.

Most difficult to discuss for at least half of the class were issues
they labeled "controversial." Both white and African American students
put racism in this category, with white males adding sexism. Class
discussions revealed that most students had little or no historical
background on issues of race, class, or gender, had no experience in
examining the origins of their beliefs, and had difficulty listening to
or accepting evidence that challenged their beliefs. At least half the
class shared what a student called "the Morton Downey model"—
that you could not talk about such issues without people screaming
at one another, a view reinforced by the television shows they watched.

The model of talk most familiar to the students was the presentational talk of previous classrooms, in which the teacher, as the
authority, would call on students for answers, a focusing on text
information. The fear of giving wrong answers was rooted in this
model, as this talk is often used by the teacher for evaluation (Barnes,
1990). The model discourages the risk taking of trying to relate ideas
or challenge ideas, behaviors needed in good collaborative planning
sessions. It was this model of talk I noted that characterized many of
the collaborative planning sessions. Even though I repeatedly modeled
the inquiry that a supporter needed to affect, it was difficult for
students to give up a model that was so strongly practiced and one
that they were experiencing in classes they were taking along with
mine. Intrinsic motivations—a need to know, an enjoyment of exploring
ideas, a feeling of growing confidence in their own thinking—seemed
to motivate those who broke with the model.

Only through collaborative planning did I see the importance
of a variable I had overlooked in my inquiry, the students' belief about

the possibility of change. Discussions revealed that half of the students shared Doug and Kara's fatalism about change: That change was possible for young children, but for high schoolers, it was "too late." Freire speaks of this kind of fatalism in political terms, noting that the oppressed cannot envision change or that they can be the instrument of change. The belief in the impossibility of change prevented students like Kara and Doug from changing learning behaviors, even in a supportive environment.

Time was another critical variable affecting whether students would employ new strategies. Those students who gave evidence of transforming learning styles employed strategies that demanded more time spent reading and writing. Generally, they estimated that they doubled the time they were spending on assignments, which meant that they had to make adjustments in other parts of their lives, such as cutting back on work hours or dropping a class, or arranging for additional baby-sitting to permit more library time. These students appeared to believe that investing more time in learning would have a deferred payoff. As Janet put it, "It will get easier." But students like Doug were tied to short-term goals defined as "do enough to pass this course."

As I indicated in the beginning of this paper, the concepts of rigidity and adaptability that motivated this inquiry were surface behaviors, behind which were hidden the factors and dynamics I have described operating in the students. The collaborative planning sessions became a powerful diagnostic tool that permitted me to see beneath the surface behaviors to gain some understanding of the students' thinking processes and consequent learning behaviors. I saw that collaborative planning was not a panacea: Students who defined their learning through their past banking/low-track education simply trans-formed collaborative planning to fit that model. But for those willing to change, even if their past educational lives had been dominated by the banking/low-track model, collaborative planning became a pow-erful model in shifting them away from an object to an actor role in the learning process, a key shift if they were to choose to transform their perceptions of learning and their image of themselves as learners.

Notes

1. The language excerpted from planning protocols and from papers and questionnaires appears as the students wrote or spoke it.

2. The collaborative planning transcripts were in response to the following assignment: Assume that you have been asked by the president of the PTA of your local high school to write an essay directed to parents of high school students that will suggest ways that the education offered by the high school can be improved and will suggest steps that parents can take at home to help their children become better students. The PTA president who knows that you have been reading about the American education system urges you to let the parents know that your suggestions are coming from researchers as well as your own analysis of your secondary education. This essay will be printed in the PTA newsletter that will be mailed to parents of all the students in the high school as well as the teachers, administrators, and school board members.

19 Supporting Students' Intentions for Writing

David L. Wallace
Iowa State University
Ames, Iowa

David L. Wallace (introduced earlier) came to his graduate work in rhetoric at Carnegie Mellon with an initial skepticism about teaching strategies at all, but with a strong commitment to tutoring and the one-on-one help writing centers can offer. He used his dissertation to explore a question tutors, teachers, and planning partners need to answer: What happens when writers try to move from (their own) intentions to text? In particular, what problems appear along the way? And how can we, as outsiders, support those intentions? This project paper, drawn from his dissertation study, tells the stories of three community college students as they journey from intention to text.

A Project Paper

When I first learned about collaborative planning, I wondered if thinking about rhetorical issues might not get some students into trouble—if collaborative planning might lead some students to write worse texts. I understood that the purpose of the planning sessions was that students would get help in defining their goals and figuring out how to use information for specific purposes and audiences. As a teacher, my instinct told me that collaborative planning would help most students, but I couldn't help wondering if some students would take on goals that they didn't know how to implement and, thus, might produce problematic texts.

My suspicion that collaborative planning would lead some students to success and others to new kinds of problems prompted me to take on a study of how 45 first-year university and community college students developed, implemented, and judged the success of their intentions for a job application letter. In this making thinking visible project, I used the initial intentions that students developed in collaborative planning sessions to look for three kinds of problems in their writing processes. First, did some of the students have difficulty developing useful initial intentions for their writing? Second, did the students have difficulty implementing their intentions in their texts? Finally, which students were able to see how their texts met or failed to meet their initial intentions?

I report the formal results of that study elsewhere (Wallace, 1991); however, in this chapter, I look closely at three of the community college students who typify the kinds of problems encountered by students in the study. Mary, Tamara, and Jeff's successes and difficulties convinced me that effective writing instruction may depend on supporting students' intentions.

Teaching writing effectively often requires teachers to play several roles for their students. As curriculum innovators, teachers adapt writing assignments to the abilities and needs of their students. As classroom facilitators, they manage numerous curricular, practical, and affective factors to create an environment where students can learn. As evaluators, writing teachers are obliged to gauge the success of students' texts as well as their development as writers, and usually they also have to assign an appropriate grade. In this paper, I investigate the question of what might be gained from making students' intentions the central focus of writing instruction, from teachers making the support of students' intentions their primary function.

Much like Freire (1970), I am suggesting that pedagogy should be student-centered and that learners should be seen as active participants in the learning process rather than vessels to be filled with knowledge. Like Bruffee, I argue that a primary task of writing teachers is to create conditions conducive to learning, and, as Bruffee (1985) argues, creating such conditions may mean many things: providing tasks that are within students' zone of proximal development, organizing students for productive conversation, refereeing differences, and evaluating students' texts as contributions to a writing community (pp. 8–9). However, I would like to extend Freire and Bruffee's positions by proposing that students' intentions can become a point of contact between teachers' curricular goals and students' understanding and appropriation of those goals. Asking students to verbalize their intentions for writing makes at least some of their goals—and the thinking that underlies those goals—available for observation and negotiation.

I offer the experiences of Mary, Tamara, and Jeff as suggestive of how this focus on students' intentions, on making a part of their thinking visible, can be beneficial for writing pedagogy. Their experiences illustrate how observing students' intentions can identify different kinds of problems that students encounter throughout their writing processes. In this paper, I briefly review the context and methods for my observations, and then examine Mary, Tamara, and Jeff's writing processes in three ways. First, I take a close look at the initial intentions that the students developed in their collaborative planning sessions to see how they responded to critical aspects of assignment. Next, I examine the texts that they wrote, focusing on how successful or unsuccessful they were in implementing their intentions and meeting the requirements of the assignment. Finally, I discuss the results of the students' *post hoc* interviews in which they judged the fulfillment of their intentions.

Context for Observations

I asked the students to write a letter of application for a job because I wanted them to respond to a task for which they could see a real purpose and because I wanted them to have ready access to the information necessary to complete the task. The letter of application met both criteria. However, I also wanted a task that would provide an opportunity for learning about writing. As a curricular goal, I wanted the students to do more than list information about themselves in their letters; I wanted them to use information to build a strong case for themselves. In more generic terms, I wanted them to *transform* information for rhetorical purposes, to select and organize information for specific purposes, and to meet the needs of their audience.

Several studies suggested knowledge transformation tasks were appropriate for these students. Burtis, Scardamalia, Bereiter, and Tetroe's (1987) study of ten- to fourteen-year-old junior high school students found that the younger students tended to make only content plans for their writing, but that with prompting, the older students began to pay attention to rhetorical concerns and thus made some transformations of topic information. However, the comparisons of experienced writers and college freshmen in Flower, Schriver, Carey, Haas, and Hayes's (1992) study suggest that college-age writers do not automatically consider content in terms of rhetorical concerns even when the task requires it. Given these results, I reasoned that Mary, Tamara, Jeff, and the other students in their basic writing course might benefit from an assignment that asked them to transform knowledge, but that they would need specific prompting and help in making these transformations.

The writing assignment was a case situation. The students were to write letters of application to a screening service that would match them with potential summer employers if their letters built convincing cases that they should be invited to placement interviews. My primary curricular goal was for the students to learn to *use* information rather than *list* it, to connect specific examples to points of generalizations that they wanted to make. In the class period that I used to introduce the assignment, I illustrated the difference between listing information and using it to build a case by showing the students examples of different kinds of job application documents, emphasizing those for which the applicant must both select appropriate information and provide the basic structure (letters of applications and personal statements).

The case information provided background information and specified the following criteria for the students' letters:

- Inclusion of appropriate personal information (PERSONAL INFORMATION)
- Demonstration that the applicant can apply high school or college courses (APPLICATION OF COURSES)
- Use of a personal, yet business-like tone (TONE)

The case information also stated that students who built a convincing case rather than just listing information in their letter would be favored by the committee; two examples with comments by committee members (actually written by the scorers for the study) were also included. After I introduced the assignment, the students spent the next class period in collaborative planning sessions with their assigned partners.

Methods of Observation

Because I wanted to see what I could learn by examining students' intentions across their writing processes, I collected three kinds of data for my observations. First, I examined the initial intentions that the students developed in response to the assignment criteria. As a part of their collaborative planning sessions, I instructed the students to discuss these criteria explicitly and to plan how they would meet them, thus, providing me a basis for comparison with the texts. Second, another writing teacher and I read the students' texts and judged how successful they were in meeting the assignment criteria. These quality judgments allowed me to compare the kinds of initial intentions that the students developed in response to the criteria with their success in meeting those criteria in their texts. Finally, I wanted to see if the students were able to judge their own success in meeting the assignment criteria. In *post hoc* interviews, I asked the students to judge how well their own and other students' texts met the criteria. I reasoned that if students had difficulty identifying their texts' success or lack of success in meeting the assignment criteria, then they would probably have difficulty making effective revisions. In short, the collaborative planning sessions allowed me to see what kinds of initial intentions the students developed, and the assignment criteria provided a means for following the students' intentions across their writing processes and a basis for comparison among the students.

From the 20 community college students who completed all aspects of the study, I chose Mary, Tamara, and Jeff to discuss in detail because their initial intentions and their texts varied greatly in quality. My rating partner and I judged Jeff's text as successful in all but one aspect of the writing task, and his initial intentions were judged as "useful" in three of the four cases. Mary and Tamara's texts received mixed ratings, but Mary had no "useful" ratings for her initial intentions, whereas Tamara's initial intentions were rated as positively as Jeff's.[1]

Developing Initial Intentions

Collaborative planning sessions can be useful as diagnostic devices because they identify the students who "get it" and the students who do not. Thus, teachers or tutors could intervene early in the writing processes of students who have difficulty developing useful initial intentions if they listen to planning tapes or sit in on the planning sessions. However, the following examples from transcripts of Mary, Tamara, and Jeff's planning sessions suggest that making such early interventions requires understanding the nature of the problem that a student faces—that "getting it" may not be as simple as it seems. Thus, the students' collaborative planning sessions were an opportunity for the students to help each other figure out what the assignment criteria meant and how they could go about meeting them. The planning sessions also allowed me to determine which students had developed "useful" initial intentions—intentions that both reflected what the assignment required and helped them use their own knowledge and experiences to meet those criteria.

In their planning sessions Mary, Tamara, and Jeff did not develop useful initial intentions for the TONE criteria; that is, none discussed

TONE as a language-use issue.[2] However, the difference between what Mary did and what Jeff and Tamara did in developing intentions for the PERSONAL INFORMATION and APPLICATION OF COURSES criteria is instructive. As I mentioned earlier, the writing assignment cued the students that they needed to do more than list information to meet these criteria; they needed to use information by connecting a specific example to a point or generalization that they wanted to make.

For the APPLICATION OF COURSES criterion, Mary's intentions suggest that she planned to list information in her text. As a first-semester community college student without a strong high school record, Mary did not think she had much to say about applying courses. In response to her partner's question about whether she was involved in any activities in high school, Mary said, "I was in marching band and that was it." Similarly, when her partner asked about her previous work experience, she responded that she had had only two jobs since high school and said about her current job, "saying that I worked at K-Mart . . . I mean I don't know how far that will get me [in the letter]." When her partner pointed out that her K-Mart work experience might be relevant for a job at Kaufmann's (an up-scale Pittsburgh department store), Mary rejected the idea, responding, "I'm assuming that we, we'd not be allowed to base our letters on our needs."

In a sense, Mary's assessment of her situation was right. If she had limited her letter to listing her past work experiences and limited academic achievements, she would probably not have been very successful. In fact, she and her partner spent part of their planning session mining the two example texts; comparing her high school experiences to those of the student in a successful example, Mary concluded that her experiences were not nearly as strong. However, neither she nor her partner seemed to see that she could do more than simply list her participation in marching band or her K-Mart work experience. Mary missed the point that listing *any* academic or work experience would not be sufficient; she did not consider that she might be able to use her experiences to support generalizations about herself.

In contrast to Mary's initial planning, both Tamara and Jeff's initial intentions suggest that they would use information; their planning made explicit connections between past academic and work experiences and points that they want to communicate to their readers. Like Mary, neither Tamara nor Jeff had strong academic backgrounds to draw on for meeting the APPLICATION OF COURSES criterion. However, both of them found ways to talk about their past academic experiences to make interesting points about themselves. Jeff said that he went to high school on drugs and slept through most of his classes, but he planned to talk about how "I realized that I wasn't going anywhere with my life and made a decision to turn my life around." Tamara reported that her academic background was not strong, but she planned to focus on the only program in high school "that was really fulfilling to me," a dental training program that helped her to decide on a career.

The contrast between Mary's limited, almost fatalistic, planning and Tamara and Jeff's proactive planning is even more pronounced for the PERSONAL INFORMATION criterion. Like Mary, both Tamara and Jeff planned to use work experiences to meet this criterion. Tamara talked about what she had learned by working at Sears. In her planning session, she linked examples to generalizations, saying that working at Sears taught her how to control herself even when "customers were very rude," and that her job taught her responsibility for tasks such as keeping her area clean—a skill that would be important when she reached her goal of becoming a dental hygienist. Similarly, Jeff established connections between points that he wanted to make about himself and what he learned at his jobs as a cook at Eat-N-Park and crew leader at Arby's. For example, as a cook, he learned to be patient and pay attention to detail even in a "very hot and tense situation" where "you've got waitresses hollering at you."

The differences between the initial intentions that Mary developed and those that Tamara and Jeff developed are striking. First, Tamara and Jeff's intentions gave them something to say. They got the message that they need to choose some points that they wanted to make about themselves and linked these points to specific experiences. Thus, the intentions that surface in their initial planning were useful because they allowed Tamara and Jeff to draw on a body of information to make a point. Also, Tamara and Jeff's initial intentions were much more detailed than Mary's. Mary's topics were sterile in terms of development because she had not moved beyond listing, while the connections that Tamara and Jeff made between generalizations and specific examples provided them abundant material for their texts. The difficulty that Mary had in developing useful initial intentions illustrates that problems in moving from intentions to text may begin very early. In this case, Mary's initial intentions did not lead her to make the connections between generalizations and specific details necessary for success in this writing task.

Implementing Intentions

In this section, I examine Mary, Tamara, and Jeff's texts to illustrate the different kinds of problems that they encountered when moving from intentions to text. In the original study (Wallace, 1991), Jeff's text was given a 3 (on a scale of 1 to 4, with 4 being best) for overall quality, and Tamara and Mary's texts were both given scores of 2. Thus, there was room for improvement in each text. The discussion of the following students' texts illustrates the different kinds of problems that these three students faced. For Mary, the problem of developing intentions that made connections between generalizations and support carries over into her text. The body of her letter comprises lists of generalizations. In contrast, both Tamara and Jeff made explicit connections between generalizations and specific details, but part of Tamara's problem was that she made these connections only within paragraphs. Jeff not only made connections between generalization and details within paragraphs but also built in some global coherence structures. His text seems to need only some fine tuning. Thus, the differences in the text structures that these three students used to implement their intentions suggest that they would face different kinds of problems in revising their texts.

Mary. Mary's text is problematic for a number of reasons; however, at least one of her problems, not making connections between generalizations and specific support, is extant from her planning session when she failed to see how she could use the information that she did have to support her generalizations. Thus, at least part of Mary's problem seems to be that her initial intentions did not cue her to make connections between generalizations and specific details.

A cursory look at the structure of Mary's text (see figure 19.1) suggests that Mary's letter has organizational problems. Her introductory paragraph and brief closing paragraph sandwich the long, single paragraph that comprises the body of her letter. The body paragraph follows a basic list structure, presenting a series of generalizations, none of which are supported with specific details. Thus, Mary responded to the assignment dictum not to present a simple list of past experiences—by constructing a list of generalizations about herself. The body paragraph of her letter can be divided into three general topics. However, Mary did not develop any of these topics; her discussion of each topic consists mainly of generalizations strung together.

> With summer time nearing and my need for a good summer job increases, I feel the need to describe my qualifications, that I am quite confident will increase my chances of finding employment in a field were my abilities, motivation, and possitive attitude will be greatly appreciated, put to good use in a variety of ways, and hold very good
> 5 chances for the possibilities of advancement.
> I am confident that I am capable of working very well with people. A possitive attitude and an out going personality are characteristics about myself that helped me to acheive both in school a variety of friends and good relationships with my teachers, and at work, the ability to make good customer/employee relationships with the public. I
> 10 graduated from high school in 1986, and not only in school but also at the two jobs that I held since I graduated, I was never late, and always did my very best. I was always against missing school. During the two years that I held my first job, I was always looking for ways and means of improving myself. I believe in always have an optomistic attitude. The position I held at these jobs were: cashier, bagger, and meat
> 15 wrapper at Kuhn's quality foods, and an apparel sales person at K-Mart. I am willing to learn anything new in order to be able to better serve my employer in any way needed. I feel that the courses I have taked so far in college, and the ones I am enrolled in how will be very helpfull for me at any time I would ever need them. Especially at a job were my writing, thinking abstractly and logically, and organizitational skills could be of great
> 25 use.
> I know up front that when you seriously consider my application for employment, you will be very pleased, impressed, and satisfied.

Figure 19.1. Mary's Text.

The first topic (lines 6–9), that she works well with people, is supported only by the vague generalization that she has a positive attitude and an outgoing personality. The second topic (lines 9–16) is comprised of a jumble of generalizations roughly related to her high school experience and the jobs that she has had since graduating high school. In support of this rather unfocused topic, Mary makes some very general points, such as "I was always against missing school" and "I believe in always having an optomistic attitude," and offers a list of her duties at Kuhn's quality foods and K-Mart. She concludes the paragraph with a vague statement that her college courses "will be very helpfull for me at any time I would ever need them," supported by a sentence fragment that adds yet another list to this unwieldy paragraph.

Mary's list of generalizations and lack of support did not impress the judges. In our comments about Mary's letter, both my rating partner and I mentioned the list-like structure and lack of specific details as major problems for the GENERAL QUALITY of her paper and as contributing to problems in meeting the PERSONAL INFORMATION and APPLICATION OF COURSES criteria. We both commented independently in our notes that we considered giving Mary's text a rating of "1" for GENERAL QUALITY, but gave it a "2" reluctantly. The TONE problems in Mary's texts are also fairly serious. Also, we both commented on the lack of topic coherence, the intrusive mechanical errors, and some poor word choices in her opening and closing. In short, the positive image that Mary attempts to create through the claims that she makes is undermined by her lack of support for those claims, by the syntax and sentence structure problems in her text, and by the lack of organization inherent in her basic list structure.

Tamara. The initial visual impression of Tamara's text (see figure 19.2) is slightly more pleasing than Mary's. Tamara's text appears slightly more organized and follows the general five-paragraph theme structure of introduction, three body paragraphs, and conclusion. In terms of the need to make connections between generalizations and specific details, Tamara's text shows some promise at both the sentence and the paragraph levels. Like Mary's letter, the body of Tamara's text has three main topics. However, rather than lumping all of her information into a single list in one long paragraph as Mary did, Tamara broke the topics into three paragraph units that center around the topics of working at Sears, other employment during high school, and high school activities. Within the paragraphs, Tamara also made some attempts to link generalizations to specific examples. The best example of this is her Sears paragraph (lines 4–8), in which she used some of the information that she discussed in her planning session. She began the paragraph with a sentence that introduces the topic, then she detailed some of her duties in the second sentence. Finally, she linked learning to be more responsible to three of her duties at Sears: "help[ing] the people in whatever they need, work[ing] with money, and it teaches you how to communicate with others." Unfortunately, Tamara tended to rely more on list structures in the remaining two paragraphs of the body of her letter.

The difference between Mary and Tamara's texts in terms of supporting generalizations did not show up in the scores that the judges gave each text for GENERAL QUALITY; they gave both texts scores of 2 (from a possible 4). However, there is a difference in the judges' written comments about Tamara's text. While both my rating partner and I put Mary's text on the border between a 1 and a 2, we were

After hearing about The College Job Screening Service I am very
interested in finding employment this summer. I know I would like the
experience of having the opportunities to be able to work for such a
organization like your.
        I have had some experience in the working field as a part-time
cashier for a year
5   at Sears and Roebuck. There I helped customers, put clothing out on
the floor, and kept the area I worked in clean. Working at Sears has
taught me responsible because there you try to help the people in
whatever they need, work with money, and it teaches you how to
communicate with others.
        While I was in high school, I worked two years in a summer
program. The
10   summer of 1986, I was a custodial at McNaugher school which require
me to clean, to work with certain cleaners and to make sure that my
fellow co-workers did what they were suppose to do. In 1987, I
worked as a child care aid, where I took care of other parent's children
and made sure that their children stay safe. Working in the summer
time would not be any problem because I am use to working in the
summer time.
15   In high school I did not join any clubs, but when I was in the
eleventh and twelfth grade, I enter into a program for dental assistant.
I liked learning the different things in dentistry and what it had to
offer. After the first semester I went to Pitt Dental School and had the
chance to work with the graduation dentists of 1988. Now that I am in
college, I have made my choice to go into dentistry and become a
dental hygienic. Being
20   in college is a whole new experience for me and I like how college lets
you be more responsible for myself.
        My past performance demonstrates my attributes, and I will
continue my good work this summer. I hope you seriously consider my
application for employment.

Figure 19.2. Tamara's Text.

both clear that Tamara's text deserved a 2. Neither of us questioned
Tamara's use or basic organization of details as we did Mary's; instead
each of us cited the lack of global coherence as the main problem. In
her comments, my rating partner asked, "Where is the overall generalization?" and commented, "The letter does not establish any
interconnectedness between the ideas." We also considered tone to be
a major problem in Tamara's paper, with both of us giving her text a
0 (on a scale of 0 to 3); in our notes, we cited the lack of coherence
and "serious" grammatical and mechanical errors as reasons for our
TONE scores.

        In her planning session, Tamara developed what we saw as
useful intentions for two of the three criteria (PERSONAL INFORMATION
and APPLICATION OF COURSES). However, in comparison with Mary,

whose initial intentions were all rated as less useful, Tamara's better intentions did not translate into much of an advantage in her text. Tamara's text did outscore Mary's by a point for APPLICATION OF COURSES, but both she and Mary received 2s for GENERAL QUALITY and for PERSONAL INFORMATION. Thus, it seems that although she developed useful initial intentions, Tamara did not succeed altogether in meeting the assignment criteria. Her text did move beyond a basic list structure by dividing topics into paragraphs, and in at least one of those paragraphs, Tamara made some attempt to connect a generalization to specific examples. However, according our judgments, Tamara's text lacked global coherence; thus, although Tamara was successful in meeting her intention to connect a generalization to an example, her text indicates that making such a connection did not solve all of her problems.

Jeff. Jeff was much more successful in meeting the application criteria than either Mary or Tamara. The main difference between Jeff's text and the texts written by Mary and Tamara is that Jeff brought a sense of global organization to his text. Thus, although the initial intentions that he discussed in his planning session are not substantively different from Tamara's, the text structures that Jeff used to implement his intentions not only coordinated his ideas at the sentence and paragraph level but also helped to build a sense of global coherence.

Jeff's text (see figure 19.3) is both longer and more complicated structurally than either Mary or Tamara's texts. Like Mary and Tamara, Jeff has introductory and concluding paragraphs; however, one basic difference in Jeff's text is that he set up a theme—leadership and administration—in his introduction that he referred to at points in the letter. The transition sentences for his second, third, and fourth paragraphs all make some kind of topical reference to leadership and/or administration (e.g., "both areas," and "leadership position"). Further, within paragraphs, Jeff made explicit connections between work and other experiences and the over-arching theme of leadership and administration, and he gave lists of specific duties and responsibilities as support for his claims.

My rating partner and I awarded Jeff's letter a score of 3 (out of a possible 4) for GENERAL QUALITY, indicating that we saw some room for improvement. For example, we noted that some of Jeff's supporting information became very list-like and that he relied very heavily on topical coherence, expecting the reader to wait until the penultimate paragraph to see how he hoped the reader would put the whole picture together. These, however, are really issues of fine-tuning

This summer I would very much like to find employment that
would best suit my talents and skills. I am capable of handling a wide
range of responsibilities and duties. However, I would like to find
something with leadership and administration opportunities in the field
of public service.

5   I do have ample experience in both areas. To start, I am currently
employed full time as Cook and Cover Manager at Eat-n-Park. As a
cook my duties include short order & prep cooking and maintenance of
the entire kitchen area. As a cover manager my duties are that of
balancing the sales register and safe, recording of all production &
sales efficiencies as well as management of the entire store and it
employees.

10   I received more of my experience however, while working at Arby's
as Crewleader. There, on a daily basis I was responsible for every
managerial task except hiring/firing. Some of my duties there included
ordering & purchasing, balancing of all sales registers, safe and bank
deposits, recording and filing of production, food efficiencies, sales and
inventory and the training and management of approx. 17–20
employees.

15   Elsewhere, I am also in a leadership position at my church. There I
am a member of the Praise & Worship Team, (I play bass guitar), and a
Support Team Councilor. I find that life is more fulfilling when I give
of myself to help encourage others and to do the right thing in life.
This is one reason why I am attending college to major in Social
Science.

           I have been independent since the age of seventeen, (I am now
21), and I am
20   presently residing with two other friends. We all share the bills,
however, I am the one responsible for the lease and payment of all
living expenses.

           These few supportive examples, along with seven years of working
experience, have shaped my character into one of paitience, maturity,
responsibility, creativity, discipline, resourcefulness and organization. I
am also very dependable; in the past three years of
25   employment I have never called off and I have a very low incident
rate of tardiness. I can confidently say that I have what it takes to
succeed at most anything I put my energies into; I would be a valuable
asset to any organization.

           Thank you for considering my application. A summer internship
would a wonderful
30   learning experience and would aid in achieving my academic goal. I
eagerly await your reply.

Figure 19.3. Jeff's Text.

in Jeff's text. He also had very few problems with TONE; in fact, we
gave his text a score of 3 (out of a possible 3), citing good sentence
structure, more than adequate coherence, and only minor problems
with punctuation and stuffy language. The one weak spot in Jeff's
paper is the APPLICATION OF COURSES criterion. Apparently, Jeff decided

not to include much information about this criterion even though he had developed an interesting point during his planning session, so his score for this criterion was low.

In short, Jeff succeeds at an ambitious task. In his introduction, he makes a sweeping claim that he "is capable of handling a wide range of responsibilities and duties," and he substantiates that claim in his text. The overall organization, the links between claims and support, and the relative sophistication of the prose all contribute to Jeff's ability to implement his initial intentions. Thus, although there was little difference between Jeff and Tamara's initial intentions, Jeff's text indicates the ability to address a wider range of issues in implementing those intentions.

Summary. In terms of the text structures that these students used to implement their initial intentions, each faced different kinds of problems, so the kinds of intervention that we would propose at this point would be different for each of these students. With Jeff, intervention is largely a local issue; his basic structure is sound but could be improved in some minor ways. In Tamara's case, intervention might begin by building on her initial intentions. Tamara has a basic understanding of what she needs to do, but she needs some help focusing and developing the points that she makes in her paragraphs and building global coherence structures. As for Mary, the data available to this point suggest that she may be missing an important intention for this assignment: Apparently, she does not see the need to make connections between generalizations and examples. Her text indicates that she needs to reconsider her overall structure and that she may not yet have realized that she needs to build more explicit links between generalizations and supporting details. These text problems are not surprising, given that her planning session suggests that she may not be aware that she needs to make those connections.

Judging the Fulfillment of Intentions

We get a final glimpse of Mary, Tamara, and Jeff's writing processes from the interviews in which they reviewed their texts. The students' judgments of their texts during these interviews provide some important clues about what kinds of problems they could see in their texts and, thus, what problems they would likely address if asked to revise their texts. Also, the students' judgments of other students' texts allow us to see if they are able to identify problems that they cannot find in their own texts.

Taken as a group, the students in the original study tended to inflate the scores that they gave to their own texts for GENERAL QUALITY and for TONE more than they did the scores that they gave to the other students' texts. In general, the students were better judges of the PERSONAL INFORMATION and APPLICATION OF COURSES criteria. These results suggest that when the students were asked to judge broad issues such as GENERAL QUALITY and TONE, they could often see problems in other students' texts that they could not see in their own. However, these general trends hide some important differences between students. As Jeff, Tamara, and Mary's interviews illustrate, students may differ widely in their ability to see problems in their own texts.

Jeff broke the general trend of students inflating the scores they gave to their own texts for GENERAL QUALITY and TONE. In fact, Jeff was a fairly evenhanded judge of his own text; he gave his text the same score that the judges gave for GENERAL QUALITY and for TONE and PERSONAL INFORMATION, the two application criteria that he judged.[3] He was also a pretty good judge of other students' texts; for TONE and PERSONAL INFORMATION, the average difference between his scores and those of the judges was very low, although for GENERAL QUALITY, he tended to rate other students' texts slightly higher than did the judges.

These measures suggest that Jeff was a fairly good judge of both his own text and other students' texts. In addition, the comments that Jeff made as he judged his own text further indicate that he was making much the same assessment of his text that we judges made. For example, we both cited a small problem with list-like development as a reason why Jeff's text deserved a 3 rather than a 4 for GENERAL QUALITY. When Jeff judged his text for this criterion, he noticed the same problem, commenting "I don't want to give it a 4 because I'm afraid it might be too list-like . . . it's a real strong 3." Also, Jeff's assessment of the tone of his letter as "smooth, consistent" and "not cocky" agrees with our assessment; we found the diction "professional" and noted only minor mechanical errors. Taken together, the data from Jeff's interview suggest that he could both judge the effectiveness of his own and other students' texts and that he could identify problems to address in revision.

In contrast, Tamara and Mary's interviews indicated they were less effective judges in terms of matching the scores that we gave their texts and identifying problems for revision. For both GENERAL QUALITY and TONE, the two judgments that required attention to multiple criteria, Tamara and Mary's judgments fit the general pattern of awarding inflated scores to their own texts more than to other students' texts. For GENERAL QUALITY, they tended to rate both their own and other students' texts more highly than we did, but both inflated the scores for their own texts more than the texts of others. For TONE, both tended to *under* rate the scores they gave to other students' texts and greatly *over* rate the scores that they gave to their own texts. They were much better judges for the simpler PERSONAL INFORMATION and APPLICATION OF COURSES criteria. In short, both Tamara and Mary fit the general pattern of difficulty in judging GENERAL QUALITY and TONE.

Given these results, we might expect both Tamara and Mary to have more difficulty than Jeff identifying problems in their own texts that would lead them to effective revisions. However, several differences in the comments that Tamara and Mary made as they judged the effectiveness of their texts indicate that Tamara may be in a better position to identify problems in her own text than Mary. First, when I asked Tamara and Mary to talk about the score that they had given their texts for GENERAL QUALITY, Tamara's response indicated that she saw a problem in her text. The main reason that Tamara cites for giving her text a score of 3 (from a possible 4) is that it was too "list-like." This list-like structure was one of the problems that both my rating partner and I cited in our rationales for giving Tamara's text a score of 2. Thus, although Tamara did not mention some other problems in her text and inflated her score by a point, she was able to see one of the weaknesses that we saw. This was not the case for Mary.

For GENERAL QUALITY, Mary gave her text a score of 4 (from a possible 4), failing to notice any of the problems that we saw in her text (e.g., lack of development and failure to link generalizations and specific details). She also gave each of the other students' texts scores of 4 for GENERAL QUALITY. During the interview, she commented that she still was not really sure what a generalization was, and the only problems that she noted in any of the texts were "a couple of spelling errors" and that some texts, including her own, "didn't mention their classes in college and high school that would benefit them throughout life." Thus, Tamara's judgment was based on at least one problem that she saw in her text, whereas Mary seemed to have no criteria for judging GENERAL QUALITY and could identify no problems for revision. Apparently, neither her initial intentions nor any goals that she might have developed later provided Mary with any means for judging the effectiveness of texts.

To summarize, looking at the interviews in which these students judged their own and other students' texts suggests some interesting differences between the students in terms of their ability to identify problems in their texts. Jeff wrote a fairly effective text and was the most successful in judging the effectiveness of both his own and other students' texts. He was also able to identify a specific problem in his own text that might lead him to a fruitful revision. In comparison to Jeff, neither Tamara nor Mary made good judgments about the effectiveness of their own or other students' texts. However, the marginal advantage that Tamara had over Mary in the measures of her ability to judge the effectiveness of texts might be critical for revision because that difference seemed to be related to identifying a specific problem in her own text.

Implications

I would like to state two implications from these observations. First, students' intentions may be important factors in understanding the problems in their texts and in intervening to help them address those problems. One interesting way to look at the experiences of these students is how they differed from the general trends in the original study. Although the overall results from the original study identify general problems for the whole group of students, these three students would clearly need different kinds of intervention.

Of the three, Jeff would probably need the least help. From the outset, the intentions that he developed indicated that he understood what was expected in this writing assignment, and in his assessment of his text in the *post hoc* interview, he identified the same problem that the judges did—some dependence on a list-like structure. Given the problems that he could already identify in his own text, Jeff may need little more than a few written comments confirming his own judgment to produce a more effective revised text. Tamara's situation is slightly different. Although she began with the same kinds of intentions that Jeff did, her text indicates that she could not implement them with the same sophistication that Jeff did, and her *post hoc* interview suggests that she saw only one of the problems that the judges identified in her text. It is likely that Tamara would need help not only in identifying some of the problems in her text but also in seeing how to address those problems.

Mary's case is the most interesting and problematic of the three. For Mary, the critical issue for intervention is more basic than for either Jeff or Tamara. While both Jeff and Tamara could see problems in their own texts, Mary saw none in hers. In fact, she had no criteria for making judgments about the GENERAL QUALITY of any of the texts that she read in her interview. This lack of judgment criteria is not surprising, given the difficulty that she had in her planning session figuring out what the assignment criteria meant. Thus, a first step in helping Mary may be to help her see that her text has problems. However, another important aspect of helping Mary would be recognizing the thinking that Mary has already done. Although she did not make the link between generalizations and support in either her planning session or her paper, she did recognize from the outset that a list of her limited accomplishments would not suffice, and she showed a good sense of her audience when she decided to take another route. If I were trying to help Mary, I would begin by acknowledging and validating her perception of the situation. However, she might need additional kinds of support. First, I would try to help her develop a new intention for her writing, to make connections between generalizations and specific examples. Then, if she ran into difficulty implementing that intention in her text, I might talk with her again about the difference between a list of generalizations and a generalization that is supported by an example. The critical factors guiding intervention here are Mary's intentions and the problems that she encounters implementing them.

The second implication that I note from these three examples is that focusing on students' intentions for writing may help writing teachers to orchestrate peer planning and review sessions. For example, in his collaborative planning session, Jeff proved quite skillful at helping his partner forge some links between generalizations and examples. Further, in a peer review session, Jeff and Tamara might be able to help each other figure out how to move away from list-like structures. However, it is equally important to note that Mary might not be of much use to another student in a collaborative planning or peer review session until she understands better what the writing assignment is about.

In conclusion, then, the experiences of these students suggest that focusing writing instruction around students' intentions may be useful for several reasons. First, when students articulate their intentions for writing, teachers, tutors, and peers have a much better understanding of what the students' writing problems are and where to begin intervention. Second, when students articulate their intentions, particularly early in the writing process, teachers, tutors, or other students may be able to help them identify and address problems. Finally, when students articulate their intentions for writing, teachers may discover which students need more intensive help and which students are likely to be able to help other students.

Notes

1. I should note that, like Jeff, many of the community college students produced very effective texts. Likewise, some of the texts written by university students in the larger study were rated as weak in several categories. Thus, my decision to focus on three community college students in this chapter should not be seen as implying that only the community college students faced the problems that I discuss. As a group, the community college students had more difficulty with the writing task, but taken individually, many of the community college students produced more effective texts than did some of the university students.

2. For the purposes of this study, tone was defined broadly to include both sentence-level issues (e.g., word choice, grammatical errors, mechanical problems) and larger issues (e.g., global coherence and discourse moves used for openings and closings).

3. Because of time limitations in the interviews, students did not judge papers for all of the application criteria.

20 Learning about Reflection

Lois Rubin
Penn State University
New Kensington, Pennsylvania

Lois Rubin, an assistant professor of English at Penn State New Kensington, has taught writing at a variety of levels over the past 27 years. Her dissertation got her interested in how students' evaluation of their own writing process can change from abstract, clichéd versions of what writers do to specific, personalized, and informed understandings. Her discovery memo records the way she used collaborative planning to support process-oriented, student-centered reflections and, at the same time, to let her evaluate for herself what this new activity was offering her students.

A Discovery Memo

Like many others these days, I believe that reflecting on one's own experience is important for learning. As Ann Brown (1978) puts it, "What is of major interest is knowledge about one's own cognitions rather than the cognitions themselves," (p. 79) and, according to Scardamalia and Bereiter (1987), "personal . . . knowledge of cognitive processes . . . enables students to take a more self-directive role in their mental development" (p. 335–36). So, in my composition courses, I am always asking students to reflect—on the value of the papers they have written and on the usefulness of the learning activities that we have performed.

When I introduced collaborative planning in two early assignments in freshman composition at Penn State New Kensington campus last fall, it seemed natural to ask students to reflect on its value—both to give them this opportunity to consolidate and to reveal to me how the new procedure was working, how useful they found it to be. And so, I asked them to reflect at different times: just after their planning session, at the time that they turned in their papers, and long after the planning session (after two papers in which they had used collaborative planning and at the end of the semester). When I looked at their reflections after the course was over, mainly to see how useful CP had been, I found that they had focused on different attributes of the process at different points in time, that the value they found in CP differed according to their distance from it. This shift tells me something important about the thinking process—that we view an experience differently, that we focus on different qualities of it at different times.

Phase 1: Reflection at End of Planning Session

Students made their first reflection at the end of the planning session for a paper about their family history and the second, in a sequence of multicultural writing assignments in which students moved from investigating their roots to exploring other cultures. When I asked them to describe what they had gotten out of the planning session, the students made comments that were, for the most part, quite specific. Given the stage in the process (notes) and the nature of the assignment (making a coherent account of fragmentary information), it is not surprising that students focused particularly on *selecting* information (what to include, exclude) and *connecting* information (finding a theme).

In both the honors and standard classes, three-quarters of the students' comments concerned either selecting information or finding a focus or theme. The comments were quite specific, especially those of the honors class.

> I need to find someone old who lives in Vandergrift to ask them if they knew anyone in my family.

> I decided not to include info on Josiah Klingensmith—doesn't fit.

> The talk helped me to unify my theme when my partner spoke about her family's three generations of coal miners. My father's side has been farmers for 100's of years.

Third in importance for both groups (about a quarter of the comments) was *organization*, as in the following comment: "She helped me put it in correct order. What should come first, last and so on."

Phase 2: Reflection upon Completion of Paper

When the students turned in their papers, I asked them to write about what CP had contributed to the paper. The students again commented largely on the *information* they had included and on the focus or *theme* of the paper. *Organization* again took third place. This time, a few comments were also made about parts of the paper: introduction, conclusion. Because students had their papers right in front of them and were asked to identify aspects in them that were the result of CP, comments were again quite specific for both groups:

> Originally I wasn't going to include the part about knowing my great-grandmother, but Andrea told me to include it, and it became one of the strong points of the paper.

> The idea of telling the story of both my grandparents' ancestors came from this session.

> I changed my introduction and split my paper into two parts.

This time, some students reported that CP had not contributed to their finished paper. Most of these critical judgments were general; two did refer to specifics: that the writer had not done enough preparation beforehand for CP to be useful and that the writer preferred to work alone.

Phases 3 and 4: Comparative and Retrospective Reflections

Using two short questionnaires, I asked the students to judge CP comparatively, along with other techniques used in the class (whole class discussion of duplicated student drafts, individual written critiques of classmates' drafts), and at a distance (retrospectively) from the planning sessions. In the comparative reflection, they commented, after experiencing CP in planning their first two papers, on whether we should continue to use it; in the later retrospective reflection on the last day of the semester, they judged the usefulness of CP along with that of all the activities of the course. In other words, students were not asked to cite particular results of CP in the retrospectives, but to comment on its overall value. As a result (of distance in time, of comparison with other techniques), these reflections focused on different aspects of CP than did the earlier ones. Far fewer comments (about one quarter) of both the honors and standard classes concerned the specifics of selecting and connecting information that had been mentioned so frequently before; instead, students talked here about more general concerns.

The Benefit of Getting a Different Viewpoint

> After talking about it you may realize that something doesn't make sense or isn't interesting by the looks someone gives you.

I liked this because it made me see my mistakes and pointed out things that were confusing for another reader.

I like this because I know how I want to write my paper, but maybe I can get a different idea from somebody else.

The Benefit of the One-On-One, Oral Medium

One-on-one [talk] seems to be more comfortable.

You got to go into more detail and depth with one person whereas in (peer critiquing) it was just a quick study.

It helped my thoughts and opinions to be stronger and gave me confidence that I was on the right track.

The Ability to Get Started On the Right Track

This helped me on the ethnic paper the most because it set me in the right direction.

Let you get an idea if your paper is on the right track.

In the retrospectives, some students made critical comments about CP, giving specific objections and suggestions:

I liked this plan, but there needs to be a time limit on each person.

I was never far enough into the paper to be able to talk about it.

I tend to get windy and only focus on myself.

I'd rather have the opinion of more than one person.

Interestingly, honors and standard students reversed the categories they emphasized in the two retrospectives: honors focusing on the reader and making specific criticisms in the first retrospective, standard students doing so in the second. And so, if I were asked which of the two retrospectives produced better results, I could not say, for productive comments of different sorts appeared on each of them, especially for the honors students. It is true, however, that a third of the standard students produced less elaborate and detailed responses on the final retrospective than they had done on the earlier one.

Reflections on Observations

It seems clear that students focus on different dimensions of CP at different points of distance from planning sessions. One might wonder which one provides the best vantage point for viewing CP. Because in the earlier reflections writers have access to so much information about their planning and writing decisions, some might say that these are the better times to reflect. On the other hand, while this kind of information is lost by the time of the later reflections, the later comments have a value of their own. Once the specific information drops off, students seem to be able to view the experience more holistically—to observe general characteristics that were overlooked in their involvement with the particulars. People see different things at different times. This shift parallels what happens to all of us when we read, where we view a text in one way when we are in the midst of reading it, another way when we have completed it, and still another way when we think back on it months or years later. The famous Virginia Woolf quote applies: "Wait for the dust of reading to settle . . . the book will return, but differently. It will float to the top of the mind as a whole" (1932, p. 290–91).

Knowing how our perception of events shifts, we should give students the chance to reflect on their experience at different points of distance from it so they can have access to the different kinds of information available at each of these times. Perhaps we can even make the data documenting the shift available to them—let them reflect on their reflections—as one way of helping them develop that personal knowledge of their mental processes that psychologists find so valuable.

Part II Observations across Contexts

Section 4
Adapting Theory and Research in University Settings

Part II Observations across Contexts

Section A
Adapting Theory and
Research in University
Settings

21 Do Supporters Make a Difference?

Linda Flower
Carnegie Mellon University
Pittsburgh, Pennsylvania

Linda Flower (introduced earlier) often talked in project meetings about how her image of collaborative planning continued to change as she moved out of her own college classroom, to teaching in a high school class, to working with teenage writers at the Community Literacy Center. Each situation called for a freshly situated "teacher's theory" of how planning and collaboration could work. In this memo, however, she takes the role of a researcher whose in-depth study asks: How are students (in this case college freshmen) themselves interpreting their instruction in collaborative planning? What happens when they put this process into practice?

A Discovery Memo

This memo is another chapter in the saga of the college freshmen collaborators I have been studying. In it I want to second the growing sense many of us share that supporters have a tremendous impact on the quality of the collaborations. And I think I can respond to the questions we raised about whether that impact stops at conversation or extends to text.

A Little Background

Let me review where our attempt to study the college freshmen has gone. When we first began to use collaborative planning in our freshman composition course, we collected tapes of three planning sessions per student from two different sections taught by graduate teaching assistants: We wanted to see what students, in the privacy of their own dorms, were really doing with this new strategy. Since then, we have all learned a great deal about how to teach collaborative planning and supporting. This study is interesting as an example of how freshmen interpreted a very simple, straightforward introduction to CP.

Since we had designed CP to help writers move from knowledge-driven planning to more rhetorical thinking, the obvious question was: Are students actually working with each other to develop purposes, points, an image of readers, and a sense of alternative text conventions? Are the rhetorical areas of the Planner's Blackboard seeing any action? My collaborators, Lorraine Higgins and Joseph Petraglia, and I answered this by counting the number of conversational "turns" on the transcript that we could code as showing evidence of one or more blackboards, consolidation, and/or reflection (Flower, in press). From previous studies of individual student writers, peer groups, and the "dorm room" protocols of our own freshmen in the Reading-to-Write study (Flower, et al., 1990), there was every reason to expect that the topic information blackboard would sweep the ratings.

The happy surprise was that these skeptical predictions were wrong. The graph in figure 21.1 shows how the freshmen were, in fact, spending their time, with nearly 40 percent of their comments devoted to purpose and key point, 20 percent to audience, and 25 percent to text conventions. For teachers using collaborative planning, this appears to be good news; this direct, in-process prompting and social support for planning is making something happen.

On the other hand, as I study these transcripts I find myself less interested in the averages and the impact of "this activity" in general and more interested in the individual students and the strategic choices they are making as they use—or do not use—CP in the way their instructors planned. These transcripts give us an opportunity to see what students are actually doing with instruction, outside of class. Also, they illustrate what I am calling writers' *strategic knowledge,* that is, (1) the *goals* writers set for themselves, including their assumptions, values, priorities; (2) the *strategies* they use; and (3) the degree of reflective *awareness* they have of their own goals, strategies, or options. Although I can teach a heuristic such as collaborative planning, what my students must really develop is the strategic knowledge—the goals and the awareness, as well as the strategies—for making rhetorical planning work. So, in this frame of mind, I began to think about some of the strategic decisions these freshmen are making.

When Supporters Ask for Rhetorical Thinking

As other people in this book have been saying, supporters make a big difference in this process, and being a good supporter calls for both skill and engagement. One of the strategic decisions a supporter can

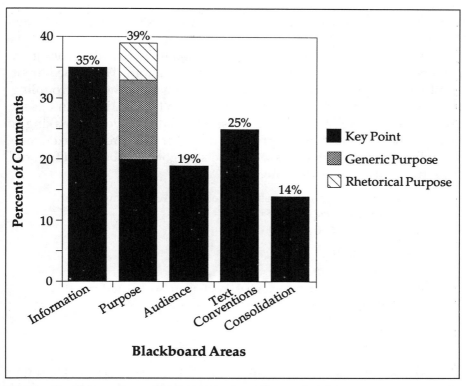

Figure 21.1. Percentage of Comments by Blackboard Areas.

make is to offer a criticism or raise a problem that cannot be answered by simply rehearsing what the planner intends to say (i.e., by replying with topic information). Such prompts might be "I don't think people will believe this" or "Can you make this seem more real?" This kind of involvement is what turns collaborative planning from just another checklist of valuable but easily dismissed "teacher questions" into a scaffold for thinking. These are interesting moments for planners as well—these moments when the supporter "puts it to them" and asks hard questions or makes requests that by their nature demand rhetorical, constructive planning. The question that naturally follows is, "What, then, does the planner do?"

We started by locating all the places in the transcripts where supporters' comments could be read (by an experienced writer) as requiring the writer to construct a plan or make a decision that involved his or her purpose, audience, or purposeful use of conventions. We found it relatively easy to agree on the comments that demanded such thinking.

As you might expect, students responded to this prompt in different ways. Some simply declined the gambit. They used their social skills to con or cajole a partner into abandoning the troubling issue. When Tomas, for instance, says, "I don't know. It doesn't seem like much of a point to me. It doesn't sound like you're making a *point*," Vince asserts that the problem does not exist. Yet the exchange that follows confirms that this was a social negotiation between friends, not a negotiation over meaning.

> *Vince:* Well, I'm just discussing something. Well, it's my—That's my purpose is to *discuss* this.
>
> *Supporter:* OK. OK. Sure.
>
> *Vince:* All right?
>
> *Supporter:* Sure.
>
> *Vince:* Thanks, Tomas. [laughs] Wish you were marking this paper. What an agreeable guy. . . . No. Well, my purpose. . . . To discuss this. This point. . . . This topic. . . . This situation.

On the surface, Paul's response in this next excerpt looks more promising, and it leads to a change in his text. Paul's partner raises an important issue: How do you integrate ideas from the book you are reading (referred to as Farb) with your own ideas?

> *Supporter:* So, how're you gonna use the Farb book into this thing?
>
> *Paul:* Hmm. I didn't really think about that.
>
> *Supporter:* Perhaps you could include that in your text convention.
>
> *Paul:* Yeah. Okay. That's a good idea. I forgot all about that Farb was. . . .
>
> *Supporter:* In writing about Farb, you should probably mention some statement of Farb's.
>
> *Paul:* Yeah. That's true. I should probably. . . yeah. That's a good idea. Can I borrow your pencil for a second and just write that down?

Paul's final text begins with a centered quotation. And neither Farb nor his ideas are ever heard from again. The track from prompt, to plan, to text is a clear one, and students are indeed sharing their knowledge of the expectations and conventions of academic discourse. However, I expect most of us would see this exchange as an opportunity not taken. The prompt to integrate Farb failed to lead Paul to reconsider his ideas or restructure his plan. He turned his collaborator's prompt into a reminder of a conventional but rather superficial text feature— it led to a plan to mention his source, rather than really use Farb's ideas. Paul subtly converted a rhetorical prompt into an invitation to add a little more topic information in a suggestive place.

I start with Vince and Paul because I think they tell us that the effectiveness of collaborative planning (or any other instructional activity we offer) is not determined by the activity or even by the social context we can create around it (like the help of a good teacher or a good supporter). It is determined by the strategic choices students make and their awareness of those choices. Is this just a case of resistance, or are Vince and Paul fully aware of the maneuvers—and the alternatives to those moves—they are making as planners? How deep does their strategic knowledge as writers go?

If this attention to students' thinking (rather than our teaching) sounds potentially discouraging (as well as realistic), there is a brighter side to this picture. Gary used his prompt a little differently. He was planning to write about problems that occur when someone has to do a translation or read text from a different dialect (his example is reading Shakespeare). His supporter poses what could be a very tough question, asking Gary for an audience-based way of presenting his ideas on translation.

> *Supporter:* Well, what's going to make this paper very interesting?
>
> *Gary:* First of all, I'm writing it. [This was probably a joke.] I think it will be interesting to people, especially people that have read Shakespeare. Because I've found that, if my English teacher wasn't there to help translate that, then I wouldn't have known what was going on. So I think it should be interesting to people who have the same problems, because they will be able to relate to it.

The question forced Gary to reflect on his own experience and the reason his seemingly esoteric information on the problems of translators had any relevance to the assignment (which was to deal with the problems freshmen writers face). What I find interesting is how he then transforms this insight into an effective text convention for not just *telling* readers that this information is relevant, but *showing* it. His text begins: "Have you even had any trouble understanding something that has been translated from another language or from a different dialect of English?" He goes on to promise an explanation of these problems.

You may be wondering who is more typical: Vince or Gary? There is some reason to hope the answer is Gary. Across the group as a whole, supporters came up with an average of nearly two-and-a-half of these significant, constructive prompts over the session, and the writers responded by constructing new ideas nearly 90 percent of the time. Moreover, this information not only turned up in the writer's text in most cases, it turned up in significant places, such as the introduction, conclusion, or major example. Even though these supporters had little or no instruction in being collaborators, much less peer tutors, they seem to be helping their partners engage in a valuable, if difficult, kind of thinking that leads to significant additions to their texts.

22 Productive and Unproductive Conflict in Collaboration

Rebecca E. Burnett
Iowa State University
Ames, Iowa

Rebecca Burnett, now assistant professor of rhetoric and professional communication at Iowa State University, brought a rich background in high school and college teaching to Carnegie Mellon where she did her doctoral work in rhetoric. As a technical communication teacher, business consultant, and textbook writer, Rebecca wanted to adapt collaborative planning to the group work and group writing required in business. Specifically, she wanted to address a problem business writers frequently face—how to deal with conflict in productive, generative ways. However, in her pilot studies, she discovered that college students were going out of their way to avoid the appearance of conflict, rather than use it. Her dissertation study used collaborative planning to make conflict visible and to draw students into a more reflective, generative use of their own differences. This discovery memo summarizes one of the key findings of her ongoing research about collaboration and then suggests ways to talk with the students about these findings.

A Discovery Memo

Lena and Jordan really should get some credit for influencing the direction my research has taken. They were excellent, highly motivated students in a junior/senior-level business and technical communication class that I taught at Carnegie Mellon during the pilot year of the Making Thinking Visible Project. During class discussions, both Lena and Jordan were confident and articulate, regularly challenging other students, especially each other. They decided to collaborate to plan and coauthor a recommendation report that was required for class, but once they had started working together, they wrote in their process journals and confided during individual interviews that they strongly disagreed with each other about the plan for their collaborative report. Lena believed her approach more accurately addressed the problem in the case situation they were solving; she had done a good deal of appropriate background research and had come up with a careful and detailed analysis. Jordan believed his approach reflected the necessary pragmatism of the workplace; he had also prepared an analysis, but he based his on experience in the workplace.

A videotape of their collaborative interaction showed them in an extended discussion that consisted primarily of what I later came to call immediate agreements and elaborations of single points. Substantive conflict—that is, considering alternatives and voicing explicit disagreements—played virtually no part in their interaction, despite their careful preparation before their collaborative planning session and despite their disagreements about each other's approaches. They were, in fact, excruciatingly polite to each other. Their prior experiences with collaboration, coupled with their preconceptions about appropriate behavior for collaborative writers, virtually eliminated any direct confrontation of their disagreements, which might have resulted in productive, substantive conflict.

I knew from reading about conflict in a variety of other disciplines that certain kinds of conflict during collaboration are not only normal, but productive. In fact, collaborative problem solving and writing processes are beneficial, in large part because of the alternatives that collaborators generate and their willingness to critically examine these alternatives. So, then, why did Lena and Jordan choose not to engage in forms of substantive conflict that would have allowed them to consider the alternatives and voice the disagreements that they obviously believed were important?

A critical influence in Lena and Jordan's behavior seemed to be the way they represented their task: They saw their goal as coming up with a workable plan, and, to them, that meant reaching consensus, even though they had learned about the benefits of brainstorming for alternatives and the risks of "groupthink." They both had workplace experience from internships as well as part-time and summer employment where they had seen and participated in collaborative groups thrashing out problems. They both had participated in a senior-level course called *Management Game*, a semester-long simulation activity that sets up teams for analyzing and resolving complex management problems. But Lena and Jordan thought of coauthoring as a cooperative activity that precluded conflict; they believed that they would be most successful by hinting at disagreement rather than being explicit, by stating alternatives as hypothetical rather than actual possibilities. During interviews, both explained that they saw direct disagreement as rude and demonstrating a lack of confidence in the other person. They thought their role as a coauthor was to persuade or manipulate the other one to agree, but certainly not to implicitly disagree by offering alternatives or to explicitly disagree by challenging the other.

Incidents such as this one with Lena and Jordan encouraged me to question the way in which collaborative writing activities were presented and taught in the context of writing classes. These students had learned the theoretical benefits of substantive conflict from a variety of perspectives, including the problem-solving focus of their undergraduate core curriculum and the emphasis on alternatives and the risks of "groupthink" presented in their technical courses. However, they seldom used this knowledge in a productive way; it was never operationalized. Some students reported that collaborative projects in other courses sometimes had serious procedural problems: Ground rules were never established, they selected a leader who was too dictatorial or too ineffectual, the time was not managed well, they did not do a great deal of group planning, but instead assumed individual parts of the project. And these experiences were compounded by their shared assumption that conflict was bad and consensus was good. The influence of their prior knowledge and experience was so strong that Lena and Jordan never reached the point of understanding that there are different kinds of conflict—some bad, some good. That students with such experiences and assumptions would not automatically engage in substantive conflict during their collaborative planning should have been no surprise, but it was—especially considering what I had learned about the value of substantive conflict.

Stimulated by Lena and Jordan, my interest in investigating the ways that coauthors interact led me first to search for factors that seemed to influence their interaction. Then, I wanted to see how one of these factors that I identified—the amount of substantive conflict they engaged in—influenced the quality of the report that the coauthors produced. I conducted a study with 48 upper-level technical and business majors enrolled in three sections of an upper-level business communications course for industrial management and technical majors at Carnegie Mellon University. Most of these students were two to six months away from accepting a job in business or industry. The training these 24 randomly assigned pairs received in planning and collaboration, as well as the complex report-writing task they completed, were part of their regular course work.

The results of this study (Burnett, 1991) showed a clear-cut, statistically significant correlation between the quality of the coauthors' reports and the amount of substantive conflict they engaged in. Simply put, coauthors who considered more alternatives and voiced more disagreements about content and other rhetorical elements (purpose, audience, and a variety of verbal and visual text conventions) produced higher quality documents than coauthors who considered few or no alternatives and voiced little or no explicit disagreements. Examining alternatives is one way to consider the strengths and weaknesses of a point. In contrast, following only one path (either by immediate decision or the elaboration of a single point) seldom exposes problems. Having more alternatives to consider gives collaborators a greater chance of making effective decisions and being able to defend those decisions. Just as considering alternatives has a positive correlation with the quality of the document that collaborators produce, so does voicing explicit disagreement about content and other rhetorical elements. Explicit disagreement (e.g., "I disagree," or "I don't think that's the right way to approach this.") gives collaborators the opportunity to reexamine their positions in the face of direct disagreement. Such opposition often generates alternatives that likely would not be considered if the explicit conflict has not been voiced.

I can see a risk, however, in blindly advising students to pose alternatives and voice disagreements during their collaborative planning because merely using a particular move does not automatically lead to a better product. Types of substantive conflict appear to be qualitatively different. To be productive, an alternative does not have to end up in the final plan or be instantiated in the document, but it does need to be offered seriously, be related to the task, be rhetorically based, and have good reasons to support it. Gratuitous alternatives, those offered just to say something, do little to strengthen the interaction or the document.

In the following excerpt, Josh and Pete present alternatives about fonts, certainly a legitimate concern when designing a document; however, they have few justifications for their alternatives other than an attitude that says, "I like mine better than yours." Josh and Pete see the choice of font as personal preference; they do not seem to recognize that such a design decision is rhetorical.

Josh: What font do you think we should use?

Pete: I personally think we should use Geneva 12-point.

> *Josh:* I kinda like Chicago 12-point. Makes it a little bit more spacious.
>
> *Pete:* I'll have to see what happens on the computer when I put it on, but I really do like the Geneva 12.
>
> *Josh:* Do you? And I prefer the Chicago 12, so—
>
> *Pete:* Chicago 12 or Chicago 10?
>
> *Josh:* Chicago 12. It's more spacious.
>
> *Pete:* Well, we'll see. Geneva comes up better and bolder.
>
> *Josh:* Yeah. Well, we'll see.

In this situation, they have offered alternatives but not considered them. Josh and Pete's question about fonts gets decided when they are drafting their report. They end up using Geneva only because Pete had control of the keyboard. The report they produced reflects the quality of their decision making. Josh and Pete wrote a document that was ranked at the bottom, 24 out of 24. During their collaborative planning session, 97.5 percent of their decision making was based on either immediate agreements or decisions about a single point. In fact, the episode above is the only instance of substantive conflict in their entire collaborative planning session.

The following excerpt is a contrasting example that also considers the alternatives of the Geneva or Times fonts. The difference with Anna and Ed's conversation, however, is that Anna and Ed use the opportunity to relate their discussion to the overall goal of their task—recommending changes to make a more effective, reader-based document.

> *Anna:* The font, so far, is not very readable.
>
> *Ed:* You don't think?
>
> *Anna:* I think like, Times or something . . . it would be easy to read.
>
> *Ed:* Yeah, that's how—I—actually that's what I've—got Times twelve. It's highly professional, too.
>
> *Anna:* This [version] is more like, um, this is more like ah—is it Geneva, or something?
>
> *Ed:* That's like a ten point, I think, actually.
>
> *Anna:* Yeah. It's not only tiny, [it's] the actual font itself. It's easier to read Times because it's more like a newspaper. That's easier.
>
> *Ed:* That, that could be something.
>
> *Anna:* So, like the font . . . not only the size but the actual font.

> *Ed:* I'd like, try like Times twelve point sounds good. I'm happy with that.
>
> *Anna:* Yeah. Times twelve point would be kind of small, but it's easier to read. Um—

Anna and Ed note specific design features of the typography, font and size, as reasons for their objections to Geneva. Anna begins this episode by saying that the original font (Geneva) is "not very readable." They consider Times as an alternative because it is so familiar to readers: "it's more like a newspaper." Unlike Pete and Josh whose stands are based on personal preferences, Anna and Ed support their alternatives with rhetorical considerations. Also, in contrast to Pete and Josh, Anna and Ed wrote a document that was ranked near the top, 4 out of 24. During Anna and Ed's collaborative planning session, 32 percent of their decision making was based on substantive conflict (as opposed to the 2.5 percent of Pete and Josh's decision making). The substantive conflict about which font to use was relatively minor in relation to Anna and Ed's overall collaborative planning session and had less impact on the quality of their final document than other substantive conflict they engaged in about content, purpose, audience, and organization.

Even though I have identified important differences in collaborative decision making, I cannot assume that my students' understanding and using a preponderance of substantive conflict during collaborative planning will automatically result in higher quality documents; the relationship is not causal. No single category of moves is inherently appropriate or inappropriate to use. Determining the value of collaborative interaction must include consideration of a variety of other factors, including the collaborators' seriousness of purpose and the relevance of the discussion to the task. If, for example, the collaborators are not on task, the alternatives they pose may be trivial, totally impractical, or obviously unworkable and, thus, probably not worth the time to make them (though, on occasion, such conversations do stimulate workable ideas). Encouraging student coauthors to elaborate points and engage in substantive conflict without emphasizing the importance of content, purpose, and other rhetorical elements defeats the potential value of the interaction. Thus, writers need to know that part of what matters in their planning is the proportion and interplay of moves as they deal with content and other rhetorical elements: Their collaborative process influences the quality of their documents.

23 Representation and Reflection: A Preservice Teacher's Understanding of Collaborative Planning

Linda Norris
Carnegie Mellon University
Pittsburgh, Pennsylvania

Linda Norris, now assistant professor of English, Indiana University of Pennsylvania, Armstrong County Campus, was the full-time educational coordinator for the Making Thinking Visible Project. Her 17 years of teaching had led to her doctoral work in education at the University of Pittsburgh and a commitment to teacher training. Her work in the project led her to ask: How do future teachers interpret and evaluate educational innovations, such as collaborative planning, that they meet in education courses? How does their own experience as students and writers affect their image of this practice? Her dissertation not only showed a remarkable connection between being a writer and learning to be a writing teacher, but suggests that reflection can exert a powerful influence on the ways students (and future teachers) reshape their own images of writing and teaching.

A Project Paper

About halfway into my second year as coordinator of this project, I became fascinated with how we writing teachers adapted collaborative planning to so many different situations and for so many different reasons. Repeatedly at our monthly seminars, I listened to other project teachers talk about how they saw collaborative planning as useful and appropriate for this student or that situation, for this particular writing assignment or that rhetorical consideration. I realized that we were interpreting collaborative planning in unique ways. The writing and conversations we shared at our monthly meetings brought about new insights to change and to help our student writers and, maybe equally important, to change and to help us as writing teachers.

This fascination with how we in the project were representing collaborative planning and reflecting on how we understood this technique naturally spilled over into the area I was most interested in—teacher preparation. I had been working with preservice secondary English teachers at the University of Pittsburgh as part of my doctoral studies, and I had been reading about "images of teaching" that preservice teachers form from their prior educational experiences, in their methods courses, and during student teaching (Calderhead & Robson, 1991; Clandinin, 1986; Elbaz, 1981; Freeman, 1991; Korthagen, 1988; Leinhardt, 1988; Tabachnick & Zeichner, 1984). I decided to focus on how future writing teachers interpret and evaluate innovations like collaborative planning. The questions I wanted to explore were, first, what is a beginning writing teacher's *representation* of collaborative planning, and, in the larger framework of learning to teach, how do teachers make sense of this new technique? (By representation I mean the information and understandings that make up a teacher's personal image of a technique including personal experiences, classroom experiences, attitudes, and reasoning.) And second, would *reflection* help a preservice teacher further understand and adapt collaborative planning as part of his or her repertoire for teaching writing? In other words, if we ask a future teacher to take a hard, close look at something he or she might be teaching, and how and why, will this reflection add something more to the knowledge base and perhaps go beyond the sometimes fleeting "images of teaching" a prospective teacher brings to his or her beginning practice? However, deliberate actions by student teachers do not necessarily mean better actions (Zeichner & Liston, 1990).

This inquiry is an attempt to redefine reflection as not just a gut reaction but as a methodology that helps prospective teachers develop a *reflective process* based on (1) making observations and comparing what they see over time, (2) taking their own attitudes into account, and (3) exploring the conflicts and considerations that arise as they are learning to teach. Therefore, I was interested in a kind of *strategic* reflection that had the power to bring the representation into full view of future teachers and let them accept, modify, or reject the practice in their developing repertoire for teaching writing.

This case study of Laura, a preservice teacher, is drawn from my dissertation study.[1] I examine Laura's representation of collaborative planning and her reflections on it from her introduction to collaborative planning in a fall semester teaching methods course through her student teaching experience in the spring semester. Studying Laura's specific representation via strategic reflection may provide some helpful information for other teacher preparation programs about how to make teacher trainees more aware of their own thinking and learning processes so that they can become more conscious of what they know and why they think it is important for them to use certain techniques in their classes.

I tracked Laura's developing representation from a number of sources, and I designed several opportunities for strategic reflection. Laura completed a variation of David Wallace's Writing Attitude Survey (see appendix at end of his discovery memo, section 2) on three different occasions: at the beginning of the fall semester before she was introduced to collaborative planning in a teaching methods course; at the end of the fall methods course, after she had done collaborative planning with her peers on several writing assignments for her course work; and at the end of her spring student teaching, during which she had opportunities to use collaborative planning with ninth-grade inner-city students. During this time, she kept a journal of responses to learning, doing, and teaching collaborative planning. Also, she discussed collaborative planning in class with her peers and with me in both informal conversations and taped interviews.

I wanted to discover how Laura represented collaborative planning to herself, and moreover, how she would decide whether or not to use this new technique in her own student teaching. Laura gave SA (strongly agree) responses to the following four items all three times she completed the writing attitude survey:

- When I have a writing assignment, I like to talk to someone about it before I write.
- People can give me useful advice about what I'm going to write.
- When I have a problem writing, I like to bounce ideas off other people.
- Telling a friend about my ideas for writing helps me write better.

And she gave SD (strongly disagree) responses all three times to these three items:

- Writing should be a very private process.
- I like to wait until I've finished a paper before I tell people about my writing.

■ It's a waste of time to talk with other students about my writing.

Laura's responses to these seven items remained consistent from the time before she first heard about collaborative planning in August to the end of her student teaching in May. She seemed predisposed to like the idea of collaborative planning from her earliest familiarity with it and continued to show that attitude on surveys in the following months.

However, Laura's survey responses are only one aspect of a much more complex representation of collaborative planning. Her journal responses and taped interview reveal important additional information on how she is thinking about the technique. In the following written and oral responses, we see Laura making several reflective points about collaborative planning and how she will incorporate it into her teaching of writing. These responses were opportunities for Laura to flesh out her representation, in this case, leading her to choose collaborative planning as part of her teaching repertoire. In the discussion that follows, I have drawn points of reflection from the data I collected which I discuss as points of acceptance, consideration, and conflict.

A *point of acceptance* confirms or agrees with the technique, strengthening the likelihood that the technique will be integrated into the teaching repertoire. A *point of consideration* weighs positive or negative aspects of the technique and might bring one closer to acceptance of or further resistance to the technique as part of the teaching repertoire. *Points of conflict* are resistance to a technique or potential problem recognition; several points of conflict will most likely result in abandoning the technique as part of the repertoire, especially if it seems impossible to resolve the problems posed by the technique. As we will see with Laura, however, some points of conflict do not mean that a teaching technique could never become part of a teacher's repertoire. Furthermore, points of conflict are important because they signal problems and allow teachers to think through why the technique should not be used.

After the first class, in which we discussed collaborative planning, Laura wrote her reactions as a writer to this technique:

> Well, I think it's very clear that this type of activity could be extremely useful in planning for writing. I think I use some sort of adapted version whenever I write. I love to talk to someone else beforehand. (Journal response, August 30, 1990)

In this early reflective response, Laura's personal experience of what she does as a writer and her responses to items on the attitude survey form an approving opinion of collaborative planning—points of acceptance—based on the notions that writing should not be a private enterprise and that talking to someone about writing can actually improve writing.

Upon further reflection, however, Laura begins to see possible problems with the new technique as she moves from her own initial acceptance of collaborative planning for herself as a writer to other student writers she will be teaching. Laura encounters points of conflict: There may be students who want privacy, who do not love to talk to others like she does, who see writing as personal rather than as something to be shared. But, she reasons, most teens do like to talk to their peers. She resolves these conflicting points by suggesting that she would consider letting each writer do what works best for him or her:

> However, I wonder about students who enjoy their privacy and might not want to talk before they write; or they may be writing about a personal subject which they would not want to share. I also think this approach fits in well with most teenagers' natural tendencies: to talk about themselves with peers. Why not work with their own preferences in helping them to learn? (Journal response, August 30, 1990)

In her second journal response, after doing collaborative planning with another class member, tape recording their planning session, and listening to their tape, Laura continues to reflect as a teacher and adds other reasons why students she will be teaching might benefit from collaborative planning:

> I can see how this aspect [being a supporter] would certainly boost a teenager's sense of self-esteem and worth. Especially someone who may not have been doing well with other aspects of the class. It was even gratifying for me. (Journal response, September 6, 1990)

Close to the end of the semester, I asked Laura to predict how she might teach collaborative planning. At this point, practical concerns surfaced about how to keep students on task, how high the noise level would be, and how much time it would take to teach collaborative planning—points of consideration. Her attitude toward collaborative planning still remained positive; however, we can see a more reflective critical attitude emerging in which she weighs the costs and benefits of time and productivity:

I think most students would talk about subjects other than their writing; at first, I would have to circulate around to see how they were progressing and keep them on track. . . . I also think some students would not participate very actively in their role. It would depend on their relationship with the other student. . . . There would be a great deal of noise. . . . I think they'd probably produce better writing—I feel pretty sure of that. More than anything, I think this activity takes time to make it productive. They'd probably need about two or three times before it would really help them, but I'm confident that it is a worthwhile project. . . . I would have one student work with me for everyone else to watch. I would be the supporter, and the student, the writer. We would go through a brief 5–10 minute collaborative planning session. I would inform them that tomorrow, they will be given half the period to do this, and the other half to write. Their papers will be due in three days. They'll do collaborative planning and begin writing— we'll probably have some discussion about how it went. (Journal response, December 6, 1990)

From Laura's writing attitude surveys, journal, and class discussions, I discovered that what triggered these reflective points were her personal experiences as a writer, her attitudes toward collaboration and planning, her reasoning as a writing teacher, and her image of the classroom, (i.e., her developing representation of collaborative planning).

By the end of fall semester, Laura learned that she would be doing her student teaching at a large inner-city school and that she would be teaching ninth-grade English With Emphasis on Reading (EWER); the students in the course are considered remedial. Laura decided to try collaborative planning with her ninth-grade EWER students while they were writing short stories.

Appendix 1 at the end of this chapter illustrates how Laura's representation of collaborative planning grows with time and experience. The excerpts are from an interview with Laura after her students used collaborative planning to write their short stories. Notice the interplay among the key elements (listed to the left of the excerpts) that contribute to Laura's representation of collaborative planning: her *personal experience* (how she sees the technique as a writer herself), her *classroom experience* (what actually happens when she tries the technique with students), her *attitude* (what she thinks, feels, or believes about the technique), and her *reasoning* (what she will do or what will happen when the technique is used again).

The excerpts also illustrate points of acceptance, conflict, and consideration (listed to the right of the excerpts). Not only do we see several points of acceptance that show Laura's willingness to use collaborative planning, but we see how she also raises points of consideration and conflict that push her to work out an adaptation of collaborative planning to fit her classroom context and her beliefs about teaching writing. Beginning with the first paragraph, notice how Laura combines her own personal experiences as a writer, "kind of a natural way to start writing," with her actual classroom experience as a writing teacher in coming to accept collaborative planning as a technique she would use for teaching writing.

Even though Laura comments in paragraph five of the interview that collaborative planning can be "intrusive," she wants to do it again because she believes that it is a "good thing to teach." She also believes, upon reflection after using collaborative planning, that she would let students choose whether they wanted to do collaborative planning or wanted to write privately. The student writing about her pregnancy reinforces Laura's vision of the writing classroom where students could have a private corner if they chose not to collaborate on a certain assignment. But ultimately, Laura wants all of her students to try collaborative planning because she believes that one of its most important goals is to allow writers authority, ownership, and responsibility for their work—that they will eventually become their own "internal supporters."

In the reflective journal she is keeping on her student teaching experiences, Laura recalls the collaborative planning classroom experience (she also refers to it as "discussion planning") and decides to add the technique to her teaching repertoire for high school English. However, she modifies the technique in ways that she thinks will work best for these students, without the planning blackboards or technical vocabulary. She downplays the blackboards and focuses the class's attention on how to be a good supporter by having students think about different types of questions and by getting them to be her supporters when she plans a piece of writing:

> The CP was the most successful part of the whole two-week unit on story writing. . . . With the discussion planning, both periods did remarkably well. I can't recall a lesson that went so smoothly with both classes. They enjoyed working with their peers in groups, and I think the idea of each person taking part in one person's work was appealing. Both ninth-grade classes have always enjoyed working in groups, and I think it's a very

important ability for these students to develop. . . . Each day I modelled the process again but focused on different types of questions. I also brought in the students as the supporters during the modeling so that they would be more involved in the process and better practiced when they began their own groups. . . . I think my students really gained a lot from this technique. They were a little less frustrated with the assignment after being able to talk about their ideas with other people in the class. Over time, I think the students who were reticent to take part in this would really come to enjoy it. I can see how this could really develop speaking skills. It also helped them to see another student's approach to the same assignment, which spawned new ideas of their own. I would do this again with writing in a heartbeat. (Journal response, April 22, 1991)

I believe Laura reaches the decision to add collaborative planning to her repertoire of teaching writing through several reflection points of acceptance; however, she also makes important points of consideration and conflict along the way. Figure 23.1 traces the path by which Laura comes to accept this writing technique and use it in her teaching repertoire. The decision to use collaborative planning seems to be a combination of Laura's early affinity for collaborative planning mixed with careful consideration and resolution of conflict over two semesters.

As a writer, Laura has meaningful personal experiences doing collaborative planning, yet she considers the importance of writers' privacy and decides to modify the Planner's Blackboard when she thinks about her students. The conflict points about the Planner's Blackboard and the consideration of writer's privacy are resolved in Laura's classroom situation. The last two features in figure 23.1 (students were much more cooperative, and students can become their own internal supporters) became part of Laura's representation of collaborative planning when she saw them emerge in her teaching in April. Obviously, a strong acceptance point for Laura was her success with collaborative planning in a situation with students who normally have difficulties with reading and writing. Couple this strong acceptance point with Laura's attitude survey responses and excerpts from her journal and interview, and we see a representation of collaborative planning that suggests that Laura will use this technique as part of her repertoire for teaching writing.

From Laura's earliest experience with collaborative planning (and even before she knew what collaborative planning was), we can see that there was a good fit between this technique and Laura's

A Feature of CP	When	Acceptance	Consideration	Conflict
Talking to someone helps	August	X		
Some writers like privacy	August			X
Peer support is important	October	X		
Planner's Blackboard is helpful structure/ metaphor	October			X
CP helps writers construct meaning	December	X		
CP could be noisy, gets students off task	December		X	
CP could produce better writing	December		X	
Students were much more cooperative with CP	April	X		
Students become own internal supporters with CP	April	X		

Figure 23.1. Features of Laura's Representation of Collaborative Planning over Time as Reflection Points of Acceptance, Consideration, and Conflict.

understandings of herself as a writer and as a teacher of student writers. Collaborative planning complemented many of Laura's personal experiences and attitudes about planning and collaboration. This match is further reinforced when Laura tries collaborative planning with her own students and experiences success in a classroom where both the students and the writing goals are challenging.

Laura's representation of collaborative planning and her reflection about ways to adapt and incorporate it into her teaching encourage us that many preservice teachers can be receptive to new ideas and practices. However, the representation and reflection of Laura and other preservice teachers like her are only part of the picture. In contrast, there were preservice teachers in the larger study (Norris, 1992) and in an earlier pilot study who came with very different attitudes toward collaboration ("I've always done well in school without the help of others"; "I wouldn't want someone to steal my ideas"; "I resent that I will be told when to collaborate and with whom") and planning ("I never plan, I just write"; "I like to be less organized"). Some came with views and experiences in opposition to the collaborative planning technique itself ("Talking is noisy, and noise is disruptive and gets students off task"; "Writing, for me, has always been a very private enterprise"). In many cases, these attitudes did not change over time. These points of conflict in their representations were not always resolved and eventually led to decisions not to use collaborative planning in their classes.

Providing opportunities for the kind of strategic reflection we have seen with Laura and other preservice teachers can help prospective teachers become more conscious of their decisions to incorporate, to alter, or to abandon certain teaching techniques. This process of strategic reflection—the combination of observation and critical contemplation on one's own attitudes, conflicts, and concerns—plays an important role in teacher preparation for two reasons: (1) it moves preservice teachers from mere exposure and "gut reactions" to a specific teaching technique to engaging in sustained written and oral responses about it, and (2) it encourages internal dialogues in preservice teachers as learners and as teachers that promote heightened awareness and informed understanding of their practices and why they adopt, adapt, or reject certain teaching techniques as part of their repertoire. Laura not only had opportunities to explain how collaborative planning was affecting her as a learner but also to imagine its impact on students she would be teaching, and further, to comment on how it affected students when she did use it, and to modify it accordingly. Strategic reflection helps us move beyond recent work in teacher training (e.g., Calderhead, 1991; Elbaz, 1987; Morine-Dershimer, 1989; Swanson-Owens, 1986) to recognize that preservice teachers' representations powerfully influence the decisions they make about what to teach, how to teach, and why they are teaching certain techniques and that these representations can change over time and in different classroom situations.

I am not suggesting that this is the only way that prospective teachers can gain insight into their teaching practices, but this type of strategic reflection is a conscious action that can bring teachers to a better understanding of the techniques they learn and then transfer to their own classrooms. And when we see their technique representations and reflection points of acceptance, consideration, and conflict, both teacher educators and prospective teachers can begin to understand what informs teaching practices and how teachers choose the techniques that best fit their pedagogy and contexts.

Note

1. The larger study was a close analysis of how seven preservice teachers in the English education program at the University of Pittsburgh represented two techniques (collaborative planning and creative dramatics) during methods courses and during student teaching and how their representations influenced their practice of these techniques (Norris, 1992). I collected eight types of data, including surveys, feature analyses, journals, lesson plans, and interviews, over an academic year from the beginning of methods courses that provided instruction in these techniques to the end of student teaching in which these practices were used. From these measures emerged each participant's representation of each of the two techniques. I discovered that student teachers' representations consisted of a variety of components including, most prominently, attitude, personal and classroom experiences, and reasoning.

Appendix 1

Excerpts from Laura's Interview after Teaching Collaborative Planning

Representation Component	Excerpt	Reflection Point
personal experience	I thought it [CP] was kind of a natural way to start writing. 'Cause I do this. . . . When I first heard about it I was just thinking, "How would this work for me if I was a student?". . . I thought, "Yeah, it would. It would probably help me a lot." And I-I liked the idea.	acceptance
	The only thing I didn't like about it was that sometimes when I write I don't feel like telling somebody about it. There's—sometimes I write stories and I don't want to talk about it because it's almost like you'll jinx it, you know? . . . I didn't want to spoil it by telling it to somebody.	consideration
attitude	And I think there are some people who do prefer writing privately and they don't want to talk about it. Especially if it's a sensitive topic.	conflict
classroom experience	I had a girl in the fifth period class who was writing about herself and her pregnancy and I was helping the guy who was the supporter of the group to ask her questions. . . . Her story stopped after the first paragraph. Like, her last sentence said, "Because my mother was giving me a hard time." But she didn't say what the hard time was and what happened. . . . She needed somebody to ask those questions, but, you know, because it's just painful or just sensitive, she didn't want to tell about it.	conflict
reasoning	For somebody like that I would probably, you know, if we did this again, and a situation like that came up . . . I would say, "Okay, people who are doing their writing privately, this is the corner for you. . . . And if you do your writing in here, you don't have to participate in this. You know, if you want to, you can sit in on a group and just listen to the questions. . . . Be an observer, or be a supporter, you know. But if the person was at that stage where they had to get some writing down, and they didn't want to be asked questions, then I would provide some time for that person to do it. . . .	consideration

attitude	It is an intrusive technique sometimes and . . . I just want to make sure that she can do this without feeling—[that she has to collaboratively plan]—Yeah. Yeah. I want them all to try it. I want them all to use it	consideration
reasoning	because what happens, I think, if they learn to do this a couple of times, then you start to be your own internal supporter . . . you start to—to gel, like—you start to kind of ask those questions to yourself. . . . And that's you know, that's definitely a big kind of benefit from this.	acceptance
personal experience	I was doing this with other people before I knew about it. . . . I used to do this with my sister who was not, I mean, she's not in English. She didn't even like to write. She's just, you know . . . she's a tough listener. I mean, she's active in a tough way. . . . She would not let me say things without elaborating or, you know, so that was good, and that was something that I started to internalize and I started to become much more hard on myself.	acceptance
attitude	I'm going to do this again, though. I really like it. I think they liked it, too. This is a good thing to teach. These are ninth graders. This is EWER. You know what people say? . . . People say you can't get them to write a paragraph. . . . So, I was happy. (Interview, April 11, 1991)	acceptance

24 Collaborative Planning: A Context for Defining Relationships

Michael A. Benedict
Fox Chapel Area High School
Fox Chapel, Pennsylvania

Michael A. Benedict has taught at Fox Chapel Area High School for 25 years, where he is department chair and a peer coach for faculty in cooperative learning. Mike was named a Christa McAuliffe fellow for the Commonwealth of Pennsylvania for his project on creating a cooperative learning environment in the writing center. He has also served as secretary for the Western Pennsylvania Council of Teachers of English and as director of public relations for the 1993 NCTE Annual Convention in Pittsburgh. Mike's experience in the computer-rich environment of a suburban high school was part of the Making Thinking Visible Project's diverse mix that included Pittsburgh's older steel mill valleys and its multicultural urban schools. But like many other members of the project, Mike was also at home in more than one educational institution in the city, writing teacher resource units in literature for the Center for Learning and teaching methods courses in secondary English for undergraduate and graduate students at Duquesne University. His discovery memo shows how transcripts of two pairs of prospective teachers' collaborative planning sessions provide insights not only about how they plan as writers, but they begin to see themselves as writing teachers.

A Discovery Memo

In "The Right Metaphor," an article I wrote (1990) for the first casebook for the Making Thinking Visible Project, I defined two different types of exchanges that could occur during a collaborative planning session. One was a *mirror* exchange, and the other was a *window* exchange. I used these two metaphors to describe what I saw happening in the transcripts of several planning sessions.

"A mirror exchange is one in which the interaction between the planner and supporter allows the planner time for consideration, reflection, and reconsideration" (p. 54). In a mirror exchange, the supporter asks questions of the planner that would allow the planner to reflect on what he or she is saying. A good supporter can set up a mirror exchange by making either of the following moves:

- Using reflective questions that cause the planner to think about the piece of writing under discussion. For example: "Are you sure that is what you want to do?" or "Is this approach the right one for your audience?"

- Restating the planner's comments in such a way that the planner has to think about the comment and then make some response to it.

In a window exchange, the planner's statements move outside the immediate area of concern. "A dialogue is a window exchange when it is transparent enough to allow the planner to see both sides of the wall and to get a clear vision of the 'outside' of his or her mind or to see concerns about the paper beyond the immediate topic of conversation" (1990, p. 55). A window exchange enables one or more of the following possibilities:

- Allows the dialogue to touch on matters that are not pertinent to the immediate question or discussion. This is analogous to stream-of-consciousness. At times it may lead away from the topic and side-track the planning session.

- Opens up an idea for the supporter for his or her paper.

- Helps the writer see concerns that are larger, outside issues or concerns. This, however, is not side tracking. By illustration of this last point, one planner's concern about a grade on a previous paper affected her planning on another.

Devising these two metaphors allowed me to conceptualize more clearly what was happening in my students' planning sessions. It then gave me another means of working with them in developing their skills, not only as planners, but also as supporters. Figure 24.1 illustrates both of these exchanges.

Although I teach English at Fox Chapel Area High School in Pennsylvania, I also teach a methods course for preservice teachers at Duquesne University. I try to expose the preservice teachers to various methods of writing instruction, including the important step of planning. During the fall semester in the final year of the Making Thinking Visible Project, I asked Linda Norris to introduce my preservice teachers

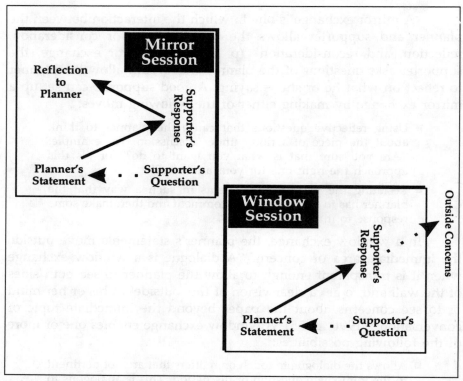

Figure 24.1. Window/Mirror Sessions.

to the various aspects of collaborative planning. She gave them a mock assignment for their first run through a planning session. They were to plan a letter of introduction to give to their ninth-grade class on the first day of school. As is our practice when students use collaborative planning, we had them tape their planning sessions so they would have a record of their planning session to review later.

I listened to these tapes later in the week. As I was listening, something struck me. There was something else going on besides the writing of a letter, besides the collaborative planning exercise. I rewound the tapes and listened again, this time focusing on what I thought was happening. Eureka! Not only were these students writing a letter to their classes—talking about what they wanted to say, what would go into the letters—they were doing something else. They were defining themselves as teachers! I started to get an image of the kind of teachers these students were envisioning themselves to be.

As I listened to the tapes from these sessions, I became aware of another type of window exchange that I had not noticed before. This new window was not concerned with the letter or what the planners were saying. This new window that opened allowed me to see the personas of these writers, to see how the writers were defining themselves by their choices of ideas or words to use in their planned piece of writing. Thus, I asked myself, *As a person is planning a piece of writing and thereby defining himself or herself as a writer, might he or she also be defining himself or herself as a person?* Would I be able to pick these definitions out of their tapes and their planning sessions? Or, would I be imposing on their planning something that I wanted to hear? I kept in mind what the physicist John Wheeler said about how an observer comes with predisposed questions to any observation. These predispositions color whatever is seen, heard, or thought during the observation session. After transcribing the tapes, I was then able to look at the words these students were using, analyzing them a little more carefully.

The following excerpts from two planning sessions illustrate how these people were starting to define themselves as teachers. The first exchange is between Maggie and Erica; the second between Christa and Nancy. In their collaborative planning session, Erica asks Maggie, the writer, questions that allow Maggie to define herself as a teacher.

> *Erica (supporter):* Okay, what were you saying?
>
> *Maggie (writer):* When I sat down to compose a letter to my new ninth-grade class, I would think about their feelings in coming in to a whole new environment from a middle school setting or a junior high setting where they were not really babied but taken care of by their teachers more than they are now . . . then think they are coming into this whole new environment . . . ahm, I'll try to be as enthusiastic as possible . . . saying that they'll be starting out a whole new part in their lives. They'll be starting out this whole new experience and that I would support them. I don't know how detailed I would get in this first letter. I would need more.
>
> *Erica:* Well, do you think you would try to give them background about yourself?
>
> *Maggie:* Um uh. I would probably most likely tell them about my family, how long I've been teaching, what made me get interested in English . . . which is not grammar (laugh). Basically because I like writing. . . . I would probably tell them

that. And tell them where I graduated from and what my experiences have been like in school.

From the outset, Maggie presents herself as a teacher who would be concerned about her students' welfare. She says that she "would think about their feelings about coming to a whole new environment from a middle school or junior high setting. . . ." Maggie indicates not only an awareness that her students would be coming into a strange, new environment, but she is also telling me that she is concerned enough about her students that she would make an effort to alleviate some of their anxieties. When she says, "I would support them," Maggie opens a window on what type of teacher she might become. I see her presenting herself as not only a concerned teacher, but also as one who would be supportive of her students in their fears and in their work. She ends this dialogue by stating, "I'll try to be as enthusiastic as possible."

What was poignant for me in listening to Maggie's opening comments is that, as a ninth-grade teacher, I am unconsciously aware of ninth grade being a transition year, but I have not consciously done anything to work with the students in my classroom the way Maggie indicates that she would do. Our school does have a ninth-grade orientation program, but I have done nothing to bolster that in my own classroom. After listening to this tape, I now realize that I should be doing something myself in the classroom to help the ninth graders make a smooth transition to the high school. Not only have I gained some insight into Maggie as a teacher, but I also now have a new window on myself.

In this next excerpt, Maggie discusses giving her students an overview of the course. While most teachers do this, I see this idea fitting into Maggie's concern about how her students see high school as a new experience. By giving them this overview, she would be alerting them to what lies ahead of them for the year.

> *Erica:* What about . . . would you give them any ideas about things you would be covering during the school year . . .
>
> *Maggie:* Probably
>
> *Erica:* . . . about activities during the school year?
>
> *Maggie:* Probably I'd mention what my curriculum would be like . . . ahm . . . like big units we would be doing, like the short story unit, novels that we'd be covering, so they would know what was ahead of them as they started out.

> *Erica:* What about fears or anything they might be having? You said you might, you might talk to them about coming from these other schools . . . or their experiences might be so different? Are you going to talk to them about, you know, being a freshman or, just like experiences that are going to be so new to them and . . .
>
> *Maggie:* I probably would talk to them about, like you said, experiences being new to them . . . and, ahm . . . I . . . how . . . oh, I really don't know . . . ahm I don't know, ask me another question.
>
> *Erica:* OK . . . do . . . you feel that including your own experiences as a freshman in high school would be important to them . . . or do you think that that would be something you would not want to include?
>
> *Maggie:* I'd probably have to think that over. Maybe that wouldn't be a good idea. . . . I would probably try to get them away from being nervous and get them to see what high school is all about. They're too young to go to a prom . . . just like simple things like ahm, the independence . . . they're growing now. They're becoming more independent people and get to, like, sort of be excited about being independent . . .
>
> *Erica:* Having something to look forward to . . .
>
> *Maggie:* . . . and not having mommy and daddy and everybody chasing them around and telling them all these things to do.

When Maggie proposes the idea of a curricular overview, Erica questions her about working with whatever fears the students might have. In looking at Erica for a moment as a prospective teacher, I see this question as something Erica might regard as important for her to work on with her students. Maggie does not know how to respond to Erica's question and just mentions that she would focus on the students' experiences in a new setting. To me, Maggie seemed unprepared to focus on this question right then. Given some time to reflect on it, she might see how she could deal with those fears in a way that would be comfortable for her and comforting for her students.

From later statements in this excerpt, I get a sense of how Maggie would view her students. She sees them as "becoming independent people" who should get excited about becoming independent. I might predict that Maggie would capitalize on this perception by designing activities and lessons that would help promote this growth toward independence. This would help to break the ties to junior high or middle school that she defines when she says ". . . not having mommy and daddy and everyone chasing them around and telling them all these things to do."

In this final excerpt from their planning session, Erica asks Maggie an important question: What point of view or voice was she going to use in her letter? As a planning prompt, Erica's question is getting Maggie to focus on her voice in the letter and on the structure or format of her letter. However, Erica's questions also afford Maggie an opportunity to define herself as a teacher.

> *Erica:* How are you going to approach the actual letter? How do you think you are going to write it? Write from "OK. I'm your teacher" kind of point of view. Or do you write it from "I understand where you're coming from. I was there once. . . . "
>
> *Maggie:* I'd probably write from more of a teacher's point of view. Because I am going to be their teacher and I would set it up like the first paragraph, I would talk about myself. The next paragraph, I would talk about them becoming freshmen. The third paragraph, I would go into what we were going to cover. So I would have, not like, a cool attitude about it, but I would not have a very strict letter like I was . . . it would be sort of casual, but not that . . . you have to keep that teacher-student relationship there.

Maggie's response is the most telling definition of herself as a teacher. She indicates that she would use a teacher's point of view. She does not want a "cool" attitude to pervade her letter, nor does she want a "very strict letter," either. I can see how she struggled to define this relationship a little more carefully, but is able to offer only polarities: not strict, but not that casual. "You have to keep that teacher-student relationship there."

The "defining-myself-as-a-teacher" theme shows up even more prominently in Christa and Nancy's planning session, probably because Christa, the writer, is an older student who is going through a career change. During the course of the semester, she kept asking questions about becoming a teacher and was expressing fears and doubts about her ability to teach and to exude self-confidence. Christa, who was mentored by one of my colleagues at Fox Chapel, had little to worry about. From all that I gathered about Christa and her mentor, Christa had a very successful student-teaching experience; however, in this planning session before her first exposure to the classroom, she is still feeling insecure.

> *Nancy (supporter):* OK. OK. You ready, Christa?

Christa (writer): I think that when I compose this letter, that, that I . . . uhm . . . I would first introduce myself and say "Welcome to ninth grade" at such and such school. And then give my name. But before . . . after I would give my name I would . . . I think I would welcome into a new, you know, if . . . it's a new school. It's a new grade . . .

Nancy: It's a new environment . . .

Christa: Very good! New fears . . . new fears.

Nancy: Good point.

Christa: And things that would. . . . "Do you know where your locker is? Do you know what hall it's in? Do you know where the principal's office is? Do you know where all the rest rooms are? Ahm . . . where the nurse's office is?" And make that transition for them before I would go . . . "Do you know who's in your classes? Do you see familiar faces?"

Nancy: I thought that this was a letter?

Christa: It is.

Nancy: Oh it is?

Christa: This is what I would put this into the letter. . . .

Nancy: Oh. Oh I see. OK. I understand.

Christa: I would put this all into the letter . . . because these things they could ask questions about in class and in discussing that they . . . you know, had worries about, or fears about . . . but were afraid to ask because nobody asked them first.

Nancy: Right.

In this excerpt, Christa emphasizes several times that she wants to alleviate her students' fears and anxieties about being in a new environment, in a new school: Christa expresses concern that her students know their way around the school, and she even wants them to look for familiar faces in order to help them feel more at ease in their new setting. Christa is aware that students may not raise certain anxieties on their own when she says that they might be "afraid to ask because nobody asked them first."

Christa: Then I would go in and introduce myself and my name. . . . Ahm, I don't think its necessary to go into my age. . . .

Nancy: (laughs)

Christa: I don't think its necessary to go into personal stuff or things about myself . . . ahm. . . .

Nancy: Why don't you think its necessary? 'Cause Mr. Benedict was saying he would give personal information or information to questions, you know . . .

Christa: It depends on . . . because, mostly because this . . . this would be sent home to parents. If the kids came into the classroom the next day . . . I may. . . . I guess that's why . . . because I'm sending these home to parents.

Nancy: OK.

Christa: So the parents could see this introduction also and know that I am allowing the kids in this class to express their fears or their anxieties or whatever. But if they would come to class and verbally say "Well, how old are you?" or "Are you married? Do you have any children?" I would answer those things, but not in a formal letter to them. I would explain some of my goals in this letter to this class. I would explain to them in this letter, that I would hope that they would have some . . . some input to give to me from them that would make the class more . . . more fun, more challenging, more creative . . . ahm. . . . I don't know where to go after that. I think I'm a little bit lost there.

In these few exchanges, I see Christa as a teacher who is going to be concerned with both the formality of her classroom presentation and also with the need of her students to know her as more than "just a teacher." Christa is also aware of the fact that there are others involved in the educational process besides the people who are in the room. She looks outside the classroom when she notes that this letter would also be sent home to parents. She is aware that the classroom context involves not only herself and her students, but also parents.

Nancy: Well, (cough) what would some of your personal goals be?

Christa: Ahhhhm . . . let's say that this is a writing course . . . OK, that I was teaching. This is a ninth-grade, you know, writing course.

Nancy: What would be the heading? Would it be English? And then writing? Or just totally a writing course?

Christa: Just writing. Ahhm . . . if this was my homeroom and my English class or my writing course, I think . . . I would go about it completely different. If this was my homeroom . . . I would not deal with the writing aspect. I would go into introduction-fears-anxieties. If this was my homeroom and my writing course, then I would definitely go to my goals, my objectives in this letter. Let's say that this is just my writing course, for now. . . .

Nancy: OK.

Christa: You asked me what my goals . . . see what they can do, see what they can't do. See how their grammar is . . . ahm have them write for me, something very easy, something simple as "What did you do this summer? What do you miss from your old school?" You know. . . .

Nancy: Umhuh.

Christa: Just as a . . . sort of . . . something I can get a sample of how they write. As one of my goals. . . . I don't know if I would put that into my letter though. As a goal I would put, first I would learn where you are at and later you will learn what new skill level you will have to come to.

If Christa's planning session had ended here, I would probably say that her classroom might be more teacher-centered than student-centered. Her focus was on her course, her goals, and so on. I can also see her groping and fidgeting as she tries to find the right words and the right ideas to express. As the planning session evolved, my perception changed.

In this next set of exchanges, Christa moves from her concern about her students being in a new setting to a concern that they might be afraid of the academic tasks that lie ahead of them. She is cognizant of any latent fears they might have about writing or grammar or essay tests. Inherent in her concern over these possible fears, is also a concern about how these fears and anxieties would affect their self-esteem. I came to realize here that my earlier concerns about Christa having a teacher-centered classroom were unfounded.

Nancy: Would you put, like, objectives you would want for them at the end of the year? Things you would want them to come out with?

Christa: To not have a fear of when a teacher says . . . ahm . . . "This will be an essay test." You know . . . "You have a paper due . . . " you know, maybe that would be little subheadings under my intro. . . . I would say things like . . . "Did you ever freeze when the teacher says 'This will be an essay test?' " or "Did you ever get sick and not come to school on the day you know that a five-page paper is due because you don't know how to write?" These are the goals I guess I would want them to learn . . . ahm . . . not be afraid of anything. Also, I want them to not be afraid . . . this is another objective . . . to not be afraid of grammar. We'll work through the grammar aspect of it while they learn how to write. That's it as far as the goals. I think . . . you know . . . I guess I want them

to learn. . . . The big thing with me is self-esteem. I want
them to learn from this letter that they have to like who
they are. They have to like what they write and how they
write it. That will be another thing they can add to their
personality . . . their . . . their . . . I don't know what word I'm
looking for . . . their . . . ahm . . .

Nancy: Attributes?

Christa: "I have nice hair. I have a good singing voice. I can
write a good paper." These are things that they can add to
their person once they realize they are not afraid to do it.

In these exchanges, Christa cycles back to the teacher I was
getting a picture of in the earlier part of her planning session—a
teacher who would work diligently to ensure that her students would
be able to overcome anxieties not just from an academic standpoint,
but also from a personal, self-esteem standpoint. In several discussions
that Christa and I had about teaching and learning, she expressed her
own anxieties as a student and the ways that overcoming them helped
her become a better person. Christa is able to translate her own
personal struggles into her concerns for her students. When she was
student teaching, Christa sometimes mentioned her frustration that
some of her students were not really taking advantage of what was
being offered them, that they wanted to be spoon-fed rather than
work through situations and problems. Because of the way she herself
struggled at times as a student, she felt frustrated when her own
students would give up so readily.

An intriguing thing happens in this final set of exchanges: In
response to Nancy's question about students behavior in the classroom,
Christa moves from talking about her goals to talking about student
goals. She says that she would change from " 'my goals' to 'your
goals' for the class." Just this change in phrasing indicates to me that
Christa envisions a student-centered classroom where students take
ownership in the goals and objectives of the class.

Nancy: What about internal things? What about "I feel confident
that I'm a good listener."

Christa: OK . . . as far as, like, a self-esteem aspect . . . that's
good, that's good. Okay I understand what you're saying
there.

Nancy: Would you put down anything about how you would
expect them to be in the classroom?

Christa: That's a good one. . . . Probably. . . . I would probably
tell them that, you know, as much as they want to be

> respected in a . . . when they speak . . . the other person
> wants to be respected when they speak. We need . . . listening
> skills. I think I would end it by saying if we work hard . . . to
> obtain your goals, not my goals, but your goals, you will be
> a better writer. I would change the objective from "my goals"
> to "your goals" for the class. This letter is something for
> them to obtain . . . not something that I expect.

Nancy: This sounds great. I would love to be in your ninth-
grade class.

Christa: Suuure. Come on in.

The one piece of advice that I might give to Christa at this point is
that she takes the next logical step toward defining herself and her
classroom. I would advise her to move from talking about "your goals"
to talking about "our goals" so everyone, teacher and student, has
some ownership in what happens in the classroom.

Both Maggie and Christa seem to be acutely aware of how
ninth-grade students might feel when coming to a new school, into a
new environment. As they worked through their respective planning
sessions, both indicated that they would try to alleviate those fears as
best they could. Christa's concern seems to grow out of her own
anxieties both about being a student herself and becoming a teacher.
Maggie, Christa, and the other students in the course found themselves
in a context in which they had to imagine themselves in relationship
to their students. Their collaborative planning sessions asked them to
envision what they would be like as teachers in front of a ninth-grade
class for the first time. In constructing their letters, they were also
constructing an image of themselves as teachers.

In one sense, the planning session acted as a mirror for both of
them, allowing them to reflect on themselves as teachers. Maggie and
Christa had to imagine their respective relationships with their students
before they could construct their letters. While we can see the thinking
of a planner as she or he is talking through a paper or letter with a
supporter in a collaborative planning session, we can also glimpse and
glean traits of the writer that allow us a sense of the person behind
the writer. In the cases above, a window opened that allowed me to
see how these two people were thinking about themselves as teachers.
I could then speculate on what type of teachers both Christa and
Maggie might become. They both approached this modeling exercise
seriously enough that I feel that my observations and interpretations
have some grounding in fact.

Martin Heidegger defines the relationship between a teacher and students thus:

> The teacher is ahead of his apprentices in this alone, that he has still far more to learn than they—he has to learn to let them learn. The teacher must be capable of being more teachable than the apprentices. (Cited in Perl and Egendorf, 1986, p. 268.)

In many ways, I see this statement as the underpinning of both Christa and Maggie's grounding as teachers. I was able to catch a glimpse of their defining themselves as teachers through their collaborative planning of a letter to their prospective students. The act of planning led to an act of defining, a process of becoming.

Part II Observations across Contexts

Section 5
Adapting Theory and Research in Community Settings

25 The Community Literacy Center: Bridging Community and School-Based Literate Practices

Wayne C. Peck
Community Literacy Center
Pittsburgh, Pennsylvania

Wayne C. Peck is executive director of the Community Literacy Center (CLC) on Pittsburgh's multicultural, urban north side. Under his leadership, the CLC is arguing for a new vision of literacy as "action, collaboration, and power" by mounting projects such as WRITE and HELP, in which teenagers (often "at risk" in school) use writings to talk about issues that affect their lives, from teen pregnancy and drugs, to housing redevelopment. In his doctoral work in rhetoric at Carnegie Mellon, Wayne combined his 18 years as director of the Community House (home of the CLC) with his questions as an educational researcher: How does "community literacy"—the collaborative, goal-directed, composing for action one finds in an inner-city neighborhood—operate? How does it differ from the academic practices we often associate with literacy? His dissertation study described a successful experiment in helping college student summer volunteers cross those boundaries and enter the rough-and-tumble world of speaking and writing as advocates for children. This memo suggests how collaborative planning became a natural part of the CLC's vision for literacy.

A Discovery Memo

In this discovery memo, I would like to use talk about using literacy as a "tool for real world change" (a phrase borrowed from my colleague Elenore Long) as a point of departure for discussing the role of the Community Literacy Center and the way its agenda has been shaped by our collective inquiry into how writers use collaborative planning in different settings. Specifically, I want to present a portrait of a literacy event in my community and show how watching my neighbor, Bob, *use* literacy to solve his housing problem can expand our current vision of literacy to include a broader range of literate practices that operate within diverse cultural settings like those of the inner city. Knowledge of how literacy functions in specific community settings can help us appreciate more fully the interplay between the social dynamics of literacy practices and the choices that writers make— writers like Rana who is described in Elenore Long's discovery memo later in this section. I am thinking of instances when Rana chose to use more informal neighborhood literacy practices over more formal school-based literacy practices. Perhaps what can emerge from the ongoing work of the CLC is a greater appreciation of the rhetorical choices some writers make from among the literacy options that are available to them in their communities. Before I present the portrait of Bob's literacy event, I want to provide some background information about the CLC and its role and mission.

The CLC: Role and Mission

The Community Literacy Center is a gathering place for people interested in exploring and supporting intercultural issues in the city. The CLC is located in a community center that for 75 years has served a diverse population of inner-city residents in one of Pittsburgh's poorer neighborhoods, adjacent to the bustling downtown business district. The center functions as a crossroads where people from diverse urban neighborhoods and the larger Pittsburgh community encounter each other and come to talk about problems and possibilities in the city. The CLC's agenda supports citizens taking action on such past issues as building better public schools by improving the ways children are taught to write, advocating before city council for decent public housing, and organizing public demonstrations to rid the neighborhood of a porn theater that operates across the street from the city's largest elementary school.

The CLC is also a community-university collaborative between the community center (the Community House) and the Center for the Study of Writing and Literacy at Carnegie Mellon. The first programs of the CLC emerged out of the Making Thinking Visible Project. Its goal was discovering how a group of high school writers would use collaborative planning to develop a brochure in which they presented other neighborhood teens with images of their community more positive than the pervasive negative ones of high crime, poor housing, and rampant drug abuse. From those beginnings, the CLC has become a project site for teaching, research, and community action involving intercultural literacy practices. The CLC's role is to expand current limited visions of literacy to include more possibilities for constructive literacy practice by supporting intercultural literate practices or those occasions in communities when people from diverse backgrounds have to negotiate such practices in order to take action on a community problem. The mission of the CLC is to build understanding of the different ways to be literate in an inner-city context. To do this, we need a new vision of literacy, one broad enough to include the powerful though nontraditional collaborative literacy practices like those of Bob in the following portrait.

Bob: A Community Literate Practice

Bob is my neighbor. His house is located in a narrow and crowded alley that runs parallel to a busy urban thoroughfare in Pittsburgh. Bob is a neighborhood handy man. For years, from the back window of my house overlooking the alley, I have watched Bob repair countless bicycles for neighborhood children who stand waiting impatiently, tapping their feet, eager to be back on their bicycles exploring similar alleys around town. Like the neighborhood children, Bob is a person perpetually in motion. Riding his own bicycle in all kinds of weather, Bob pursues his peculiar avocation. He is a collector of sorts. At first glance, it is possible to mistake Bob for a street person as he pedals frantically through downtown traffic with odd-sized bundles strapped to his bicycle. But there is a logic to what Bob collects. Bob buys his groceries with the money he gets from collecting and selling recyclable materials. Some people in the neighborhood accuse Bob of being a "junk man." There is some truth to their claim: While he does sell some of his collection, much of it he saves. The alley around his house is strewn with treasures that Bob has retrieved from trash disposal points all over the city. Anything that Bob can lift and cart home on his bicycle is fair game to wind up as an asset in his expanding collection.

Bob is a gentle man with a puzzling lifestyle. Having the appearance of a character who has escaped somehow from the pages of a Ken Kesey novel, Bob is middle-aged, "fifty or sixty something," he says. He sports a long, shaggy gray beard and a baseball cap pulled down to his ears. Bob's manner is direct and engaging as he converses with other neighbors who live and work or walk in the alley. Time and again, I have had to learn there is no such thing as having a private conversation with Bob. For no matter what the topic, Bob's deep resonant voice booms forth, echoing off the brick houses in the alley.

A few years ago, a fire destroyed the interior of Bob's house and all his possessions. Rather than choose to go and live in a neighborhood shelter for homeless people, Bob responded to the fire by removing the damaged wall board from within his house. Now all that remains inside his home are charred, bare studs, an empty shell filled with "junk" or "recyclable materials," depending upon your perspective. An overpowering smell of smoke still lingers in Bob's house and permeates his clothes. Without running water or heat in the winter, Bob sleeps in his basement in order to keep warm. From all outward appearances, Bob appears positive, almost upbeat, about his circumstances. His neighbors, though, those people who have known him for years, worry about Bob. They fear he may be losing touch with reality.

Given the condition of his house, it is not surprising that Bob has had many brushes with city housing officials. Numerous complaints have been filed by another alley resident regarding the health and safety hazards created by Bob's style of living. For a number of years, Bob has successfully weathered attempts by city officials to condemn his house by making promises to renovate his home; promises that Bob has yet to fulfill.

A couple of months ago, city housing officials finally took action by dispatching a city work crew with two dump trucks to remove what they considered "refuse" from within Bob's house and from around the alley. As the men from the-city loaded the materials onto their trucks, Bob tried to convince the men that these were indeed the very supplies he needed to renovate his house. Unable to convince the men to desist, Bob became agitated and finally belligerent. The police were called and patrolmen arrived in squad cars with lights flashing and pistols drawn. Bob was arrested and was forced to spend the night in jail.

Given the trauma of the arrest, many of Bob's neighbors were concerned about how Bob would respond once he was freed. Driven by anger, would he make good on the threats he had hurled at the city's officials as the police were carting him away? Or, ashamed and possibly disoriented, would Bob withdraw further into the protective cocoon, the shell his house had become?

Bob surprised us all. Immediately after being freed, instead of withdrawing, Bob began to talk with his neighbors. He began organizing support for himself from other alley residents who, he was convinced, could become similarly disenfranchised. Bob went door to door in the neighborhood, alerting people to the action the housing authority had taken against him and warning them, in conspiratorial tones, "*They* could be next." As he talked with his neighbors, Bob recorded both his thoughts and feelings and those of his neighbors who identified with Bob and were angry about what had happened to him. Moreover, he began to speculate with neighbors about trends in housing in the community and what was happening to the neighborhood as a whole. Wherever he went in the neighborhood, Bob asked questions, he took notes. The pockets of his parka bulged with bits of paper on which he had scribbled key facts he was assembling into a document from which he would argue his case at his upcoming hearing before the city housing board. Bob cajoled a secretary in a neighborhood church to type ongoing drafts of his argument that Bob periodically distributed to residents in the neighborhood asking for input and for ways his case could be strengthened. The latest revision of Bob's document reads as follows:

Appeal to the Housing Authority of the City of Pittsburgh

I have lived here 32 years in that house.

No one wants it to be beautifully restored more than I do.

No one knows more about what it needs to get the job done than I do.

In this declining central city neighborhood 17 houses have already been torn down in my block alone since 1952. Most of the buildings are 100 years old. Speculators and commercial interests eye this area like sharks.

Some have already moved in and are pressing hard on the remaining owner occupied homes. In the entire block there are only five remaining owner occupied houses, all of whom, are, I believe, are now in favor of me.

I have been repeatedly robbed and vandalized.

The local impressionable youth have as role models the invading army of totalitarian plundering pillaging destroyers of my property. What lessons are we teaching them?

Recycling was always desirable, but in recent times has become mandatory, it should be encouraged, not sneered at or derided.

Self-reliance is to me a virtue. My upbringing during the depression made thrift necessary, not just a virtue. To me, the destruction of property valuable to me in restoring my home is not merely wrong, it is abominable, and to seize it at gunpoint, is a violent criminal unjustifiable wrong.

The real battle involved is economic. To force me to pay for a legal defense is to force me to lose—even if I would win the legal battle. Why make it a battle—playing games is not the bottom line answer—we all want the same thing—the betterment of Pittsburgh and citizens that trust the mayor and the administration sufficiently that they do not flee from the suburbs but try to live harmoniously and in peace here in the city.

I ask for two things:

1. An investigation to clarify the issues and clear my name;
2. Reappointment of Ms. Matthews, of the housing clinic, to assist me; she was very valuable and helpful to me in the past and knows the situation and knows that the solution does not lie in merely increasing the pressure and temperature but in getting SOLUTIONS to problems.

With all the help that Bob received from his neighbors who collaborated with him in the writing process, Bob took to describing his document as a "neighborhood manifesto" and convinced other residents to stand with him at his upcoming hearing before the housing authority.

Building Bridges of Understanding through the CLC

Bob's uses of literacy as *a tool for real world change* gives us insight into some of the social dynamics of literacy practice at a grass roots level in the city. As Bob's actions show, a community literacy practice such as organizing support for a case before the city housing officials is a complex (oral and written) one. It grows out of dilemmas in the lives of neighborhood people and depends on a conversational, collaborative process. Bob took the lead in composing himself and his neighbors for action and used his text both to interpret the increasing trend of displacing residents like himself from their homes and to offer a critique of the fairness of the city's policies. Going door to door, first in the alley and then in the community at large, Bob wove a document that invited neighbors to join with him in response to his dilemma and, at the same time, allowed neighbors to voice their own concerns about housing in the community. When I asked him about certain phrases and sentences in his document that did not seem to make sense at first reading, Bob disclosed that certain parts of his text—for instance, the sentence, "The local impressionable youth have as role models the invading army of totalitarian plundering pillaging destroyers of my property"—emerged from a conversation with a neighbor. By placing his voice alongside other voices within his text, Bob created a community document through which others could come and stand with him at the hearing and have a say about what they perceived was happening in the neighborhood.

My purpose in presenting a portrait of Bob's literacy event in this discovery memo has been to draw attention to "hidden literacies," those collaborative literate practices that operate at a grass roots level in urban communities but have yet to be celebrated as literacy per se. One of the roles of the Community Literacy Center in the future will be to make these working literate practices more visible. Perhaps by becoming more aware of the social dynamics in which literate practice operates in the community, classroom teachers can begin to build bridges between collaborative literate practices in the classroom and the practices that operate beyond its walls.

Postscript

Bob's case recently came before the city housing board. A judgment of $1,000 was rendered in Bob's favor. City housing officials are appealing the ruling. A new hearing date has been set.

26 Reflecting on HELP at the Pittsburgh Community Literacy Center

Philip Flynn
Community Literacy Center
Pittsburgh, Pennsylvania

Philip Flynn is director of programs at the Community Literacy Center. He came to this position by an interesting chain of events, after working with Linda Norris as a part of the collaborative planning study mentioned in her project paper, while he was teaching in a north side high school. In his current doctoral work in cultural studies at the University of Pittsburgh, he hopes to situate critical theory in the practical work and exploratory, observational practices of the CLC. As a long-time community activist and coordinator of sports and community service programs for youth, Phil saw collaborative planning as part of the larger process of "action and reflection" behind the HELP project he describes below.

A Discovery Memo

Note to Readers

If action is the lifeblood of community literacy projects, then reflection is certainly the circulating pump that ensures the health and vitality of the work we do as community educators. Post-action reflection is an opportunity to interrogate ourselves in a productive way, to ask the kinds of questions that can enable us to continue to be effective planners and teachers of innovative community learning projects. Each project at the Community Literacy Center is rigorously and systematically evaluated upon completion, and our reflections often take the form of written explorations of key aspects of individual projects. We ask ourselves what we have done well, what we could have done better, where and when were the significant critical incidents taking place over the course of the projects. How well did we plan? How well did we adapt when things did not go as we planned? Did we achieve the kinds of learning outcomes we had intended to achieve? What kinds of relationships did we build? How do the students feel about having worked in the project? Did we set realistic goals, and were we able to meet them? Any or all of these kinds of concerns can be addressed in a post-action reflection.

I want to share with you the reflection I wrote after I had finished my first Summer HELP project. The Housing Empowerment and Literacy Project was a pilot effort to combine literacy and action in community work that would help teenagers and an even more often neglected segment of the population, senior citizens. This reflection was written as an internal evaluative document to be discussed with the other members of the Community Literacy Center as a basis for planning the next project. Another purpose was to discover what kinds of literacy practices were taking place in the course of the eight-week project and to identify what was unique and valuable about the kinds of literacies that are possible in a community context.

The first Summer HELP project of the Community Literacy Center concluded with a public celebration, a community conversation that included Pittsburgh Mayor Sophie Masloff, State Representative Tom Murphy, as well as other city and school district officials. At the reception following the dedication ceremony at the Perry South Senior Center, Fay, a patron of the Senior Center, remarked to me, "This is a real pleasant surprise. I didn't think teenagers could be like this anymore."

Fay had good reason to be surprised, for she was witness to the culmination of a remarkable community project executed by urban teenagers over an eight-week period that summer. During those eight weeks, eight teenagers had planned and built a landscaped courtyard at the Senior Center, complete with steps and railings, an attractive walkway, trellises, and a new bench. They had planted eight new full-size trees as well. What is more, these same teenagers had written an impressive eight-page newsletter that they published and distributed at the community dedication ceremony and reception. The community gathering itself was impressive; the eight teenagers had planned and conducted the celebration attended by more than 100 people. One thing is clear—there was a whole lot of literacy going on in those eight weeks.

It will be difficult to assess all of the literacy practices that were engaged in during the course of this eight-week project, but I will try to evaluate some of them. I propose to assess four basic components of the Summer HELP project: work, writing, interaction, and pedagogy.

Work

The physical labor turned out to be a problem. Not only did we overextend ourselves by taking on a task that required sophisticated carpentry skills, but we picked a difficult site. Simple tasks such as digging a hole for a tree became monumental work projects that required three or four people using pry bars, a mattock, a pick, and two kinds of shovels. It took one of our four-person crews three hours to dig one of these holes. We were truly fortunate to get help from a group of students at Oliver High School who were looking for some work and who joined us in the fifth week of the project. These students dug a lot of holes and put in a lot of time and labor on this part of the project.

The HELP kids could not do all of the carpentry tasks that the project required, especially potentially dangerous ones that involved large power tools, and so a carpenter-mentor and our construction coordinator did a lot of things for them. The kids did not mind that they were getting help, but we have to remember that the adults need no practice, and our budget would not stand the strain of paying for the long hours a carpenter-mentor must put in on this type of project. In the future we will be wise to limit the amount of advanced carpentry work that will be necessary to complete a project. We thought it was important that this first HELP project be successful in every way, so this time we could justify spending the extra money and putting in the extra time. It is probably smart to remember, too, that we are not primarily interested in teaching students how to use power tools or to learn extensive building trades skills. We are not a "jobs" program, nor are we an apprentice program for the building trades. An elementary but clear understanding of the rudiments of using basic tools is useful for everyone, though, and all of the HELP kids seem to have made real progress in this area.

Writing

Creating the eight-page newsletter turned out to be the most interesting part of the project for me. I watched the kids' attitudes toward writing evolve over the eight weeks, beginning with a general reluctance to write and gradually moving toward a basic tolerance of writing. Then, as the building part of the project progressed, the team members became more interested in telling about what they were doing and how they thought it might be valuable to others. Clearly, the kids needed to believe in their work in order to write with feeling, to write with the sort of commitment that comes from a clear sense of purpose. Drafts of their segment of the final newsletter started to emerge as their goals gained clarity and finally came together toward the end in a spirited flurry of revision with the adult mentors.

Now that the project is finished, we have a newsletter that we all can be proud of; it has been fascinating to hear the reactions of the participants as they show other people the HELP document. All of them seem to be proud of helping to produce such an attractive and impressive piece of writing. Linda Flower talks about the power of writing, which most of us can appreciate. But most teenagers have not had the opportunity to experience that power first hand. For many of them, school writing has been a succession of random assignments based on an assigned text that was selected by someone else. More often than not, these writing activities have had little connection to their lives outside of school. As the HELP document is passed around to family members, friends, teachers, and school officials, these eight inner-city students are beginning to understand that the things they write can make a difference in their own lives. Now that they have a newsletter that they planned and produced themselves, this sense of power is becoming real. Most of the people they know will not be able to see the work they have done at the Senior Center, but they will be able to see their work through their newsletter. It *is* a powerful document if it is read carefully. These teenagers are starting to get some genuine recognition as a result of the writing they did during the Summer HELP project. This recognition, I think, also helps them understand what we mean when we talk about the power of writing.

We have a lot of writing resources we can tap at the CLC; we used some of them in this project. We took advantage of the fact that the Research Associates from the Center for the Study of Writing at Carnegie Mellon bring an abundance of writing experience to the CLC. Lorraine Higgins used her experience in public relations to conduct a successful session writing a news release (it must have worked, judging from the impressive media response to the release composed by two student writers, Ronrieka and Theresa). When Pam Turley, a composition instructor at the Community College of Allegheny County, related the story of the "shock effect" suffered by new students when they begin writing in college after a high school writing career full of term papers and five-paragraph themes, the kids were all ears. They were relieved to hear that the sort of writing they were doing for the HELP project was a lot like the problem-oriented writing tasks they would be asked to do in college.

Having available six or seven writing professionals who are all proficient in using collaborative planning is probably the most valuable resource the CLC has at its disposal. Staff and associates were able to serve as supporters for Kelly and Monita, two HELP writers, as they generated a plan that served them throughout three revisions. When Rondale, another student writer, was stalled and "couldn't think of anything else to say" midway through his section, collaborative planning supporters were able to help him extend and clarify his section in the newsletter by simply asking him, over and again, to "explain what you mean by that." All of the writers thrived with the considerable support and attention their planning and writing could get as a result of one-to-one collaborative planning. Even with the attendance problems that we managed to ride out in the middle of the writing activities, we were able to work quickly and effectively because each writing pair had at least one adult supporter for each writing session. Collaborative writing is well suited to this sort of problem-posing and problem-solving instruction.

Using adult supporters as mentors in our projects appeals to me for a number of reasons. First, it allows us to invite interested writing professionals into the CLC to share in our work. Second, our writers benefit from a lot of close attention that is difficult to duplicate in most other settings. Third, it enables us to use collaborative planning efficiently in our writing projects with teachers who have already used collaborative planning successfully in classrooms. We can refine this process to work even more effectively for us and the writers in future projects.

Interaction

Teenagers who worked on the HELP project interacted with all sorts of people and situations that were new to them. At first, some of them related to me as they might relate to their English teacher (maybe because some of them knew me as an English teacher at their high school). But this arrangement changed gradually over the eight weeks of the project as we planned the design, dug holes, pounded boards, lugged around heavy trees, and did many more non-school tasks together. Soon they were acting as if I were a normal human being.

Very early in the project, the HELP team members had to figure out a way to adapt to HELP Construction Coordinator Kevin Mc-Cartan's blindness. They did this quickly as they learned to joke about Hondo, Kevin's seeing-eye dog, and Kevin put them at ease by laughing with them. It was clear as the weeks went by that the teenagers respected Kevin's uncanny ability to "see" details related to building and design. They began to rely on his expertise as a former professional contractor and community developer whenever construction problems arose. Kevin could explain in exhaustive detail what measures needed to be taken, and the team members never hesitated to consult Kevin. (Even on "writing days" when Kevin would be at the site preparing for the next day's work, they wanted to know where he was.)

Kevin led the HELP team through an especially productive and instructive session when they priced materials using the plans we had worked up in consultation with an architect. They worked up a lot of enthusiasm in this session, and they managed to estimate costs of materials within twenty dollars of the amount we would actually spend on the project ($2,200.00). It was during this session that I heard one teenager remark to another, "Wow, I never thought I'd have to use geometry after the tenth grade!" We would often hear comments similar to this at the building site.

Working with the architect was another novel interactive experience. It helped that our architect, Diane LaBelle, characterized her job as "90 percent planning" because this assertion impressed the HELP kids with the essential nature of planning in a working professional's context. It was interesting to watch as HELP team members very quickly got comfortable with the architect's drawings. They were eager to revise the original set of drawings on their own copies; many of them added features we had not thought of. They had suggested we begin with two sets of drawings of the site: a "simple" version of the features we could build on the site, and a more elaborate set of features that were more interesting visually, but also substantially more difficult to build. Clearly, they enjoyed working with the two separate sets of plans; their copies of the plans seemed to take on the character of a chalkboard they could draw on. They were not afraid to dream a little bit on these copies of the plans, and offered a number of novel ideas for the site. Diane was patient in explaining why she planned the way she did, and she was glad to agree to all of the changes that the HELP team prescribed. All of this planning was taking place on paper away from the actual site. But everything changed when we took them to see the site for the first time. This was the first critical point of instruction for all of us.

This was an occasion for writing to flex its muscles for most of the team members. In the session directly after our initial visit to the site, we had what might have been our best session of the eight weeks. This was one of those wonderful occasions when discord led to insight. The disjunction came about because prior to visiting the site we had been working exclusively on a set of architect's drawings—drawings done in rich colors and sharp precision—in contrast to the downright cruddy reality of the actual space we were going to build in. The actual site was much smaller than they had imagined, and the rubble and weeds that dominated the space were not represented on Diane's site plans. When we reflected on the reasons for this disparity in perceptions, we began to realize that Diane was not "on drugs" (as some of the teenagers had exclaimed upon first seeing the site), but that although her plans were drawn to scale (1/4 inch = 1 foot), they were not meant to render a faithful "snapshot" of the space. We needed to learn how to "read" this scale and "see" that the site would look different after we worked to make it look different. The skeptics got the architect's rule out and checked Diane's drawings (we found a few small discrepancies), but we all learned a valuable lesson—site drawings only approximate the real thing (what you see is *not* what you get).

It helped for everyone to register their reactions to this experience through writing. We started by writing down our impressions as we saw the site for the first time. As we were writing, many of us began to work out *why* we reacted the way we did. We shared our written work with the group; the discussion that accompanied the writing helped all of us understand the work that lay ahead of us and reaffirmed our commitment to successfully complete the project. But we needed to become conscious of our doubts and reservations, and this writing occasion provided that opportunity. (In this instance, talking and writing complemented each other; writing made talking about the problem easier.)

We were also fortunate to have the services of a tree expert, Fred Galvez of Parklets for Pittsburgh, who showed us the right way to plant new trees and explained the kinds of things we needed to do to ensure that the trees would grow and last over time. The HELP team learned that we needed a plan for choosing the location and properly planting the trees we placed at the site. Again, the essential nature of planning was clear and the HELP team was beginning to believe that anything worth doing was worth planning carefully.

Pedagogy

What sort of pedagogical strategies did we use in a community literacy project? We had students who were coming from a full year of classroom instruction to work on the HELP project. I knew that this could not be like school; this would have to be different. I was new to the CLC, but I knew there was support for an approach to teaching that empowered learners to direct themselves in a structured environment that offered learners support rather than imposing constraints on them. This meant that when we asked questions, we really did not know the answers. Some people's ideas counted more than others at various times—but only for good reasons, like "I've done this before, and last time . . ." or "I measured that part and it's not long enough. . . ." No one pronounced from on high.

What roles did the project leaders assume? Certainly we were co-learners, as most of us were finding out a lot of things with the students as we went along. We were planners too, as we tried to figure out ways to allow good things to happen in each of the twice-a-week sessions. We were writers as we wrote with the students in each phase of the project. We were friendly adults, not an insignificant role for teenagers whose interactions with adults are frequently hostile. But we were teachers, too.

We are all teachers. It is easy to lose sight of this in the middle of a community project such as the Summer HELP project. I think this happens partly because we shed our traditional notions of "teacher" in this kind of work; we are truly co-learners in a project such as the Perry South Senior Center. I feel more like an organizer when I am working with groups like this one. Decision making is a shared activity, goals are set by consensus, and conditions of work are negotiated. During the Summer HELP project, a real Freirian "dialogue" was enacted as the adults were forced to abandon their "expert" stance for one that fit the occasion—we were people together working to a common end, an end we had worked out together. We were real partners in community learning.

27 Rana's Reflections . . . and Some of My Own: Writing at the Community Literacy Center

Elenore Long
Carnegie Mellon University
Pittsburgh, Pennsylvania

Elenore Long is a researcher with the Center for the Study of Writing and Literacy at Carnegie Mellon. Her work with collaborative planning led her to the Community Literacy Center as a place where the teaching of writing, linked with research in literacy, was dedicated to substantive, local social change. Her dissertation is a study of the Carnegie Mellon mentors who are working as collaborative planning supporters for teenage CLC writers. It tracks the ways these two groups—with their different images and expectations of writing—negotiate these different discourse conventions and come to understand the practice of community literacy. Elenore's memo, written about one of the early pilot projects at the CLC, documents a young woman's emerging view of her own text as a context for action.

A Discovery Memo

In a recent newsletter, directors at the Community Literacy Center explained that "planning, writing, reading, and taking action at a community level enable teenagers to make connections between literacy and community involvement" (*Community*, 1991, p. 2). Literacy and community involvement merge, for instance, when teens like Rana use writing first to analyze some of the challenges they face as urban youth and then to initiate a conversation that fosters support from leaders in the community regarding those issues. Emphasizing that purposeful literacy is tied to real-world action, the CLC works to build a context for change, both by enriching the ways people think of literacy and by making physical changes in the neighborhood through literate action, changes such as the addition of a community garden or the elimination of a porn theater next to an elementary school.

My comments here focus on the reflections of a teenage writer named Rana. I am suggesting that Rana's reflections indicate that her own use of written language parallels the goals of the center: Both strive to build contexts for change. As I bring my own reflection to a close, I will discuss what I see as a challenge, not only for Rana but also for people like me who plan literacy programs at such places as the CLC.

Each semester the center sponsors a WRITE project, involving eight to twelve high school students who meet twice a week for several months to research and to write about issues that affect their lives, such as teen pregnancy, street-corner hang-outs and their alternatives, and problem solving in the workplace. Together, collaborative planning and reflection are used at the center not solely to promote text production but also to foster awareness about oneself as a thinker and writer. In each project, collaborative planning serves to support and structure writers' plans for a text in progress; reflection helps writers articulate their goals, examine plans for achieving those goals, anticipate difficulties, and reconcile competing ideas (cf. Bereiter & Scardamalia, 1987; Flower & Hayes, 1980; 1981).

This memo is in response to a discourse-based interview I had recently with Rana in which she reflected on the writing and thinking she had done as a member of two literacy projects. This interview was characterized by prompts requesting Rana to read segments of her text and to discuss the goals, options, and obstacles that she considered to be connected with that piece of writing (Odell, Goswami & Herrington, 1983). What Rana's reflection illuminates is her literate awareness at work. We get her story of how she constructed textual cues designed to bring about change, specifically, changes in her readers' attitudes and actions.

Both of the projects in which Rana participated focused on the issue of teen pregnancy. In Allegheny County, the county in which the Center for Community Literacy is located and in which Rana lives, the rate of teen pregnancy is one of the highest in the nation. The effects of such a high teen pregnancy rate are highly problematic. Statistics from the Family Health Council of Allegheny County (1987) reveal that infant mortality is highest among infants born to teen mothers. Statistically, it is rare for teen mothers to finish high school;

it is common, on the other hand, for teen mothers to remain dependent upon public support. Rana was first involved in the Teen Stories Project, which entailed interviewing teen parents and writing their stories. Then Rana was involved in the Issues & Information Project, in which the team of writers used interviews to identify primary questions that teen mothers had about parenting. After researching issues of child development, nutrition, and parenting skills, the writers published an informational booklet addressed to these young parents—a resource pamphlet for teens by teens.

A Question of Godliness: Transforming Textual Information

Rana's story as a member of Teen Stories Project began when she heard her own disregard for teen parents voiced even more strongly by a member of her community. At the beginning of the project, Rana's own view of teen parents was less than compassionate: "At the beginning, I thought they were stupid and I was brushing them off. But I never got in depth as to why they were pregnant. I just though they were stupid." Through a survey distributed to the congregation of a nearby church, members of Teen Stories Project investigated how many neighborhood residents viewed the issue. Of all the responses to the surveys, that of a woman named Nan rose to the top for being the most opinionated. Rana described Nan's response to the survey:

> She turned it [the survey] in and everything on hers was negative. Everything was bad. Nan just dogged them [teen mothers]. She said they were stupid. She just went on and on. Everything was negative. And I was like . . . I thought the same thing, but I didn't think it could be that bad.

Nan's extreme stance made Rana question her own position. As a result, she began to defend the teen mothers whom Nan had condemned outright. Rana explained in the interview that after doing research, which involved interviewing teen mothers from the neighborhood, her own views and those of other members on the Teen Stories Project began to change: "We did our research, and we began to see that it wasn't like that. It was nowhere near to what Nan said."

Through the confrontation with Nan's views on teen pregnancy, an exigency emerged for the project's brochure, *Teen Pregnancy*. The general purpose of the brochure, Rana explained during the interview, was "to . . . tell the stories of teen mothers to people who thought it was all bad." So, as Rana commented, the audience for the brochure included more readers than just Nan. Rather, Nan's response to the survey worked to represent a larger, more general audience. And, as that conception of audience was stretched, it became more diversified and less concrete. In Rana's words, the brochure was directed at "people who didn't think anything could come out of it [teen pregnancy]."

Rana described her role in WRITE's Teen Stories Project as encompassing, on a larger scale, her role as a member of her community; likewise, her conception of the audience stemmed from her conceptions of the community:

> [I]n this community, there are old people, well, I hate to say old people, there are people who think, every time they see a pregnant teen walk by their house and they say, oh, she's bad. And like I wanted them to think, "Well, maybe she's not so bad."

For Rana, public disregard for teen mothers was an injustice. She articulated the end she hoped to achieve through her text: "To stop it [the public disregard]. Because they [teen mothers] aren't all bad people. It's a stereotype. They get thought of in that way just because. It's wrong." As Rana's comments made clear, the rationale behind the purpose for her text in the *Teen Pregnancy* brochure, which she called "Tammi's Story," was intimately tied to her conceptions of her audience. For her as a writer, the purpose and audience formed the context in which she began to compose her text.

During her reflection, Rana pointed to several places in her text where she found herself talking to Nan (and those that Nan represented) most directly. The first passage described Tammi as a particular kind of high school student: (The text is italicized to indicate Rana's written prose.)

> *Tammi Thomas . . . was very popular and on almost every committee, club, and team possible, both in school and at the church she attended every Sunday. She was a model for Gimbels Department Store, had a B+ grade average in school, her first real boyfriend, and a family that loved and supported her. . . .*

She then explained her rationale for beginning the story with, essentially, a list of Tammi's "credentials":

> When I said she was popular, on every committee and team. All that stuff. Nice family. Some people think that only people who get pregnant are those that didn't have anything else to do. And that were dumb and, you know, weren't going anywhere. But she was smart and she had a nice family.

Asked to state the argument framing this part of "Tammi's Story," Rana responded:

> It could happen to anybody. Not just dumb people or people
> they consider to be dumb, so to help people understand better.
> Not just say, "Okay. Oh, she's dumb," or something like that.

For Rana, information regarding Tammi's life before and after she had her child provided much more than a way of describing Tammi. Material from the interviews provided rich ways of prompting her readers to build a new context for thinking about the biases they may have been holding against teen mothers. Getting her audience to build that new context and to begin changing their stereotypical images of teen mothers went hand in hand.

Rana cited a final place in her text where she had focused her prose to respond to the people whom Nan had come to represent. The passage works perhaps more subtly than the other sections she had identified. The text she pointed to (in bold below) is embedded within a larger paragraph.

> *She got pregnant. Yes, pregnant, and she didn't know what do do.
> She had never talked with her parents about sex or anything that
> had to do with sex. What had happened? She didn't know, one thing
> that she knew, however, was that she wasn't going to give the baby
> up; nor was she going to let it ruin her life. **She figured that
> since it had happened it must have been something God
> wanted, something that was meant to be. God was the head
> of her life and she thought, who was she to rebel?***

During Rana's reflection, she explained that this passage regarding Tammi's religious perspective linked back to the first paragraph. In the earlier passage she had made sure to include that Tammi was not only a member of a church, but also that she attended every Sunday. For Rana, this information regarding Tammi served a rhetorically powerful purpose:

> Tammi said it was something God wanted. She wasn't going to
> do anything [like have an abortion]. . . . And the lady [Nan],
> she goes to church, and she's suppose to be godly or whatever,
> and she's thinking, "Well, you wouldn't do that if you were
> godly," but Tammi *was*. . . . She went to church. I wasn't going
> to leave this part out. It would mean a lot to people in the
> church.

It appears from Rana's above commentary that the juxtaposition of Nan's survey and Tammi's interviews prompted Rana to speculate on Nan's position on God, sex, and teen pregnancy. Rana speculated that the stance Nan voiced in her survey response extended to include the position that young women "wouldn't do that if [they] were godly." In selecting parts of Tammi's interview that challenged this stance, Rana apparently used a strategy to spur her readers to confront the falsity of those premises which they perhaps had held to be true.

Asked to read "Tammi's Story" from Nan's perspective, Rana mentioned what might be Nan's response: "She might say, 'This is just her. Everyone else. This might just be an exception. . . . Not everyone else is like this.' " Rana realized the limits of "Tammi's Story" as an argument to persuade her audience to change its views regarding teen pregnancy. Indeed, the limitation Rana cited parallels the drawback often cited within academic communities when a researcher attempts to generalize from a case study. But so does her response to counter the criticism. The numerous stories within the *Teen Pregnancy* brochure portray the lives of many teen parents. No one story is the same. Indeed, Tammi's story is much happier and more inspiring than one condensed from a troubling interview with an apparently confused and lonely fifteen-year-old mother. Collected together, however, individual descriptions become especially significant. In the case of the *Teen Pregnancy* brochure, they challenge the notion that one blanket response is adequate to respond to and understand the situations of teen mothers in Rana and Nan's community. Getting her audience to recognize this inadequacy is what Rana's version of "Tammi's Story" is all about.

Employing Text Conventions: Motivating Action

Rana's choice of text conventions, especially rhetorical questions, makes her prose read interactively. As Rana explained during the interview, these conventions work to energize her texts with a dynamic more typical of oral discourse:

> I think about talking . . . out loud . . . because . . . when you talk, you use your voice more than when you write. There's more that you can do with your voice than with a pencil. So when I write I have to put on little things to make it have more . . . you know, voice. That's how come I put in little things. So when it's going through their heads, they're making it sound this certain way.

Rana credited a teen magazine, *Sassy*, with teaching her these techniques, a magazine, she was quick to comment, that is not "for dumb, oh, how-does-my-hair-look girls but for intelligent teens who care about what's going on." What Rana's extended reflection made clear, however, is that she had expectations for the text conventions she employed that went beyond getting a text to "sound a certain way . . . when it's going through [a reader's] head." Those expectations relate directly to her sense of the audience and purpose for each text. Rana explained that in writing "Tammi's Story" she used rhetorical questions to make readers confront their "built-in" expectations about teen parents. Rhetorical questions (in bold below) are crafted into two passages of the story. One passage is embedded in the paragraph describing Tammi's credentials as a "together teen":

> *She was a model . . . had B+ average in school, her first real boyfriend, and a family that loved and supported her. . . . **This sounds like the perfect teen, doesn't it?***

The other passage is in the paragraph that announces Tammi's pregnancy and her decision to keep the baby: *"She got pregnant. . . . **What happened?** She didn't know . . . "* During the interview, Rana articulated the rationale behind these questions:

> I asked them questions to get them interested because they might have had their own little thing about what happened. *And I gave an answer that was probably totally different from what they thought* [emphasis added].

These prompts, then, model on a small scale what the entire story works to achieve. Both the questions and "Tammi's Story" itself work to provoke readers to acknowledge and question their preconceived biases regarding teen pregnancy.

Regarding the texts Rana wrote for the Issues & Information Project, rhetorical questions not only make these pieces more like interactive discourse, but, according to Rana, they also serve another function—one not called for in the *Teen Pregnancy* articles. The difference in function has to do with the difference in audience and purpose. In the interview, Rana described the audiences for the two texts. For *Teen Pregnancy,* she explained, the writers "were talking to the grown-ups that thought it was bad." But in the Issues & Information Project brochure, *Teen Parents: Questions and Answers,* the writers "talked to the actual teens." Rana continued to describe the purpose behind this document addressed to teen parents:

> [T]o help pregnant teens get back on their feet. They had fallen, or whatever, and we're helping to get them back on their feet, so later on they can help themselves. So that they could be more like what we saw in [Issues & Information Project brochure,

Teen Parents: Questions and Answers], more like the [positive] stories we gave. And make their lives better.

Ostensibly, *Teen Parents: Questions and Answers* simply provides readers with the information in which they had indicated an interest. However, as Rana explained during the interview, to her "help[ing] pregnant teens get back on their feet" required more than simply being some go-between in an information transaction. It required building a context that would encourage the audience to make use of the information provided. "Encouragement," Rana explained, "I think they [teen mothers] can use all the encouragement they can get."

The passage below is one example of how Rana prompted a response from her audience. (The rhetorical question is in bold.):

The Neighborhood Tenants Reorganization is an organization that encourages home ownership. It is not specifically designed for teen parents, but it is original, creative, and worth checking out. In order to qualify for this program you must be at least 18 years old, if not 18 then at least 16 and emancipated or "on your own," financially independent (from parents or guardians), low income, and you must have a child. **Got it?**

Rana explained her rationale behind using the question:

Usually you just get information. That's all you see. You just read, and read, and read. And it's up to you to get it all. This lets them [readers] stop and gives them a rest, and asks if they "got it."

From Rana's perspective, adding the question, "Got it?" was a way of encouraging her audience to make sense of—and to use—the material she was presenting. Asked to anticipate her audience's response to the question, Rana continued:

I would probably think, "Wow, she wants me to get it." She cares. I mean [laughter] she cares if I get it or not.

Rana explained that the response she anticipated from her audience was connected to her own experience as a reader working to make sense of the prose:

That little "eighteen if not eighteen, sixteen and emancipated." That was a lot, too. That's really why. Because it was like, that whole concept was confusing to me—who was writing it down. . . . When I was checking over it and I read "got it," I stopped to check that I "had it." [laughter] It was a lot.

As a teen herself, Rana indicated more of a tendency when reflecting on *Teen Parents: Questions and Answers* to merge her own experiences as a reader with those responses she expected from her own audience. As Rana described them, rhetorical questions and other interjections work as textual cues urging readers to take the provided information and to put it to use. For Rana, getting her readers to decode her text was not enough. Through her use of text conventions, she worked to motivate teen parents to take action—to make the phone calls, to take the steps, to put the information from her texts to use.

Conclusion

Within her texts, Rana constructs contexts for change, contexts that aim to change the reader's view of the issue or the reader's sense of herself as an active, assertive problem solver. For Rana, this literate activity has required her to integrate what she knows from writing at school, the text conventions she has noticed while reading at home, and strategies such as collaborative planning and reflection that she has learned to use at the Community Literacy Center.

Yet Rana's reflection brings to the fore a disturbing question regarding her prose style. What she articulates are the presumptions she has made—and hopes her readers to make—while interpreting what she has written. Rana's reflection at this point, however, considers only hypothetical readers, products of her own imagination. Neither Rana nor I know how the actual readers whom she intended to reach would actually interpret her texts. I do know, however, that at least a couple of readers, albeit older and from backgrounds different from Rana's targeted audience for *Teen Parents: Questions and Answers,* responded negatively to the comment, "Got it!" These readers considered the comment to be condescending, to set up a patronizing artifice between Rana and her readers. If additional readers, especially those whom Rana thought she would affect, would find the comment offensive and off-putting, Rana, especially as a writer striving for change, would be in for real trouble. In instances such as the textual cue isolated here, she may be creating an effect contrary to the one she intended.

But I am going to emphasize that what we do get from Rana is confirmation that she sees her writing as a tool for making changes. This may be a first and critical step in developing an empowering relationship with written language. Furthermore, such a perspective may sustain her as she works toward another step: that of learning to negotiate meaning with real—not just hypothetical—readers. Yet if the CLC is to foster literate action effectively directed at real-world change, then it may need to do more. It may need to extend provisions to include a context in which Rana can experience and explore the presumptions that real-world readers bring to her text. As someone who is in on some of the planning of literacy projects at the CLC, I know how difficult it is to work in that response from intended readers. Several times we have scheduled activities aimed at hearing from real-world readers. But as time runs short (and it always does), those activities are some of the first to go. They require contacting still more people and complicating the revision process, which the young writers already find arduous. I am beginning to see now that it may be important for us to reconsider our priorities when we pare down our plans for literacy projects.

And I am realizing that, for Rana, the study of how various readers respond and use her text would most assuredly take her on a journey that confronts the social rules that, as Gumperz (1982) writes, "reward or punish, reinforce or sanction verbal behavior" (p. 203). I am beginning to see that such a study, though one that most assuredly will be fraught with frustrations, obstacles, and that will confront many injustices, may in the long run be necessary to provide Rana with the rhetorical options required to instigate real changes in her neighborhood. Thus, perhaps it is during such an exploration that Rana would most benefit from the kinds of support the CLC has to offer.

Works Cited

Aston, J., Norris, L., & Turley, P. (Eds.). (1991). *Collaborative planning: Concepts, processes, and assignments.* Pittsburgh, PA: Center for the Study of Writing at Carnegie Mellon. (ERIC Document Reproduction Service No. ED 334 594)

Atwell, N. (January, 1982). Class-based writing research: Teachers learn from students. *English Journal, 71,* 84–87.

Barnes, D. (1990). Oral language and learning. In S. Hynds & D. L. Rubin (Eds.), *Perspectives on talk and learning* (pp. 41–54). Urbana, IL: National Council of Teachers of English.

Bartlett, F.C. (1932). *Remembering: A study in experimental and social psychology.* Cambridge: Cambridge University Press.

Benedict, M.A. (1991). The right metaphor. In J.A. Aston, L. Norris, & P. Turley (Eds.), *Collaborative planning: Concepts, processes, and assignments, a casebook* (pp. 49–59). Pittsburgh, PA: National Center for the Study of Writing and Literacy at Carnegie Mellon. (ERIC Document Reproduction No. ED 334 594)

Bereiter, C., & Scardamalia, M. (1987). *The psychology of written communication.* Hillsdale, NJ: Erlbaum.

Bissex, G.L., & Bullock, R.H. (1987). *Seeing for ourselves: Case-study research by teachers of writing.* Portsmouth, NH: Heinemann.

Brown, A.L. (1978). Knowing when, where, and how to remember: A problem of metacognition. In R. Glaser (Ed.), *Advances in instructional psychology, volume 1* (pp. 77–167). Hillsdale, NJ: Erlbaum.

Bruffee, K.A. (1984). Collaborative learning and the "conversation of mankind." *College English, 46,* 635–52.

Bruffee, K.A. (1985). *A short course in writing.* Boston: Little, Brown.

Bruner, J. (1978). The role of dialogue in language acquisition. In A. Sinclair, R.J. Jarvella, & J.M. Levelt (Eds.), *The child's conception of language* (pp. 241–56). Berlin: Springer-Verlag.

Burnett, R.E. (1990). Benefits of collaborative planning in the business communication classroom. *The Bulletin of the Association for Business Communication, 53*(2), 9–17.

Burnett, R.E. (1991). *Conflict in the collaborative planning of coauthors: How substantive conflict, representation of task, and dominance relate to high-quality documents.* (Doctoral dissertation, Carnegie Mellon University, 1991). *Dissertation Abstracts International, 52.4:* p. 1286-A.

Burnett, R.E. (1993). Conflict in collaborative decision-making. In N.R. Blyler & C. Thralls (Eds.), *Professional communication: The Social Perspective* (pp. 144–62). Newbury, CA: Sage.

Burtis, P.J., Bereiter, C., Scardamalia, M., & Tetroe, J. (1983). The development of planning in writing. In B.M. Kroll & G. Wells (Eds.), *Explorations in the development of writing* (pp. 153–174). Chicester, England: John Wiley & Sons.

Calderhead, J. (1991). The nature and growth of knowledge in student teaching. *Teaching & Teacher Education, 7,* 531–55.

Calderhead, J., & Robson, M. (1991). Images of teaching: Student teachers' early conceptions of classroom practice. *Teaching & Teacher Education, 7,* 1–8.

Calkins, L.M. (1985). Forming research communities among naturalistic researchers. In B.W. McClelland & T.R. Donovan (Eds.), *Perspectives on research and scholarship in composition* (pp. 125–44). New York: Modern Language Association of America.

Carey, L., & Flower, L. (1989). Foundations for creativity in the writing process: Rhetorical representations of ill-defined problems. In J.A. Glover, R.R. Ronning, & C.R. Reynolds (Eds.), *Handbook of creativity* (pp. 283–303). New York: Plenum Press.

Clandinin, D.J. (1986). *Classroom practice: Teacher images in action.* London: The Falmer Press.

Clifford, J. (1981). Composing in stages: The effects of a collaborative pedagogy. *Research in the Teaching of English, 15,* 37–53.

Collins, A., Brown, J.S., & Newman, S.E. (1989). Cognitive apprenticeship: Teaching the craft of reading, writing, and mathematics. In L.B. Resnick (Ed.), *Knowing, learning, and instruction: Essays in honor of Robert Glaser* (pp. 453–94). Hillsdale, NJ: Erlbaum.

Community literacy center: A community-university collaborative. (October, 1991). (Available from Wayne Peck, Executive Director, 801 Union Avenue, Pittsburgh, PA 15212).

Daly, J.A. (1979). Writing apprehension in the classroom: Teacher role expectancies of the apprehensive writer. *Research in the Teaching of English, 13,* 37–44.

Daly, J.A., & Miller, M.D. (1975). Further studies in writing apprehension: SAT sources, success expectations, willingness to take advanced courses, and sex differences. *Research in the Teaching of English, 9,* 250–56.

DiPardo, A., & Freedman, S. (1988). Peer response groups in the writing classroom: Theoretical foundations and new directions. *Review of Educational Research, 58,* 119–49.

Elbaz, F. (1981). The teacher's "practical knowledge": Report of a case study. *Curriculum Inquiry, 2,* 43–71.

Elbaz, F. (1987). Teachers' knowledge of teaching: Strategies for reflection. In J. Smyth (Ed.), *Educating teachers: Changing the nature of pedagogical knowledge* (pp. 45–53). London: The Falmer Press.

Emig, J. (1971). *The composing processes of twelfth graders.* Urbana, IL: National Council of Teachers of English.

Family Health Council of Allegheny County. (1987). *Fact Sheet.* (Available from Family Health Council of Allegheny County, 625 Stanwick Street, Pittsburgh, PA 15222).

Flower, L. (in press). *The construction of negotiated meaning: A social cognitive theory of writing.* Carbondale, IL: Southern Illinois University Press.

Flower, L. (1989). Cognition, context, and theory building. *College Composition and Communication, 40,* 282–311.

Flower, L., Burnett, R., Hajduk, T., Wallace, D., Norris, L., Peck W., & Spivey, N. (1991). *Making thinking visible: Classroom inquiry in collaborative planning.* Pittsburgh, PA: National Center for the Study of Writing and Literacy at Carnegie Mellon. (ERIC Document Reproduction Service No. ED 334 593)

Flower, L., & Hayes, J.R. (1980). The dynamics of discovery: Defining a rhetorical problem. *College Composition and Communication, 31,* 21–42.

Flower, L. & Hayes, J.R. (1981). The pregnant pause: An inquiry into the nature of planning. *Research in the Teaching of English, 15,* 229–44.

Flower, L., Schriver, K.A., Carey, L., Haas, C., & Hayes, J.R. (1992). Planning in writing: The cognition of a constructive process. In S. Witte, N. Nakadate, & R. Cherry (Eds.), *A rhetoric of doing* (pp. 181–243). Carbondale, IL: Southern Illinois University Press.

Flower, L., Stein, V., Ackerman, J., Kantz, M.J., McCormick, K., & Peck, W.C. (1990). *Reading-to-write: Exploring a cognitive and social process.* New York: Oxford University Press.

Freedman, S.W. (1987). *Peer response groups in two ninth-grade classes* (Technical Report No. 12). Berkeley, CA: Center for the Study of Writing, University of California at Berkeley and Carnegie Mellon.

Freeman, D. (1991). "To make the tacit explicit": Teacher education, emerging discourse, and conceptions of teaching. *Teaching & Teacher Education, 7,* 439–54.

Freire, P. (1970). *Pedagogy of the oppressed.* New York: Herder and Herder.

Gargaro, J.Z. (1991). Transferring talk to text. In J.A. Aston, L. Norris, and P. Turley, (Eds.), *Collaborative planning: Concepts, processes, and assignments* (pp. 81–90). Pittsburgh, PA: National Center for the Study of Writing and Literacy at Carnegie Mellon. (ERIC Document Reproduction Service No. ED 334 594)

Gere, A.R., & Stevens, R.S. (1985). The language of writing groups: How oral response shapes revision. In S.W. Freedman (Ed.), *The acquisition of written language* (pp. 85–105). Norwood, NJ: Ablex.

Giroux, H. (1988). *Teachers as intellectuals: Toward a critical pedagogy of learning.* Ganby, MA: Bergin & Garvey.

Goswami, D., & Stillman, P.D. (Eds.). (1987). *Reclaiming the classroom: Teacher research as an agency for change.* Upper Montclair, NJ: Boynton/Cook.

Graves, D. (1983). *Writing: Teachers and children at work.* Exeter, NH: Heinemann.

Gumperz, J. (1982). *Discourse strategies.* Cambridge: Cambridge University Press.

Higgins, L., Flower, L., & Petraglia, J. (1992). Planning text together: The role of critical reflection in student collaboration. *Written Communication, 9,* 48–84.

Jones, B.F., Palincsar, A.S., Ogle, D.S., & Carr, E.G. (Eds.). (1987). *Strategic teaching and learning: Cognitive instruction in the content areas.* Alexandria, VA: Association for Supervision and Curriculum Development.

Kagan, D.M. (1990). Ways of evaluating teacher cognition: Inferences concerning the Goldilocks principle. *Review of Educational Research, 60*(3), 419–69.

Korthhagen, F.A.J. (1988). The influence of learning orientations on the development of reflective teaching. In J. Calderhead (Ed.), *Teachers' professional learning,* (pp. 35–51). London: The Falmer Press.

Leinhardt, G. (1988). Situated knowledge and expertise in teaching. In J. Calderhead (Ed.), *Teachers' professional learning.* London: The Falmer Press.

Matsuhashi, A., & Gordon, E. (1985). Revision, addition, and the power of the unseen text. In S.W. Freedman (Ed.), *The acquisition of written language: Response and revision* (pp. 226–49). Norwood, NJ: Ablex.

Mohr, M.M., & Maclean, M.S. (1987). *Working together: A guide for teachers.* Urbana, IL: National Council of Teachers of English.

Morine-Dershimer, G. (September-October, 1989). Preservice teachers' conceptions of content and pedagogy: Measuring growth in reflective, pedagogical decision-making. *Journal of Teacher Education, 40,* 46–52.

Murray, D.M. (1985). *A writer teaches writing.* Boston, MA: Houghton Mifflin.

Myers, M. (1985). *The teacher-researcher: How to study writing in the classroom.* Urbana, IL: National Council of Teachers of English.

Neuwirth, C., Palmquist, M., & Hajduk, T. (April, 1990). *Collaborative writing and the role of external representation.* Paper presented at the annual meeting of the American Educational Research Association, Boston, MA.

Norris, L. (1992). *Developing a repertoire for teaching high school English: Case studies of preservice teachers.* (Doctoral dissertation, University of Pittsburgh, 1992). *Dissertation Abstracts International,* 53.5: p. 1486-A.

Norris, L., Brozick, J., & Gargaro, J. (Eds.). (1992). *Discoveries and dialogues.* Pittsburgh, PA: Center for the Study of Writing at Carnegie Mellon. (ERIC Document Reproduction Service No. ED 348 670).

Norris, L., & Burnett, R. (Eds.). (1992). *Planning to write, notes on collaborative planning* (3 newsletters). Pittsburgh, PA: Center for the Study of Writing. (ERIC Document Reproduction Service No. ED 335 682).

North, S.M. (1987). *The making of knowledge in composition: Portrait of an emerging field.* Upper Montclair, NJ: Boynton/Cook.

Odell, L., Goswami, D., & Herrington, A. (1983). The discourse-based interview: A procedure of exploring tacit knowledge of writers in nonacademic settings. *Research on writing: Principles and methods* (pp. 221–36). New York: Longman.

Palincsar, A., & Brown, A.L. (1984). Reciprocal teaching of comprehension-fostering and comprehension-monitoring activities. *Cognition and Instruction, I,* 117–75.

Peck, W.C. (1991). *Community advocacy: Composing for action.* (Doctoral dissertation, Carnegie Mellon University, 1991). *Dissertation Abstracts International,* 53.2: p. 431-A.

Perl, S., & Egendorf, A. (1986). The process of creative discovery: Theory, research, and implications for teaching. In D.A. McQuade (Ed.), *The territory of language: Linguistics, stylistics, and the teaching of composition* (pp. 251–68). Carbondale, IL: Southern Illinois University Press.

Perl, S., & Wilson, N. (1986). *Through teachers' eyes: Portraits of writing teachers at work.* Portsmouth, NH: Heinemann.

Phelps, L.W. (1988). *Composition as human science: Contributions to the self-understanding of a discipline* (p. 207). New York: Oxford University Press.

Phelps, L.W. (1991). Practical wisdom and the geography of knowledge on composition. *College English, 53*(8), 863–85.

Piaget, J. (1932). *The language and thought of the child.* (M. Gabin, Trans.). New York: Harcourt Brace.

Putnam, L.L. (1986). Conflict in group decision-making. In R.Y. Hirokawa & M.S. Poole (Eds.), *Communication and group decision-making* (pp. 175–96). Beverly Hills, CA: Sage.

Rogoff, B. (1990). *Apprenticeship in thinking: Cognitive development in social context.* New York: Oxford University Press.

Scardamalia, M., & Bereiter, C. (1987). Knowledge telling and knowledge transforming in written composition. In S. Rosenberg (Ed.), *Advances in applied psycholinguistics, Volume 2* (pp. 142–75). Cambridge: Cambridge University Press.

Scardamalia, M., Bereiter, C., & Steinbach, R. (1984). Teachability of reflective processes in written composition. *Cognitive Science, 8,* 173–90.

Schecter, S., & Ramirez, R. (1991). *A teacher-research group in action* (Tech. Rep. No. 50). Berkeley: National Center for the Study of Writing and Literacy, University of California.

Schecter, S., & Ramirez, R. (1992). A teacher-research group in action. In D. Nunan (Ed.), *Collaborative language learning and teaching.* New York: Cambridge University Press.

Schon, D. (1987). *Educating the reflective practitioner.* San Francisco: Jossey Bass.

Schultz, L.M., Laine, C.H., & Savage, M.C. (1988). Interaction among school and college writing teachers: Toward recognizing and remaking old patterns. *College Composition and Communication, 39,* 139–53.

Slavin, R.E. (1990). *Cooperative learning: Theory, research, and practice.* Englewood Cliffs, NJ: Prentice-Hall.

Spivey, N.N. (1987). Construing constructivism: Reading research in the United States. *Poetics, 16,* 169–92.

Spradley, J. (1980). *Participant observation.* New York: Holt, Rinehart & Winston.

Swanson-Owens, D. (1986). Identifying natural sources of resistance: A case study of implementing writing across the curriculum. *Research in the Teaching of English, 20,* 69–97.

Tabachnick, B.R., & Zeichner, K.M. (1984). The impact of the student teaching experience on the development of teacher perspectives. *Journal of Teacher Education, 35*(6), 28–36.

Trimbur, J. (1989). Consensus and difference in collaborative learning. *College English, 51,* 602–16.

Vygotsky, L. (1986). *Thought and language* (A. Kozulin, Trans.). Cambridge, MA: MIT Press. (Original work published 1934)

Vygotsky, L.S. (1987). *Mind in society.* Cambridge, MA: Harvard University Press.

Wallace, D.L. (1991). *From intention to text: Developing, implementing, and judging intentions for writing.* (Doctoral dissertation, Carnegie Mellon University, 1991). *Dissertation Abstracts International, 52.4*: p. 1242-A.

Walvoord, B., & McCarthy, L.P. (1990). *Thinking and writing in college: A naturalistic study of students in four disciplines.* Urbana, IL: National Council of Teachers of English.

Watson, S. (1989). *Writing in trust: A tapestry of teachers' voices.* Southeastern Region, National Writing Project.

Watson, S. (1991). Letters on writing—A medium of exchange with students writing. In K.H. and J.L. Adams (Eds.), *Teaching advanced composition: Why and how* (pp. 133–50). Upper Montclair, NJ: Boynton/Cook.

Woolf, V. (1932). How should one read a book? *The second common reader.* New York: Harcourt Brace.

Zeichner, K.M., & Liston, D.P. (1990). *Traditions of reform in U.S. teacher education.* (Issue Paper 90–1). East Lansing, MI: The National Center for Research on Teacher Education.

Selected Bibliography on Collaborative Planning

Aston, J., Norris, L., & Turley, P. (Eds.). (1991). *Collaborative planning: Concepts, processes, and assignments.* Pittsburgh, PA: National Center for the Study of Writing and Literacy at Carnegie Mellon. (ERIC Document Reproduction Service No. ED 334 594).

Collects 14 papers written by project members during the 1989–90 academic year as a casebook about collaborative planning. The discovery papers focus on clarifying the concepts behind collaborative planning and classroom inquiry, tracing the processes by which project fellows used collaborative planning and made discoveries about their writing classrooms, or adapting collaborative planning to specific writing assignments and writing goals.

Burnett, R. E. (1991). *Conflict in the collaborative planning of coauthors: How substantive conflict, representation of task, and dominance relate to high-quality documents.* (Doctoral dissertation, Carnegie Mellon University, 1991). *Dissertation Abstracts International,* 52.4: p. 1236-A.

Reports a study of collaborative planning in three junior-level, college technical communication courses, focusing on the role of conflict in coauthoring.

Burnett, R. E. (1990). *Technical communication* (2nd ed.). Belmont, CA: Wadsworth.

Discusses using collaborative planning in technical writing courses.

Flower, L. (in press). *The construction of negotiated meaning: A social cognitive theory of writing.* Carbondale, IL: Southern Illinois University Press.

Discusses the strategic knowledge that first-year college writing students bring to collaborative planning.

Flower, L. (1992). *Problem-solving strategies for writing* (4th ed.). Fort Worth: Harcourt Brace Jovanovich.

Discusses using collaborative planning in college writing courses.

Flower, L., & Ackerman, J. (in press). *Writers at work.* Fort Worth: Harcourt Brace Jovanovich.

Discusses using collaborative planning in business writing courses.

Higgins, L., Flower, L., & Petraglia, J. (1992). Planning text together: The role of critical reflection in student collaboration. *Written Communication, 9,* 48–84.

Reports a study of the role that reflection plays in collaborative planning in two sections of first-year college writing courses.

Norris, L. (1992). *Developing a repertoire for teaching high school English: Case studies of preservice teachers.* (Doctoral dissertation, University of Pittsburgh, 1992). *Dissertation Abstracts International,* 53.5: p. 1486-A.

Reports a study of how reflection helped preservice teachers develop their representations of collaborative planning and creative dramatics.

Norris, L., & Burnett, R. (Eds.). (1992). *Planning to write: Notes on collaborative planning.* Pittsburgh, PA: National Center for the Study of Writing and Literacy at Carnegie Mellon. (ERIC Document Reproduction Service No. ED 335 682).

Includes three newsletters written by project members in February, 1989; Fall, 1989; and Fall, 1990. Each newsletter contains 12 pages of articles about background on collaborative planning, how project members adapted collaborative planning for their particular classroom use, the kinds of writing tasks students were asked to do, and what discoveries they made about themselves and their student writers.

Norris L., Brozick, J., & Gargaro, J. Z. (Eds.). (1992). *Discoveries and dialogues.* Pittsburgh, PA: National Center for the Study of Writing and Literacy at Carnegie Mellon. (ERIC Document Reproduction Service No. ED 348 670).

As a second casebook on using collaborative planning, presents 15 discovery papers, written during the 1991–92 academic year, about making discoveries about collaborative planning and students. Also included are summaries and photographs from five open dialogues hosted by the project members on a variety of issues concerning teaching and learning, such as adapting collaborative planning to an already existing curriculum, community literacy, learning to teach, success with collaborative planning in different contexts, and how collaborative planning can be useful in nonacademic and workplace situations.

Peck, W. C. (1991). *Community advocacy: Composing for action.* (Doctoral dissertation, Carnegie Mellon University, 1991). *Dissertation Abstracts International,* 53.2: p. 431-A.

Describes the collaborative nature of community literacy.

Wallace, D. L. (1991). *From intention to text: Developing, implementing, and judging intentions for writing.* (Doctoral dissertation, Carnegie Mellon University, 1991). *Dissertation Abstracts International,* 52.4: p. 1242-A.

Uses collaborative planning to examine how first-year community college and university students develop, implement, and judge their intentions for writing.

Index

Student intentions, supporting, 204-222
  developing initial intentions, 208-211
  fulfillment of intentions, 217-220
  implementing intentions, 211-217
  implications for, 220-222
Students, assumptions of, 4
Student-teacher conference, 126, 157
Student teaching, 244, 245
Substantive conflict, 79, 237-242
Supporter engagement, 68
Supporters
  attitude, 68-71
  behavior, 71
  differences made by, 231-236
  examples of engagement in, 76-81
  first-time experience as, examples of, 111-114
  importance of in collaborative planning, 67-68
  prompts by, 49, 73-74, 104
  qualities necessary in, 18-19
  strategies for, 60
  verbal moves, 73-76
Supporting skills, development of, 49, 57-58
Swanson-Owens, D., 252, 302

Tabachnick, B. R., 244, 302
Teachers
  as practitioners, 6
  as researchers, 26
  as transformative intellectuals, 7
Teacher's self-reflection, 7
Teacher training, 17, 35-36
  understanding of collaborative planning, 243-253
Teaching
  role of research in, 11-13
  and theory, 5-8
  as theory building, 3
Teen Stories Project, 286-295
Tetroe, J., 206, 298
Text conventions, 30, 48, 56-57, 107, 117, 173, 291-294
Thematic Apperception Test, 145

Theory building
  defined, 3
  observation-based, 17-22
  research in, 11-13
  tensions between teaching and research, 14-16
  See also Situated theory
Tracking, 66, 184
Transforming textual information, 206, 288-291
Trimbur, J., 68, 302
Turley, P., 33, 54, 281, 297, 304

Validity, 14
Verbal moves, 73-76, 82
Videotaping, 30, 54, 59, 66, 238
Vincent, Jim, 30
Vygotsky, L., 37, 38, 39, 49, 73, 302

Wallace, David, 16, 48, 64, 67, 69, 91, 101, 137, 145, 147, 204, 205, 211, 245, 299, 302, 306 307
Wallace, Richard, 26
Walvoord, B., 26, 303
Watson, S., 8, 27, 303
Weaver, Dee, 133
What-if scenarios, 17
Wilson, N., 26, 301
Window exchange, 256, 257, 259
Woolf, Virginia, 227, 303
WRITE Project, 286-295
Writer's Maze, 126, 127
Writing across the curriculum, 26
Writing apprehension, 146
Writing Attitude Survey, 143-144, 245
  case studies, 148-153
  development of, 137-140
  using, 141-142, 145-146
Writing centers, 204

Zeichner, K. M., 6, 244, 302, 303
Zone of proximal development, 49, 73, 205

Editors

Linda Flower is a professor at Carnegie Mellon and co-director of the National Center for the Study of Writing and Literacy at Berkeley and Carnegie Mellon. She was director of the Making Thinking Visible Project.

David L. Wallace is an assistant professor of rhetoric and composition at Iowa State University and was part of the Carnegie Mellon team.

Editors

Linda Norris, now assistant professor of English at Indiana University of Pennsylvania, Armstrong County Campus, was the full-time educational coordinator for the Making Thinking Visible Project.

Rebecca Burnett, now an assistant professor of rhetoric and professional communication at Iowa State University, was a member of the Carnegie Mellon Making Thinking Visible Project.

Contributors

Jean A. Aston is professor of English at Pittsburgh's Community College of Allegheny County.

Michael A. Benedict has taught English at Fox Chapel Area High School for 25 years, where he is department chair and a peer coach for faculty in cooperative learning.

Marlene W. Bowen is a reading specialist with the Iroquois School District in Erie, Pennsylvania. She team teaches a ninth-grade English course for basic students.

James R. Brozick has been a teacher for 27 years at North Hills High School where he is currently department chair.

Leonard R. Donaldson has been teaching social studies at Pittsburgh's Peabody High School for 25 years.

Leslie Byrd Evans teaches at Steel Valley High School in the Monongahela Valley on Pittsburgh's south side.

Philip Flynn is director of programs at the Community Literacy Center in Pittsburgh.

Jane Zachary Gargaro has taught English in Pittsburgh Public Schools for 24 years, 14 of which she spent as the Instructional Teacher Leader at Peabody High School.

Karen W. Gist teaches English in grades 9–12 at Peabody High School.

Thomas Hajduk, who has taught college English since 1986, at Carnegie Mellon, the University of Pittsburgh, and Community College of Allegheny County, is completing his doctorate in the rhetoric program at Carnegie Mellon.

Elenore Long is a researcher with the Center for the Study of Writing and Literacy at Carnegie Mellon.

Theresa Marshall has taught at Iroquois High School in Erie, Pennsylvania for the past 19 years.

Andrea S. Martine has taught high school English at Allderdice High School in Pittsburgh for the past 26 years.

Wayne C. Peck is executive director of the Community Literacy Center (CLC) on Pittsburgh's multicultural, urban north side.

Lois Rubin, an assistant professor of English at Penn State New Kensington, has taught writing at a variety of levels over the past 27 years.